TIMELY RENEWED

Amendments to Restore
the American Constitution

James W. Lucas

All human constitutions are subject to corruption
and must perish, unless they are timely renewed
and reduced to their first principles.

Algernon Sidney, copied by
Thomas Jefferson into
his Commonplace Book

ISBN 145383916X
EAN 13-9781453839164

Constitution Renewal Initiative
www.TimelyRenewed.com

This book is dedicated to:

Pv2 A. J. Z.
SrA J. L. P.
and
Special Agent J. L. C.

and all others who protect and defend
our Republic and Constitution

TABLE OF CONTENTS

Chapter 1

The Republic and its Constitution

A republic, if you can keep it

Benjamin Franklin, when asked if the
Constitutional Convention had created
a republic or a monarchy[1]

Consider three years: 1787, 1913, and today.

From May to September 1787, delegates of twelve of the thirteen
independent united States of America gathered in Philadelphia,
Pennsylvania to revise the arrangements under which they had
cooperated since declaring their independence from the Kingdom of
Great Britain eleven years earlier. This declaration had been
negotiated in the same hall in which they were now meeting, the
Pennsylvania State House. The agreement which was proposed by
that gathering, the "Constitution," created a new national government
for the recently independent States. The government thus created,
and its governing document, are now in their third century. As long
as they endure, that government will be the longest continuously
functioning constitutional republic of any size in the world, and that
document will be the oldest written constitution in the history of
humankind.

Today the idea of a written constitution, thought rather odd and
novel in 1787, is considered along with a flag as an essential of any
newly independent sovereign nation. Almost every nation in the
world now has a written constitution. All look back in one way or
another to the document written in 1787.

1

The nation governed by that government and constitution has changed enormously since 1787. Its population has gone from three million to over three hundred million. It has expanded from the easternmost coast of North America (in 1787 already thought too unwieldy an area to govern) to cross the continent and beyond. And, that nation has been at the forefront of economic, technological, and social changes unimaginable to the framers of 1787.

None of those men thought that the Constitution they had written was perfect, even at the beginning. Benjamin Franklin began his famous address in support of the Constitution by saying that "I confess that there are several parts of this constitution which I do not at present approve."[2] They certainly contemplated that it would be changed over time. However, that change was to be careful and calibrated. James Madison, called the "Father of the Constitution" for his extensive involvement in its creation and adoption by the States, warned that changing laws too quickly "poisons the blessings of liberty itself." According to Madison, if no man "knows what the law is to-day" he can only "guess what it will be to-morrow. Law is defined to be a rule of action; but how can that be a rule, which is little known and less fixed?"[3] Consistent rules enable people to plan for the future, and planning for the future is the source of all prosperity. Indeed long-range planning is one of the fundamentals of what makes humanity distinctive among the inhabitants of our planet.

This book is about how we have changed our constitutional rule of law, how we ought to make such changes, and what we can do to bring the two closer together. It is about how we can restore the rule of law by repairing the damage that has been inflicted on our Constitution in the more than two centuries it has served as the foundation of our government.

To begin, consider the following cases of how our Constitution has been changed since 1787:

A young couple have left the hectic life of modern urbanity, and become organic farmers. They do not use pesticides or other chemical treatments on their crops, instead applying natural fertilizers produced on their own or neighboring farms. They grow most of their own food. Some of their excess production is fed to their free range chickens. They sell the organic produce they do not eat along with their free range chickens to secure cash for items they can not produce themselves. However, seeking to minimize their carbon footprint, they only sell these at the local farmers market.

The Constitution of 1787 had a clause that empowered Congress to "regulate Commerce with foreign Nations, and among the several States, and with the Indian Tribes." If you had asked the men leaving the Pennsylvania State House in September 1787 after completing the Constitution what "Commerce ... among the several States" meant, they would have thought you a bit of a naif. To them it obviously meant the sale of goods across state lines. One of the main reasons for calling the convention to review the arrangements among the States was that the States were putting restrictions and taxes on the import of goods from the other States.[4] This impeded the development of a common market among the American States to promote a strong, prosperous continental economy. If you had suggested to them that a local farmer just selling his goods locally could be subjected to national control because he was in "interstate commerce," they would have thought you daft, and the notion absurd.[5]

And yet today, that is the constitutional law of the United States. Our organic farming couple are considered to be in "interstate commerce" and subject to regulation by the national government because they impact the national market for food. How? By growing their own food and their own feed for their free range chickens they are not buying it from someone else who might be in another State.[6]

Therefore, if Congress, or more likely a regulatory agency run by unelected bureaucrats, decides that local organic food growers have to comply with expensive labeling and testing regulations, they can do so because these local farmers are in "interstate commerce." In our modern government, the bureaucrats who promulgate these rules have substantial input from lobbyists for big agribusinesses and major manufacturers of artificial fertilizers and pesticides, all of whom see local organic farmers as a growing competitive threat.

Of course, our organic farming couple and others like them are unlikely to have a large Washington lobbying firm on retainer, nor are the bureaucrats making the regulations likely to be looking for a job with the organic farmers when they leave the government. Instead, they will be hoping for a high-paying job with one of the major companies who are lobbying them regularly, or maybe one of the lobbying firms themselves. Unsurprisingly, the regulations will impose a lot of expensive, complicated requirements on our organic farming couple. How they can complain? After all, they are the ones who chose to get into "Commerce ... among the several States."

Consider another case. You are in your home and you text your friend who lives nearby about your opposition to US military intervention in the Middle East. Under a law called the Foreign Intelligence Surveillance Act of 1978 Amendments Act of 2008, government agents can intercept your conversation without a warrant.[7] You might assume that they base their power to do this under the Constitution on some very expansive claim of national security, but you would be wrong. The constitutional basis used to authorize government agents to intercept your text messages is that, when you text your friend down the street about your political opinions, you are in "Commerce ... among the several States"!

And what of the gentlemen leaving the convention at the Pennsylvania State House in September 1787? For them the idea that the federal government's authority to regulate "Commerce ... among the several States" would empower the government to intercept two gentlemen's private political correspondence not only absurd, but horrifying.

4

Consider another case. A young child dies. The deceased child's elementary school classmates are upset as they talk about it. They seek out the hugs of their kindly teacher. Seeking to comfort the distraught children, she says a little prayer, making it clear that the children do not have to participate if they do not want to. Upon learning of this, the school authorities immediately fire the teacher. The administrators explain that they have no choice, the teacher's conduct was not only illegal, but unconstitutional.[8]

The Constitution proposed in 1787 was very controversial, and was only approved by the States after extensive debate. Several of the States conditioned their approval on the immediate passage of amendments assuring that this new national government would not infringe on certain basic rights. In the First Congress James Madison promptly prepared the requested amendments, now known as the Bill of Rights.

The first phrase in the first of these Bill of Rights amendments in our Constitution says that "Congress shall make no law respecting an establishment of religion." If in September 1789 you had asked the men leaving the First Congress at Federal Hall in New York City after voting in favor of Mr. Madison's amendments what an "establishment" of religion meant, they would have pitied your lack of education. Everyone knew what an "establishment" of religion was. This was when the government preferentially supported one particular religion. In England it was the Church of England, or Anglicans, in Scotland it was the Presbyterians, in the Scandinavian and northern German states it was the Lutherans, in Spain it was Roman Catholicism, in Russia it was the Orthodox Church. Having an officially approved national religion was hardly limited to Christian Europe. In Japan, Shinto was the official religion, and the emperors of China had promoted Confucianism for millennia. And, of course, across broad swaths of the globe Islam was sustained by kings, shahs, and caliphs. This amendment prohibited the new national government from picking one religion to be supported as the official

"Church of the United States of America."[9] If you had suggested to these members of the First Congress that their amendment would require the dismissal of a teacher for saying a prayer in school, even under the most innocent of circumstances, they would have considered you worse than ignorant, and the idea a threat to the public well-being.

And yet today, that is exactly the constitutional law of the United States. If you were to ask most Americans today what the first amendment says about religion, few would recognize the term "establishment of religion," much less understand its correct historical meaning. Far more would reply that the first amendment says that there is a "wall of separation between church and state." However, for most of our history, let alone in 1789, no one would have recognized that phrase. It is not in the Constitution, nor does it appear in any official document relating to the adoption of the first amendment. Indeed, for most of our history no one would recognize it at all, for in fact it only comes from a letter Thomas Jefferson wrote in 1803 which was, until recently, lost in obscurity. You might also note that, although Thomas Jefferson is an honored founder of the nation, he was not a framer of its Constitution. He was in France serving as ambassador during the 1787 convention, and had not yet returned to America when Congress completed the Bill of Rights amendments and sent them to the States for ratification.

However, this throwaway phrase, from a simple piece of correspondence from a man who had nothing to do with creating either the Constitution or the Bill of Rights, now defines the meaning of the very first phrase of the very first amendment. Under the "wall of separation" understanding of the "establishment of religion," it is not enough that there is no official national church. Religion must now be wholly absent from the public sphere. Of course, any public employee who comes even close to the wall must be dismissed. How can she complain? After all, with her little prayer she is "establishing" state supported religion in clear violation of the "wall of separation" required by the Constitution of the United States of America itself!

Consider another case. Someone living in a dangerous neighborhood wants to own a handgun for self-protection. The city council, believing that the presence of handguns increases the risk of someone getting killed or seriously injured in violent confrontations, has passed a law banning the ownership of handguns by private individuals.

The second amendment to the Constitution voted by that First Congress in 1789 reads, "a well regulated militia, being necessary to the security of a free state, the right of the people to keep and bear arms, shall not be infringed." Again, if you had asked those first members of Congress what they meant by that, they would have probably assumed you to be a foreigner newly arrived in our country, and uninformed about America and her struggle for liberty. In 1789 every State had a militia, and thus everyone knew what a militia was about. Every able-bodied adult man was assumed to be available for militia service in defense of his State and community and most were, in fact, participants in the militia to some extent or another. It was an important social and political organization in most communities.

In order for this force to work, every man had to have his own firearms at the ready. In the war with the British, having an armed citizenry ready for immediate militia service was seen as an important element of the colonists' readiness to resist the imperialists. Disarming the local citizens so they could not form militias was one of the abuses committed by the British to control the colonists. The second amendment assured that the national government would not repeat this tyrannical abuse.[10]

Today, the militia no long exist as official State organizations. They have been superseded by the National Guard, which no longer considers its membership to be every able-bodied adult in the community. Does that mean that the right to bear arms has disappeared with the old-fashioned universal State militias? Or is the second amendment's reference to the militia merely a prefatory statement leading to the broader principle that it is a mark of a free society that it does not fear that its law-abiding citizens possess firearms? Both sides are very passionate in their interpretations. So how do we decide which is right?

In school you were taught that it is the Supreme Court that decides. For example, in 2008 the Supreme Court addressed the meaning of the second amendment in a case called District of Columbia vs. Heller.[11] In the *Heller* case the Supreme Court decided by a 5-to-4 vote that the second amendment prohibited the District of Columbia government from banning Mr. Heller from having a handgun in his home. In 2010 this ruling was extended to state and local governments in the case of McDonald vs. Chicago, again by a complicated 5-to-4 vote.[12] Advocates of the right to bear arms were very pleased and advocates for gun control were very displeased. However, the advocates of gun control could take heart in the narrowness of the vote on the Supreme Court. A shift of one vote in some future gun control case in the Supreme Court would change the constitutional interpretation they did not like.

The media, lawyers, and issue advocates are all avid Supreme Court vote counters. Especially watched are so-called "centrist" justices, whose votes swing unpredictably back and forth between voting with either what are considered the more consistently "liberal" and the more consistently "conservative" justices.[13] And, of course, Supreme Court justices occasionally die or retire, which in our times always sets off a furious storm of vicious political battling over the replacement. Although much criticized, this intense fighting is not so unreasonable when one considers that the swing of one vote on the Supreme Court can profoundly change the meaning of our two hundred twenty-plus year old Constitution.

Is this what the framers intended? They clearly knew that there would be, in Madison's words, "useful alterations...suggested by experience" to the Constitution.[14] However, when Madison wrote these words, he was not referring to judicial interpretation of the Constitution. He was referring to Article V of the Constitution, which sets out the process for amending the Constitution. The Constitution says nothing about the Supreme Court being the final judge of the Constitution's meaning. That principle was not established until more than a decade after the Constitution came into effect, in the Supreme Court's decision in 1803 of the case called Marbury vs. Madison.[15]

In the *Marbury* case, Mr. Marbury was suing James Madison as the Secretary of State in the administration of newly elected President Thomas Jefferson. Although we think of the Secretary of State as being in charge of foreign relations, the Secretary of State is also in charge of issuing official government documents, and Marbury wanted Madison to deliver to him a certificate confirming his appointment as a justice of the peace by outgoing President John Adams. Jefferson had defeated Adams for re-election as President in 1800, and Mr. Marbury was one of a number of federal judges who had been appointed by Adams in the interim between the election and when Jefferson took office. Jefferson and Madison (who is truly ubiquitous in American constitutional history) declined to deliver the certificate to Marbury, who was from the party of their political opponents led by the defeated Adams.

In the *Marbury* decision the Chief Justice of the Supreme Court, John Marshall (who himself had recently been appointed by Adams) declared that it was "emphatically the province and duty of the Judicial Department to say what the law is. Those who apply the rule to particular cases must, of necessity, expound and interpret that rule. If two laws conflict with each other, the Courts must decide on the operation of each."[16] He then went on to decide that the section of the law setting up the procedure under which Marbury was suing was contrary to the Constitution, and therefore Madison did not have to follow it and give Marbury the certificate of appointment.

Technically the Jefferson administration had won. However, Thomas Jefferson vigorously rejected Marshall's argument that judges could decide that a law was unconstitutional, because that also made them the final arbitrators of what the Constitution meant. Jefferson, who himself had been a practicing lawyer before the Revolution, wrote that "the doctrines of that case were given extra-judicially, and against law."[17] The Supreme Court could not "usurp" the right "of exclusively explaining the Constitution." To do so turns the Constitution into "a mere thing of wax in the hands of the judiciary, which they may twist and shape into any form they please." The only check in the Constitution against abuse of this power by the Supreme Court was impeachment, which "experience has already shown...is not even a scare-crow."[18]

The major alterations in the meaning of "Commerce...among the several States" and "an establishment of religion" are the result of Supreme Court decisions, and these are only a few of many major changes in the understanding of the plain language of the Constitution between the time of its creation and today. Even if on policy grounds one likes these changes, one would be hard-pressed to convince Mr. Jefferson that they do not show the Constitution being twisted and shaped into a form decided by, and only by, a handful of Supreme Court justices "unelected by and independent of the nation." For the rest of his life Jefferson protested this assumption of power by this most undemocratic branch of the government, whose members serve for life without ever having to answer to the people. The year before his death on July 4, 1826 (the fiftieth anniversary of the Declaration of Independence which he wrote) Jefferson wrote that the Supreme Court was "at first considered as the most harmless and helpless" of the three branches of government. However its exclusive power of declaring what the Constitution means "by sapping and mining, slyly, and without alarm, the foundations of the Constitution, can do what open force would not dare to attempt."[19]

Consider three years: 1787, 1913, and today. So far we have looked at things that happened in 1787 and shortly thereafter, and where things stand today. What of 1913?

In 1913 the most disliked provision of the United States Constitution, the sixteenth amendment, was ratified. The sixteenth amendment removed a constitutional impediment to certain aspects of the income tax. (By the way, in today's dollars the income tax rates that were enacted after the Amendment was approved were 1% on the first $350,000 of income rising to 7% on annual income of over $10,000,000.[20]) So what does the sixteenth amendment have to do with this?

Like his close friend and colleague James Madison, and all of the other founders, Thomas Jefferson recognized that "nothing is more likely" than that aspects of the Constitution would be found to be "defective. This is the ordinary case of all human works." So what do we do about it? Are we locked forever into a Constitution written for the world of 1787? Of course not, wrote Jefferson, "let us go on perfecting it, by adding, by way of amendment to the Constitution those powers which time and trial show are still wanting."[21]

The sixteenth amendment of 1913 represents the last time any new governmental power was added to the Constitution by amendment. There have been a number of amendments since then, but they were all about either expanding voting rights or fiddling, in one way or another, with how the President is selected. Expanding voting rights is tremendously good and valuable, but does not really impact the powers and operation of the governmental structure created by the Constitution. Fine-tuning the mechanics of selecting the President has been going on since the twelfth amendment of 1804, but again does not impact the authority of the national government under the Constitution. The last amendment changing the language of the Constitution effecting the authority or reach of the national government was in 1913 with the 16th Amendment authorizing the income tax.

In 1930 when the government first started officially measuring gross domestic product (GDP) the federal government constituted 3.5% of the nation's economy.[22] Based on other historical estimates of the size of the economy, in 1913 the federal government consumed 1.8% of the nation's economy.[23] In 2009 that figure was over 28% with a deficit equal to 13% of total GDP.[24] In 1913 the federal government had 396,000 employees compared to over 2 million today.[25] That 500% increase is far greater than the three times increase in the total US population over that same period. And that 2 million federal employee figure does not count contractors, grantees, and state and local government employees working to fill federally mandated functions, which are estimated to number almost 13 million.[26]

An even more astonishing measure of the expansion of the national government is the sheer number of laws and regulations each American is subject to. It is difficult to estimate how many federal laws and regulations were in effect in 1913 because they were not collected in any single publication. However, when the first official collection of the federal laws was made in 1926 they fit in a single volume. The most recent official collection of the federal laws in 2006 filled 33 volumes, *each* well over a thousand pages long.[27] And that was before the addition of the recent mammoth healthcare law and other major legislation promoted by the current administration. As for regulations promulgated by federal agencies under those laws, when the first official annual publication of federal regulations was made in 1936 it was 2,620 pages long. The one for 2008 was 80,700 pages long.[28]

In the almost one hundred years since the ratification of the sixteenth amendment, the number of workers either in the federal government or operating under federal direction has increased at ten times the rate of population growth, the share of the national income consumed by the federal government has increased about fifteen times, and there are over thirty times as many laws and regulations as measured by simple page count. And these quantitative figures can not begin to take account of the impact on the quality of American freedom of the regulatory reach of an alphabet soup of federal bureaucracies into every aspect of American life.

Some might be tempted to blame this massive change on the income tax, but the fact is that the exponential expansion really began two decades later in the 1930s. Although it is true that the expansion could not have occurred without the revenue from the income tax, that does not explain why or how it occurred.

How could this amazing expansion of our national government occur without any expansion of the powers vested in the national government by the Constitution? The year 1913 is the last time the Constitution was amended to give the national government any new power. Instead, this vast expansion in the power and scope of our national government in the century since then has been entirely authorized by decisions of the United States Supreme Court, interpreting the Constitution to allow the national government to do things which would have left most of its framers aghast.

Of course, there are many Americans who have no problem with this expansion of the national government by Supreme Court decision. A large national government helps people, courts need to interpret the Constitution in light of changing conditions, and we need a strong national government to deal with global challenges and threats. However, every coin has two sides, and many coins consist only of a thin veneer of valuable-looking metal designed to hide a base interior. Let us consider what our national government has become. How well does our unlimited national government really serve true human needs? Was Thomas Jefferson wrong?

Chapter 2

A Progressive Case for a More Jeffersonian Government I:
We are all Republicans, we are all Federalists

But every difference of opinion is not a difference of principle. We have called by different names brethren of the same principle. We are all Republicans, we are all Federalists..... Let us, then, with courage and confidence pursue our own Federal and Republican principles, our attachment to union and representative government...entertaining a due sense of our equal right to the use of our own faculties, to the acquisitions of our own industry, to honor and confidence from our fellow-citizens, resulting not from birth, but from our actions and their sense of them; enlightened by a benign religion,...with all these blessings, what more is necessary to make us a happy and a prosperous people? Still one thing more, fellow-citizens--a wise and frugal Government, which shall restrain men from injuring one another, shall leave them otherwise free to regulate their own pursuits of industry and improvement, and shall not take from the mouth of labor the bread it has earned. This is the sum of good government, and this is necessary to close the circle of our felicities.

Thomas Jefferson, from his
first inaugural address[1]

In our times, complaints about judicial activism and excess government usually come from those currently labeled "conservative." However, looking back to the beginning, back to 1787 and the first decade of the Republic, throws an interesting light on our modern disputations. Among the founders were two amazing men who stood

14

at the head of two powerful currents which have ever since flowed through the American polity. One was a scion of prosperous Virginia planting gentry. The other was an immigrant from the West Indies, born out of wedlock to a serving girl and the ne'er-do-well son of a Scottish laird who, although well-born, abandoned the family. One gave voice to the ideals which have defined us as a nation. The other began the practices that would make us an empire. One was Thomas Jefferson. The other was Alexander Hamilton.[2]

Alexander Hamilton was in many ways the classic American immigrant. Effectively left an orphan upon his mother's death when he was 13, he worked full time as a clerk while diligently studying on his own. Impressed by his hard work and bright mind, his employer and other local merchants paid for him to go to the British American colonies to pursue a college education. Arriving in New York City in 1773 at the age of 17 without family or acquaintances, he plunged into an accelerated course of study at King's (now Columbia) College. However, his studies were interrupted by the growing conflict between Britain and her North American colonies. Hamilton joined the Continental Army and served with distinction as both an artillery officer and as an aide to George Washington. He finished his war by leading an infantry charge against one of the last British defenses at Yorktown. Returning to New York City he gave himself a crash course in the law and was admitted to practice after less than a year. He also served in the Continental Congress.

As a former military man, he grew concerned about the ability of the loosely affiliated American States to cooperate sufficiently to defend their independence against continuing intrigues by European powers. He promoted the convention of 1787 to improve on the arrangements among the independent American States, and was elected a delegate from New York. However, the other members of the New York delegation were opposed to creating a national government, so Hamilton was absent for much of the convention because he could not cast New York's vote alone. When he did appear, he made an oration of several hours length advocating the abolition of the States and that the President and Senators serve for life. The other delegates listened politely and then ignored his recommendations.[3]

Nonetheless, when the Constitution emerged from the convention Hamilton became a staunch supporter, and led the tough fight for its ratification by the state of New York. In the course of that battle he enlisted James Madison and fellow New Yorker John Jay to write a series of newspaper articles promoting ratification of the new Constitution. As was the custom of the day, they were published under a pen name, with all three using "Publius." Collected as *The Federalist Papers* they are still considered some of the most brilliant American political writing.

In them, Hamilton began to lay out his vision of the American future. Here he argued that the security of the new republic was enhanced by "the ENLARGEMENT of the ORBIT" of the republic which would supersede the interests of many "little, jealous, clashing, tumultuous commonwealths, the wretched nurseries of unceasing discord, and the miserable objects of universal pity or contempt," although still leaving "in their possession certain exclusive and very important portions of the sovereign power."[4] With this enlarged scope, the national government would give vent to "the adventurous spirit which distinguishes the commercial character of America" which "has already excited uneasy sensations" in the European powers. However "under a vigorous national government, the natural strength and resources of the country, directed toward a common interest, would baffle all the combinations of European jealousy to restrain our growth."[5] A further object of this Union would be "a prosperous commerce," which "is now perceived by all enlightened statesmen to be the most useful as well as the most productive source of national wealth." This would serve "the assiduous merchant, the laborious husbandman, the active mechanic, and the industrious manufacturer," who all "look forward with eager expectation and growing alacrity to this pleasing reward of their toils."[6]

George Washington named Hamilton the first Secretary of the Treasury, a post which he filled with such energy that his portrait appears on the current ten-dollar note. (He has also become the subject of a hit musical.) Although he performed many critical roles in the Washington administration, two are of especially lasting importance. The first was to establish the new national government's creditworthiness by having it assume all of the liabilities for the promissory notes which had been issued to finance the Revolutionary War. Further, he had them paid at full face value, even though most of them were then held by speculators who had acquired them for pennies on the dollar from the veterans who had originally received them as pay for their service in the Continental Army. Since that time the United States of America has never defaulted on its debt. This fact lies at the foundation of our nation's ability to borrow trillions of dollars to fund our enormous modern budget deficits.

In the second role Hamilton was initially unsuccessful but, as we shall see, ultimately prevailed. In 1791 he sent Congress a report on the development of American manufacturing. In parts of it he almost sounds like a modern human potentiality guru. People's minds "fall below mediocrity and labour without effect, if confined to uncongenial pursuits. And it is thence to be inferred, that the results of human exertion may be immensely increased by diversifying its objects. When all the different kinds of industry obtain in a community, each individual can find his proper element, and can call into activity the whole vigour of his nature..... To cherish and stimulate the activity of the human mind, by multiplying the objects of enterprise, is not among the least considerable of the expedients, by which the wealth of a nation may be promoted." He envisioned not just "a nation of mere cultivators" but "a nation of cultivators, artificers and merchants" pursuing a full spectrum of human endeavor.[7]

In many respects Hamilton personally epitomized the modern American entrepreneurial spirit. He founded a bank and newspaper which still exist today, and planned the creation of the United States' largest industrial complex at the Paterson, New Jersey site of the largest waterfalls on the eastern seaboard. (Factories used water power before the development of steam power in the early 1800s.)

However, in his *Report on Manufactures* Hamilton also began another American tradition. He called for an energetic national government to subsidize projects like the Paterson factory complex.[8] He also proposed spending federal funds for projects, such as improvements in the transportation system, which would benefit business and financial interests, under the rationale that these would increase overall national prosperity. He also sponsored the creation of a federally chartered Bank of the United States, a forerunner of the modern Federal Reserve Bank and the national banking system which relies on it.

If Alexander Hamilton were to rise today from his grave at Trinity Church in lower Manhattan at the intersection of Broadway and Wall Street, of all the founders he would probably be most pleased by what he saw. America as the world's preeminent power both economically and militarily, governed by a strong national government, would fulfill his grandest dreams for his adopted homeland. Everything he had and became in his life Alexander Hamilton owed to America. He loved America passionately, and he sought to build her might and power in every way he could.

Thomas Jefferson loved America also. If he were to rise from his graveyard on the site of his old family plantation in central Virginia, he would undoubtedly be pleased to see that his beloved Monticello had been so carefully preserved, including the bust of Hamilton in the front foyer (there, the guides say, so that Jefferson could keep an eye on him). However, beyond the pleasant woods of the Monticello historical site, Jefferson would not be happy with the America he saw. For as much as Jefferson loved America, he loved liberty also.

As George Washington's Secretary of State, Jefferson opposed the steps proposed in his cabinet colleague Hamilton's report. He told

Washington that the decision on the *Report on Manufacture's* recommendations would "let us know, whether we live under a limited or unlimited government.... The *Report on Manufactures...*under color of giving *bounties* for the encouragement of particular manufactures, meant to establish the doctrine that the power given by the Constitution to collect taxes to provide for the *general welfare* of the United States permitted Congress to take everything under their management which *they* should deem for the *public welfare* and...that the subsequent enumeration of their powers [in the Constitution]...did not at all constitute the limits of their authority."[9]

Jefferson was referring to Section 8 of Article 1 of the Constitution, which lists 17 specific powers granted by the Constitution to the national government. However, the first clause of Section 8 gives Congress the power to lay taxes "to pay the Debts and provide for the common Defence and general Welfare of the United States." Hamilton argued that, although the first clause appeared to be simply an authorization to collect taxes for the following 17 specific purposes, the phrase "general Welfare" in this clause was an independent grant of authority for the national government to do things which were not included in the 17 powers specifically authorized by the Constitution.

Jefferson saw this interpretation as an open-ended empowerment of the national government to do anything it wanted without regard to the rights of states, localities, or the people. He warned that "when all government, domestic and foreign, in little as in great things, shall be drawn to Washington as the centre of power, it will render powerless the checks of one government upon another, and will become as venal and oppressive as the government from which we separated [Great Britain]."[10] For Jefferson, it was "not by the consolidation or concentration of powers, but by their distribution that good government is effected."[11] And it was John Marshall's Supreme Court, "installed for life responsible to no authority," which was "advancing with a noiseless and steady pace to the great object of consolidation" of power in the national government.[12]

The history of the United States of America from then to our time can be interpreted as a conflict between these two views of the proper role of government. Hamilton's immigrant energy and entrepreneurial drive led him to invest government with the same "can-do" spirit he brought to his private enterprises. Jefferson's love of liberty and independence led him to cherish the people's ability to be self-reliant and to distrust any power concentrated too far away from the people. These contradictory viewpoints laid the basis for our first political parties, Jefferson's Republicans and Hamilton's Federalists. And, as Jefferson said in his first inaugural address, we all possess some of both tendencies. For almost two and half centuries we have struggled to reconcile our Jeffersonian souls and our Hamiltonian spirits.

State Capitalism

It has been often said that America's government is Jeffersonian in rhetoric and Hamiltonian in practice. Initially the Jeffersonian view was powerful. Jefferson, Madison, James Monroe, and Andrew Jackson each held the presidency for two terms, almost always opposing Hamiltonian schemes to increase the economic power of the national government. Unfortunately, the Jeffersonian approach was pulled into the service of the cause of the States which sought to preserve the practice of slavery. There are many complex reasons for the Civil War, but on one level it can be seen as a conflict between an increasingly Hamiltonian North and a resisting Jeffersonian South.

Of course, both then and now this is an oversimplification. There were and are many northerners with a powerful Jeffersonian dislike for Hamiltonian meddling from Washington, and plenty of southerners who can, and do, far surpass their northern brethren in grabbing Hamiltonian pork barrel government spending, all while spouting Jeffersonian pronouncements about government frugality.

Nonetheless the nation took a decidedly Hamiltonian turn after the Civil War. This was most clearly reflected in massive government subsidies to railroads along with favorable government regulation.[13] A policy of high tariffs on imports also protected powerful manufacturing interests at the expense of consumers, as well as supplying revenue to the national government to continue its Hamiltonian subsidies and spending.[14] The United States also began to build a permanent military and assert itself internationally. In a war with Spain at the end of the 1800s, the United States acquired an international empire by seizing the Philippines, Puerto Rico, and other overseas possessions.

All of this was under the guidance of the new Republican Party which had been established in the 1850s. The Democratic Party of this era still had a strong Jeffersonian streak. The one Democrat to be elected President between 1860 and 1912, Grover Cleveland, frequently vetoed spending which he felt was beyond the proper scope of the national government. His hundreds of vetoes, more than any of his predecessors, even included an appropriation to help drought-stricken farmers because he could "find no warrant for such an appropriation in the Constitution." In his view, such government aid "encourages the expectation of paternal care on the part of the government and weakens the sturdiness of our national character, while it prevents the indulgence among our people of that kindly sentiment and conduct which strengthens the bonds of a common brotherhood." He pointed out that there had already been substantial private relief efforts for the farmers, and that other general government funding was available for the relief if members of Congress were willing to give up their own pork barrel claims on it (Cleveland did not use the term "pork barrel," but it is clear enough what he was talking about).[15]

However, in the late 1800s a political shift began. Frustrated with the national government's Hamiltonian support of big business, many began to demand that the national government turn to "paternal care," even if it meant Hamiltonian government activism. A champion of these demands was the man who followed Cleveland as the Democratic presidential nominee in the election of 1896, William

Jennings Bryan of Nebraska. Bryan was the Democratic presidential nominee in 1900 and 1908 as well, losing by ever-increasing margins in each successive race. Despite these defeats, Bryan commanded a broad and devoted following. A legendary orator, he was seen as a passionate Christian and representative of the common man. He was even referred to as the "Great Commoner." Bryan revered Jefferson and saw himself standing in the Jeffersonian tradition of looking out for the common folk against the wealthy and powerful.[16]

Finally, with Bryan's support Woodrow Wilson was elected President in 1912 after Theodore Roosevelt ran as a third party candidate and split the Republican vote. Wilson, who had no affection for the boisterous Nebraskan, nonetheless named him Secretary of State out of political expediency.[17] They immediately set about implementing what Bryan thought was a bold agenda to empower his common people. One of their most far-reaching steps was the creation of the Federal Reserve Bank in 1913. However, now the Wilsonian path began to diverge from Bryan's. Bryan naively thought that the Federal Reserve would stand as a bulwark to protect the common people from banking and financial interests. However, from the very beginning New York banking interests controlled the appointments to the Bank's Board, and used the Bank to reverse a decentralizing trend which had seen the growth of banks in other parts of the country. With the Federal Reserve in place, control of the nation's financial sector was decisively pulled back to the major New York banks.[18]

Similarly, Bryan thought that the new Federal Trade Commission would provide protection to regular consumers. However, again, it immediately came under the control of major business interests, which instead used it to suppress upstart competitors who sought to compete by offering lower prices.[19] In fact the legislation creating the Commission was written by an attorney for the US Chamber of Commerce, who Wilson then named one the first FTC Commissioners.[20] Wilson also put US foreign policy in the service of major US corporations, adjusting tariffs to favor them over smaller producers and consumers and applying pressure, even military intervention, to protect US corporate interests in Latin America. For Wilson, imperialism was fine as long as it was economic domination rather than permanent political annexation.[21]

Bryan did not understand that a regulated economic interest would inevitably take control of any powerful governmental institution which was important to it. Such business interests have a very focused interest in the regulator, whereas the general public's interest is dispersed. Unlike the general public, the regulated industry will devote its attention and resources to influencing the regulator and supporting politicians who facilitate that influence.[22] This process began with the earliest federal regulatory agency, the Interstate Commerce Commission. When a new Democratic Attorney General, who was a former railroad attorney, was asked by his old clients to eliminate the agency, he replied that instead "The Commission . . . is, or can be made, of great use to the railroads. It satisfies the popular clamor for a government supervision of the railroads, at the same time that that supervision is almost entirely nominal. Further, the older such a commission gets to be, the more inclined it will be found to take the business and railroad view of things.... The part of wisdom is not to destroy the Commission, but to utilize it."[23]

This turn to a Hamiltonian approach to government was not disturbing to Wilson.[24] The cool, erudite former president of Princeton University was quite comfortable mixing with the elites who Bryan saw as his enemies. Indeed, in his days as a university professor Wilson had written a highly influential article called "The Study of Administration." Here Wilson complained that efficient government administration was impeded because the "bulk of mankind is rigidly unphilosophical, and the bulk of mankind nowadays votes."[25] Wilson's solution was to treat public administration as "outside the proper sphere of politics."[26] Government administration should be left to professionals who are given "large powers and unhampered discretion."[27] For this to work,

Americans would have to get over "that besotting error of ours, that of trying to do too much by vote.... The problem is to make public opinion efficient without suffering it to be meddlesome."[28]

Instead specially educated officials must administer the government. Concerns that this might lead to "a domineering, illiberal officialdom" were misplaced where the "bureaucracy...is removed from the common political life of the people, its chiefs as well as its rank and file" because those department chiefs would still somehow be subject to scrutiny by public opinion so they "really served the people."[29] This was simply a bald assertion on Wilson's part. He offered no methods to assure that bureaucrats would listen to the public, or any explanation as to why they would do so if they were as insulated and powerful as Wilson proposed. Of course, the modern technocratic view, in the words of one scholar, is that the "pivotal roles of public opinion and citizen participation are seen as artifacts of an earlier time .... Politics must be administratively centralized, much more technocratic, and largely elitist. Democratic government, as conventionally understood, must inevitably wither under these arrangements, a process well underway."[30]

Wilson may well be seen as the founder in the United States of the modern bureaucratic state administered by a professional technocratic elite.[31] Hamilton would have approved of Wilson's close attention to the needs of major corporations as well, and would not have cared much that Wilson's programs did little for workers, Native Americans, or poor whites. The Wilson administration was also actively racist, refusing to hire African Americans for federal jobs above the level of janitor and dismissing many who had achieved higher level positions.[32]

While Bryan did not understand the anti-democratic potential of his initiatives, he was soon disabused by other events of any notion that Wilson was as committed to the same sincere, if misperceived, Jeffersonian idealism as the Great Commoner. As Secretary of State, Bryan strenuously resisted Wilson's growing militarism regarding the

First World War then raging in Europe. Unable to persuade Wilson to maintain a neutral stance in the hope of brokering a peace between the warring European states, he resigned in protest.[33] With Bryan gone, Wilson quickly moved the nation steadily towards war. In the period leading up to the United States' entry in to the First World War, in the words of one progressive historian, Wilson "was sucking power into Washington (and the White House) as if he were a corporation executive on a binge of vertical integration."[34] During the war Wilson ferociously suppressed civil liberties, jailing even those engaged in strictly non-violent opposition to the war.[35]

When the United States entered the war, Bryan patriotically volunteered to serve in any capacity, but was spurned by Wilson.[36] After the war, Bryan turned to causes like women's suffrage, prohibition, and opposing the application of Darwinist ideas to society. Later called "social Darwinists," elite scientists and men of affairs advocated eugenics and other measures, even warfare, to eliminate the weaker elements of the human race.[37] Bryan saw the philosophy as an attack on his beloved common man.[38] Like other educated men of the established elites, Wilson openly advocated eugenics. As governor of New Jersey, immediately before his election as President, Wilson had supported and signed a law providing for the sterilization of the "feeble-minded, epileptic, certain criminals and other defective inmates" of state institutions.[39] This period also saw a major cultural shift in progressive politics, as religious rural populists like Bryan gave way to urban sophisticates like the journalist John Reed, the hero of the Warren Beatty movie *Reds*, who instead idolized the cool, intellectual Wilson.[40]

Bryan died in 1925, a few days after prosecuting a Tennessee teacher for violating a law against teaching the theory of evolution which underlay the social Darwinist philosophy. Bryan's opponent in this famous trial was agnostic Wilson supporter Clarence Darrow, who had come for the express purpose of humiliating the Great Commoner.[41] By this time Bryan was universally mocked by the elites, who now deified Wilson and his aggressive Hamiltonian approach to domestic and international affairs.[42] With Bryan's death, the Democratic Party lost its last tenuous link to its long Jeffersonian heritage.[43]

This shift by progressives to the Hamiltonian approach reached full fruition in the 1930s. The nation had plunged into a severe depression caused, many economists argue, by ham-handed actions by the Federal Reserve Bank before and after one of the nation's periodic stock market downturns.[44] Franklin Roosevelt, who had been a cabinet under-secretary in the Wilson administration, expanded government in ways which would have astonished even his fellow New Yorker Hamilton. Of course, the received wisdom is that Roosevelt challenged big business and used government to protect the people from its depredations. Jefferson, not Hamilton, was presented as the inspiration for the Roosevelt administration. Indeed, it put up a beautiful memorial to the third President carved with his famous words in Washington, D. C., near the Washington Monument and Lincoln Memorial.[45]

However, as is usually the case, the truth is more complicated. In the 1960s New Left historians began to reexamine Roosevelt's New Deal programs. These clearly showed the New Deal as Hamiltonian, root and branch.[46] It was run in true Hamiltonian/Wilsonian fashion by a select elite group of advisors known as the "Brain Trust." The centerpiece of the recovery efforts in Roosevelt's first term was the National Recovery Administration (NRA). Under the NRA, government-sponsored industry associations were supposed to coordinate the efforts of the government, businesses, and labor to rebuild the economy. These associations were supposed to promote fair wages and working conditions, and businesses which were members got to display a blue eagle. Huge publicity campaigns urged all citizens to only buy government approved Blue Eagle goods.

However, the associations were universally allowed to fall under the control of the largest companies in each industry who instead, in the words of one the New Left historians, "raised prices, limited production, narrowed the leeway of small businesses, and failed to produce any general recovery."[47] The larger companies were thus able to enjoy government enforced monopoly profits. The NRA allowed the "erection, extension, and fortification of private monopolistic arrangements, particularly for groups that already possessed a fairly high degree of integration and monopoly power."[48] This extended to the agricultural sector as well, where the New Deal programs were dominated by, and thus supported, larger farming operations at the expense of smaller farmers, sharecroppers, tenant farmers, and farm laborers.[49] For example, when the larger farming operations received government payments to restrict the acreage they farmed, it was usually land used by tenants and sharecroppers that got taken out of production, while the large farming operations used their production allotments for their own land.[50]

Large companies and farming operations were not the only major business groups assisted by the New Deal. Emergency support for the major banks was rushed through Congress as soon as Roosevelt took office. One of the New Left historians of the 1960s described the action to support the major banks in 1933 in terms that may be eerily familiar to modern readers. "So great was the demand for action that House members, voting even without copies, passed it unanimously, and the Senate, despite objections by a few Progressives, approved it the same evening. 'The President,' remarked a cynical Congressman, 'drove the money-changers out of the Capitol on March 4th - and they were all back on the 9th.'"[51]

In 1935 the Supreme Court ruled the NRA unconstitutional in the case of Schechter Poultry Co. v. United States.[52] In this case, which we will come back to in a later chapter, the Supreme Court ruled that the national government's power under the "interstate commerce" clause of the Constitution (mentioned in Chapter 1) did not extend to a poultry producer which only operated in Brooklyn, New York. The NRA was a shambles by then anyway, so Roosevelt was not adverse to seeing it fall. However, he was concerned about the implications of the Supreme Court ruling for other aspects of his efforts to achieve what one historian describes as the Roosevelt "administration's program for state capitalism."[53] With most New Deal programs ineffectual and only a modest recovery since his election in 1932, Roosevelt knew it would be difficult to run on his record in the 1936 election. He therefore turned to a campaign of militant anti-business rhetoric, blaming "economic royalists" for the failure to achieve any significant recovery from the Depression. This approach succeeded spectacularly, with Roosevelt winning by a landslide and major Democratic gains in Congress as well.[54]

However, later historians found Roosevelt's 1936 anti-business campaign rhetoric largely illusory.[55] Although the NRA was dead, the Roosevelt administration continued to create and enforce monopoly cartels for any industry where the major companies requested them. One historian describes how "as Democratic party leader James Farley collected cash contributions from oil companies, Roosevelt overruled Interior Secretary Harold Ickes and established a compromise oil price control scheme. With its implementation, the greatest of major American industries achieved near complete price control for a generation."[56] Monopoly cartels run by the largest companies were also set up for coal and transportation.[57]

These schemes all served to hold prices and profits up at the expense of the consumer, and to suppress or eliminate smaller or new competitors. New agricultural programs based on soil conservation had the same results as the old programs, aiding large agricultural operations over the rural poor. In all cases the objective was to keep prices and profits up, not to increase production or employment.[58] As another historian summarizes, "most New Deal planning was in the nature of government-sponsored cartelization. It came at the behest of organized economic groups intent on strengthening their market positions through legal sanctions or government supports."[59]

At this point you are probably rebelling. This is not what I was taught in school about the New Deal. FDR was a great friend of the working man and opponent of Big Business, and the New Deal

28

promoted social welfare programs and workers' rights. However, yet again, as the historians dug past decades of pro-New Deal conventional wisdom, a rather different picture has emerged. Consider Social Security, the largest and most enduring of the New Deal social welfare programs. Surely this was a great victory for the common man over Big Business? Hardly. The fact is that Social Security was invented by Big Business. The proposal was put together not by New Deal Brain Trusters, but rather by a Rockefeller funded committee of the nation's largest corporations and passed with only some modifications to accommodate southern agribusiness.[60] Notice who pays for Social Security. The workers themselves through highly regressive payroll deductions which, for many lower-income workers, are larger than their income taxes. It is true that these payments are matched by employer contributions. However, large corporations who dominate their markets can pass these costs on to their customers, something which is much more difficult for smaller companies.[61]

Similarly, the Wagner Act, which supports labor's right to organize, was also promoted by the major corporations, who found it easier to deal with one industry-wide union dominated by a politically-connected professional leadership than the many smaller crafts unions which had often proven unmanageably democratic.[62] Roosevelt was actually uninterested in further expanding rights to labor organization, and only supported the Wagner Act at the last minute when it looked like it might pass Congress without him getting credit for it.[63] Even then, expanded collective bargaining rights did nothing for the large majority of workers who were in the service and agricultural sectors rather than industry.

The truth behind Social Security and the Wagner Act illustrates the most important secret of the New Deal. Major corporations were a major element of the New Deal -- it served them well. The top executives of the largest corporations shared social class and educational backgrounds with the New Dealers, and most especially with the patrician Roosevelt. It is true many business groups did oppose much of the New Deal. However, these were business groups who were not "in the know," smaller and regional businesses who did not have the class and educational connections to the Roosevelt administration enjoyed by the top corporate leadership.[64] They only had Roosevelt's virulent anti-business rhetoric to go by, and it frightened them.[65] But those major corporate and financial powers, especially in the well-connected financial and capital-intensive industries, supported Roosevelt politically, earning themselves praise for being "moderate" and "enlightened" all while successfully turning government action to their own uses.[66]

Of course, not everyone had to wait decades for scholars to ferret out these connections. There were eyewitnesses. After Roosevelt's landslide victory in 1936, many progressives were very enthused, led by the campaign rhetoric to believe that the New Deal was finally going to implement real social change. Progressive Governor Philip La Follette of Wisconsin, brother of the legendary Progressive leader Robert La Follette, organized a delegation of state governors to visit Roosevelt after the election to discuss the exciting new possibilities. La Follette left an account of the meeting in his autobiography:

> Roosevelt, having been elected by an enormous vote, did not feel beholden to any governor or congressmen. I stayed a moment after lunch to appeal personally to the President on behalf of those in distress.... the genial mask dropped as he said, "Phil, there have always been poor people; there always will be. Be practical!"

> If I had had doubts before, they disappeared in that moment. I knew then what I had only feared before: Roosevelt had no more real interest in the common man than a Wall Street broker. He was playing the same game as Big Business, only he sought, got and intended to keep *power*, rather than money.

La Follette concluded that he "would never again support [Roosevelt] politically; he was just not aiming at the ends that Bob and I had been taught from childhood were the objectives of progressive government." Instead La Follette turned his attention to working on the state level back in Wisconsin.[67]

The events which followed Roosevelt's reelection lend credibility to La Follette's judgment, for the next major thrust of the New Deal was an assault on the one institution which Roosevelt still did not control, the Supreme Court. As noted above, the Supreme Court had been finding many New Deal programs unconstitutional. In 1868 the fourteenth amendment to the Constitution had been ratified. With the admirable goal of assuring the rights of the slaves freed by the Civil War and the thirteenth amendment, it had included some very vague general language forbidding any State from denying "any person of life, liberty, or property, without due process of law; nor deny to any person within its jurisdiction the equal protection of the laws." The Supreme Court eventually neutered the real purpose of this amendment by upholding racial segregation in the notorious Plessy v. Ferguson decision.[68] However, it did find a use for the amendment when it determined in the 1880s that a corporation was a "person" entitled to "due process" and "equal protection."[69] It thereafter began to strike down efforts to regulate businesses, and was still doing so in the 1930s to Roosevelt's New Deal. (Even though the Court reversed itself on economic regulation, corporate personhood is still alive and well, such as in the 2010 *Citizens United* decision.[70])

Roosevelt was so frustrated by this that in 1937 he advanced a scheme to expand the number of Supreme Court justices so that he could name justices favorable to his desire to expand the role of government. This was too much Hamiltonianism even for his own party, and the effort failed. However, the Supreme Court began to shift its views. A New Deal law which the court had overturned a year earlier was approved by the Court when Justice Owen Roberts changed his vote to uphold it. Soon a number of justices retired, and the Roosevelt appointees who replaced them went on to interpret the Constitution to sanction regulation by the national government of all aspects of national life.

Although he ultimately prevailed in forcing the Supreme Court to conform to his views, in the short term the "court-packing" fight was a major political setback for Roosevelt. Then later in 1937 a slow economic recovery was aborted by a new "depression within the Depression." The stock market fell further than it had in 1929 and unemployment began to rise again. There were many possible causes for this new economic collapse, but among them were the across the board tax hike created by the new Social Security program, which drained spending power from the economy, and uncertainty created by Roosevelt's anti-business rhetoric.[71]

Roosevelt had to do something to respond to the new political and economic crises. His response was to blame monopolies for the downturn and to launch a massive antitrust campaign. The antitrust staff of the Justice Department was increased and put under a dynamic and aggressive leader named Thurman Arnold. In addition, a massive investigation was begun under the Temporary National Economic Commission (TNEC). However, as with earlier New Deal efforts, the antitrust campaign generated a great sound and fury but came to nothing. The administration would generally not allow serious antitrust action to go forward against any well-connected major corporation. The TNEC worked for several years and generated massive reports, but in the end nothing was done with them.[72]

Thus, the New Deal not only left the major corporations in place but, through government regulation, even strengthened their position toward smaller competitors. It is tempting to imagine big business and New Deal insiders sitting about smoking cigars, twirling their waxed mustachios and cackling about how they had put another one over on the little people. However, the New Deal and major corporate interests came together in a form of "state capitalism" due to much deeper influences, influences which continue to have tremendous importance..

The economic crisis of the 1930s was worldwide, and there was worldwide agreement that government economic planning was the solution. In Italy Benito Mussolini's government had been directing corporate activity for a decade, and the economic planning of the Soviet Union, now in its second decade, was widely admired.[73] New Deal Brain Trust member Rexford Tugwell had toured the Soviet Union and, while denouncing its repression of political liberties, wrote in 1934 that in the United States "poverty and suffering exist on a tremendous scale." Tugwell argued that we must give up our allegiance ideals like "individualism and competitive profit-seeking" and instead "mold our social and economic environment...to act in the public interest on a national scale.... For many years the technical task of devising plans for regulating our complex economic interests was too difficult...but today we know that...Russia has shown that planning is practicable."[74] Prominent liberal newspaperman Walter Lippman wrote that Roosevelt "may have no alternative but to assume dictatorial powers."[75]

In Germany the funny little man who had become chancellor at the same time Roosevelt was first elected, Herr Hitler, was also using government direction of the German business establishment to combat the Depression. Similar attitudes were found in France and Britain.[76] Particularly influential in the English-speaking world were the British Fabian socialists, who advocated national economic control by an elite specially trained government bureaucracy. The Fabian socialists counted among their numbers such august figures as Bertrand Russell, George Bernard Shaw, and H. G. Wells.[77] The Fabians' views jived nicely with Wilson's promotion of control by professional government bureaucrats. For aspiring national economic planners in the Roosevelt administration, it was much easier to direct economic activity through a few large corporations rather than many smaller companies, even if that meant reduced competition.[78]

As we have seen, the leaders of many of these large corporations in turn saw advantages in economic planning and deficit spending.[79] Also, since the top managements of the large corporations were more likely to share social class and educational backgrounds with the government administrators, personnel increasingly began to regularly move back and forth between the two realms.[80]

According to progressive historian Barton Bernstein, this system of interlocking and interchanging management of the national government and the major corporations "also heralded the way of the future -- of continued corporate dominance in a political structure" although some formerly outlying groups were allowed a subsidiary role. "Many liberals did not understand the dangers in the emerging organization of politics...of leaders not representing their constituencies, of bureaucracy diffusing responsibility, of officials serving their own interests,... of unrepresentative leadership and the many millions to be left beyond" the new order.[81]

Another famous progressive historian, William Appleman Williams, summed up the New Deal by observing that "from the outset the New Deal strengthened the convergence and coordination between the government and the large corporations. Whatever the rhetoric of liberalism, the substance of the political economy was a corporate state capitalism increasingly financed by the taxpayer and controlled by a bureaucratic and political elite drawn from the upper classes."[82]

During Roosevelt's second term unemployment remained astronomically high. The New Deal did not solve the Great Depression, and it has been argued that it prolonged it.[83] At a private meeting in May 1939 with Democratic members of the House Ways and Means Committee, Roosevelt's own Treasury Secretary, Henry Morgenthau, lamented that the government had "tried spending money. We are spending more than we have ever spent before and it does not work.... we have just as much unemployment as when we started...and an enormous debt to boot!"[84] However, the New Deal did leave a national government vastly expanded in scope and power, and ever more tied to the nation's major corporations.

In 1940 Roosevelt finally found a government program to solve unemployment – universal military conscription. In 1940 there were about 8 million unemployed. By 1943, 8.5 million men had been drafted and unemployment was minimal. The Second World War, however, did not mark the return of prosperity. Universal wage controls and rationing still kept most at a standard of living similar to that of the Depression 1930s.[85]

On the other hand, the war did cement the close relationship between big business and big government which was begun during the New Deal. The largest corporations dominated wartime production and their executives took over government economic operations.[86] The power of big business continued to grow ever stronger after the war.[87] In addition, as with Wilson in the First World War, police powers of the national government were expanded beyond economic activities and used to severely curtail civil liberties. The worse example of this was the mass internment of Americans of Japanese ancestry.

Fat Cats

Prosperity did return after the war. The Democratic Party was now indelibly the party of FDR. When they had a choice, they selected suave, well-educated Presidents like John F. Kennedy, Bill Clinton, and Barack Obama, men who fit the FDR image and who could operate comfortably in the post-New Deal nexus of national government and multinational corporations.[88] The "accidental" Presidents, Truman and Johnson, only broke the mold in style, not substance. The title of one of the New Left historian's books in the 1970s neatly summarizes the state of the post-New Deal party -- *"Fat Cats and Democrats: The role of the big rich in the party of the common man."*[89]
Unsurprisingly he concludes that "the Democrats are hardly the party of the common man." Policy decisions are made by a "power elite of

the big rich and their corporate hirelings, who work through an interlocking and overlapping maze" of organizations supplemented by masses of corporate lawyers working the regulatory agencies and lobbyists working the Congress. The Democratic Party is "little more than an unending series of broken promises" by "sweet-talking Democrats who are bought and paid for by the big rich."[90]

Of course, for the record, let us not leave out the Republicans. Although there was some pushback against certain aspects of this ever-expanding national regulatory state under Ronald Reagan, no one could deny that the national government expanded enormously in scope, expense, power, and ties to big corporate interests under George W. Bush.[91] No one could deny either that "inside-the-Beltway" Republicans are as much a part of the big business/big government complex as the Democrats.

Today the system is well understood. Lobbyists, lawyers, and politicians travel through a "revolving door." They pass from Congress or regulatory agencies, which make laws and regulations, to lucrative jobs at the corporations for whom the laws and regulations were made, or for law firms and lobbying firms in the service of those corporations or other special interest groups. Periodically they will leave and return to government "service" for a while to renew their influence and contacts. The fuel which makes this system run is campaign contributions. A law or regulation which gives a large corporation an advantage over its smaller competitors, a tax break, or a government subsidy can be worth many times the cost of the contributions.[92] Similarly, money spent lobbying for regulatory advantages, subsidies or tax breaks can yield returns far beyond any other "investment." In one case, $280 million in lobbying expenditures resulted in a tax break worth $88 billion![93] Of course, the average taxpayer or small business usually can not afford to spend $280 million for lobbying. This is strictly a game for the big players.

All of this depends on a massive, pervasive national government which goes far beyond anything envisioned even by the ambitious

Colonel Hamilton. Today we live in a wholly Hamiltonian state, a state which took almost a century and a half to overcome its Jeffersonian resistance, but which was finally fully realized in the first half of the 20th century under Woodrow Wilson and Franklin Roosevelt. It has aspects which many find attractive. The United States has had, until recently, a strong economy, and is militarily the most powerful nation in the world. A constantly expanding social safety net offers at least some protection to the most vulnerable, and extensive government regulation supposedly polices bad behavior by businesses.

On the other hand, our Hamiltonian country is also home of an ever-expanding national security state and almost constant foreign military aggression. It is dominated by global corporations which exercise massive influence on the national government, which despite its pervasive regulatory power consistently fails to attend to regular working Americans. And, of course, it is our Hamiltonian regulated and subsidized economy which has produced dangerously accelerating environmental degradation. We still live with the rhetoric that government activism is opposed to corporate interests. However, if we look into how Washington really works, we can readily see that Big Business has learned how to use Big Government to live very well under what Ralph Nader aptly calls "a government of big business, by big business, and for big business. In summary, *corporate socialism.*"[94]

So now we come to today. We have a President who has eloquently promised to change the way government works. Let us see how he is doing by looking at the signal achievement of his administration, health care reform. The Affordable Care Act was presented as a triumph over the health insurance industry which would halt its rapacious practices and provide excellent health insurance to numerous uninsured Americans. Here is an analysis of this picture by progressives who have been actively working on health care reform, supplemented by non-partisan sources:

- Jane Hamsher of the progressive website firedoglake.com has shown that the bill "is almost identical to the plan written by AHIP, the insurance company trade association in 2009. The original Senate Finance Committee bill was authored by a former Wellpoint vice president." The Congressional Budget Office estimates that 24 million will still be uninsured under the bill. That the main point of the Affordable Care Act was the care of insurance companies can be seen from the fact that "since Congress released the first of the health care bills...health care stocks have risen 28%."[95]

- After the Senate bill which was the basis for the final bill was passed, the *New York Times* reported under the heading "Corporate Glee" that the "insurance companies were probably among the merriest of industries last week. Because the legislation mandates that everyone buy insurance, those companies stand to gain 30 million new customers."[96]

- Progressive activist Dave Lindorff sees this mandatory insurance as further consolidating "the death grip that the insurance industry has over health care access and delivery in America....by mandating that everyone buy health insurance, on pain of being slapped with a heavy fine by the IRS." This measure will "hand the private insurance industry a huge captive customer population who will be stuck with high-cost, low-benefit insurance that will generate huge profits for the industry. The industry will be further enriched by nearly half a trillion dollars in subsidies needed to help low-income people or small businesses buy their mandated health insurance -- subsidies which will end up going directly to insurance companies, which will be offering in return wretched bare-bones plans that will only cover some 60% of actual medical costs."[97] Lindorff says that the bill should properly be referred to as the "Health Industry Enrichment Act."[98]

- Jane Hamsher's analysis also notes that the health care bill will not bring down health insurance premiums, "leaves out nearly every key cost control measure," has no mechanism to enforce the restrictions against dropping people when they get sick, "does not limit insurance company rate hikes" and, because they keep their anti-trust exemption, the health insurance companies are "free to raise rates without fear of competition in many areas of the country."[99]

The health insurance industry was not the only to benefit from the health care bill. The pharmaceutical industry also makes out very well. Importation of lower cost drugs is prohibited, Medicare and Medicaid are forbidden to negotiate volume discounts for prescription drugs, generic drugs can no longer be purchased with health savings accounts and certain classes of generic drugs are barred from sale altogether.[100] The pharmaceutical industry did agree to some discounts and rebates, but they are a tiny fraction of the revenues from prescription drug sales, especially considering all the ways that full-price prescription drugs are now mandatory.[101]

The hospitals made a token cost contribution in exchange for having all uninsured patients covered by Medicaid, and the physicians got a promise of a major increase in Medicare reimbursement, although that had to be left out of the health care bill to disguise its true cost and maintain the fiction that it was fully paid for.[102]

Oh yes, and the single payer option which was at the center of progressive efforts for health care reform? That lasted about as long as a snowball in a Chicago summer. In Lindorff's words, "I'm with Marcia Angell, editor of the New England Journal of Medicine. The Obama plan for health care "reform,"...[is a] devious disaster..... This whole effort was never about reform from the day last March when the new president called on Congress to begin deliberations on health care reform. It was about catering to the wishes of the big players in the Medical Industrial Complex -- the big pharmaceutical multinationals, the hospital companies, the physicians and, most of all, the insurance industry. People and their health care needs had little or nothing to do with this."[103] Even mainstream Democrats like columnist Howard Fineman describe the health care bill as an example of the political view that "big business deserves to make a lot of money (a lot of it from the government itself) in the name of doing some good for the citizens."[104]

How could this have happened? Consider the following:

- According to the Center for Public Integrity about "1,750 businesses hired about 4,500 lobbyists, total -- eight for each member of Congress -- and spent at least $1.2 billion to influence health care bills" and other "health reform" related issues.[105]

- In the 2008 presidential campaign, Barack Obama received 263% more campaign contributions from the health industry sector than John McCain and almost four times as many contributions from "lawyers/lobbyists."[106] The Obama campaign's contributions from the pharmaceutical industry were more than three times those to McCain.[107] Contributions to Obama from donors affiliated with the drug maker Pfizer were alone almost five times greater than those to McCain.[108]

- The leading Democrats in the House and Senate in charge of the health care bill, Charles Rangel and Max Baucus, were each the third highest recipients of health care industry campaign contributions in their respective houses of Congress.[109]

- Overall in the 2008 elections Democrats received twice the amount of campaign contributions from the health care industry as Republicans and almost four times as many contributions from the category "lawyers/lobbyists."[110]

Unfortunately, this appears to be a pattern, not an aberration. Consider the bank bailouts. They were initiated by George W. Bush. However, then Senator Obama voted for them, and not only continued the bailouts as President, but filled his economic team with Clinton administration veterans who were behind the financial deregulation which many believe contributed to the 2008 meltdown.[111] He made hundreds of billions of dollars available to preserve the major Wall Street banks even as over 300 local community banks were closed.[112] Under Obama, the three largest banks' share of the nation's bank deposits has gone from one-fifth to one-third, roughly a 60% increase.[113] Beyond the direct bailouts to the big Wall Street banks, the Obama administration encouraged the Federal Reserve to make trillions of virtually interest-free funds available to the big banks, and did nothing to stop them from returning to their trading in exotic financial instruments, which yielded huge profits and bonuses and which had facilitated the crash of 2008 in the first place.[114] That could not be related to the fact that Barack Obama received 70% more campaign contributions from the securities and investment industry than John McCain, including four times as many from Goldman Sachs, three times as many from JP Morgan Chase, and other multiples from other major Wall Street firms, could it?[115]

President Obama promulgated a policy against appointing lobbyists to his administration, and then issued dozens and dozens of waivers so that his administration has been as lobbyist-ridden as any.[116] Surely, this is unrelated to the fact noted above that Barack Obama received almost four times as many campaign contributions from the category "lawyers/lobbyists" as John McCain, right?

It is true that Barack Obama raised more money overall than John McCain. Indeed he raised so much money that he declined presidential campaign funds. Public financing of elections has been one of the central demands of progressives to counteract corporate influence. Yet Barack Obama was generally excused for turning against this fundamental progressive election reform measure because

41

supposedly his donations came from many small donors. The problem with this excuse is that it is not true. While Obama did receive more contributions from small donors, that is simply a function of having more donors overall. In the end Obama received over 60% of his campaign contributions from donors of more than $4600, which is not much different than John McCain's 65%.[117] And, as seen above, he received far larger donations than McCain from many corporate interests with issues before the government. (This continued in 2012, when Obama received almost twice as many contributions from lobbyists as did Mitt Romney.)

Of course, these are not the only campaign promises on which Barack Obama has proven flexible. As summarized by progressive writer Chris Hedges, Obama had promised to oppose "the FISA Reform Act that retroactively made legal the wiretapping and monitoring of millions of American citizens without warrant; instead he supported passage of the loathsome legislation. He told us he would withdraw American troops from Iraq, close the detention facility at Guantanamo, end torture, restore civil liberties such as habeus corpus and create new jobs. None of this happened" (and these are some of Hedges' milder comments about the supposed progressive hope for change).[118] Although many supported Obama because of his supposed opposition to the war in Iraq, on the broader policy level Boston University professor and former Army officer Andrew Bacevich writes that Barack Obama has "proffered his full-fledged allegiance to the Washington consensus" for "maintaining a global military presence" which delivers "profit, power, and privilege to" politicians, policy intellectuals, and defense contractors and their lobbyists, who are often "retired US military officers hired by weapons manufacturers or by consulting firms appropriately known as 'Beltway Bandits.'"[119]

Hedges is not the only progressive to see Barack Obama and his administration as a continuation of Washington business as usual, or worse. Roger Hodge has written a book about Obama's "betrayal of American liberalism." Hodge argues that Obama's "change-hope vision was always a mirage" from "a man with the character of a common politician, whose singular ambition in life was to attain power." To this end "Obama and his Clintonian advisors now embody the worst traits of both parties. As terrible as the [Obama] administration has been with regard to finance and health care, its record on torture, detention and executive authority is even worse. Obama has institutionalized the usurpations and abuses of the Bush regime..... Our constitutional system may never recover."[120] Veteran civil liberties activist Nat Hentoff believes that "Obama has little, if any, principles except to aggrandize and make himself more and more important.... This is a man who is causing us and will cause us a great deal of harm constitutionally and personally. I say personally because I am 84 years old, and this is the first administration that has scared me.... I can't think of a single area where Obama is not destructive."[121]

Today's Democratic Party proudly traces its institutional antecedents back to Thomas Jefferson's Republican Party. However, since Woodrow Wilson supplanted William Jennings Bryan at its head, it has betrayed its Jeffersonian heritage with the very Hamiltonian combination of Big Business and Big Government that our third President so vigorously opposed. One of the New Left historians who exposed the long roots of this combination back to the New Deal reflected that even then the "fatal circle was closed ... the national Democratic party was permanently committed: it was now a party of the comparatively advantaged" even though it still held itself out as the party of the "people" as opposed to the Republicans as the party of "big business." This perception "created illusions that ran very deep. Cultivated by the press, nourished by increasingly affluent business groups, and fiercely protected by two generations of (often handsomely rewarded) scholars, this view of the Democrats and the New Deal left ordinary Americans alternately confused, perplexed, alarmed, or disgusted, as they tried to puzzle out why the party...so often betrayed the ideals of the New Deal. Little did they realize that, in fact, the party was only living up to them."[122]

Chapter 3

A Progressive Case for a More Jeffersonian Government II: The Depositary of the Powers, or Politics as if People Mattered

The higher level must not absorb the functions of the lower one, on the assumption that, being higher, it will automatically be wiser and fulfill them more efficiently... The burden of proof lies always on those who want to deprive the lower level of its function, and therefore of its freedom and responsibility.... If the freedom and responsibility of the lower formations are carefully preserved ...the organization as a whole will be 'happier and more prosperous.'

E. F. Schumacher [1]

No, my friend, the way to have a good and safe government, is not to trust it all to one, but to divide it among the many.... What has destroyed the liberty and the rights of man in every government under the sun? The generalizing and concentrating all cares and powers into one body.... The secret [to liberty for man] will be found to be in the making himself the depositary of the powers respecting himself, and delegating only... so as to trust fewer and fewer powers in proportion as the trustees become more and more oligarchical.

Thomas Jefferson [2]

In 1973 a German-born British economist named E. F. Schumacher published a small book entitled *Small Is Beautiful: Economics as if People Mattered.* This book was enormously influential. It played a significant early role in raising consciousness about the environment, and also launched the resulting movement for sustainable technology.

However, Schumacher's concern was for humanity as well as humanity's environmental impact. He describes how he "was brought up on an interpretation of history" which began "with the family; then families got together and formed tribes; then a number of tribes formed a nation; then a number of nations formed a 'Union' or 'United States' of this or that; and that, finally, we could look forward to a single World Government."

However, he noticed a tendency which ran counter to this trend toward ever larger and more centralized government. This was that "large units tend to break up into small units" as evidenced by the ever increasing number of new nations in the world.[3] He also noted that these small units could be quite economically viable. For example, historically the German-speaking lands which did not unite with the German Empire in the late 19th century, Switzerland and Austria, did perfectly well even though the accepted wisdom was "that in order to be prosperous a country had to be big – the bigger the better."[4] Beyond that, he noted that "while many theoreticians -- who may not be too closely in touch with real life -- are still engaging in the idolatry of large size, with practical people in the actual world there is a tremendous longing and striving to profit, if at all possible, from the convenience, humanity, and manageability of smallness."[5] While there are appropriate uses for larger organizations, "today we suffer from an almost universal idolatry of giantism. It is therefore necessary to insist on the virtues of smallness."[6]

What are these "virtues of smallness"? They are the virtues of "democracy, freedom, human dignity, standard of living, self-realization, fulfillment...of people. But people can be themselves only in small comprehensible groups." This is not possible with a "political and organizational structure" based on the "giantism' which is "a left-over of nineteenth-century conditions and nineteenth-century thinking and...is totally incapable of solving any of the real problems of today." Thinking which cannot "grasp this is useless" and should be scrapped so that we can "start afresh."[7]

How do we achieve such a fresh start? First, we have to put off "experts." "The case for hope rests on the fact that ordinary people are often able to take a wider view, and a more 'humanistic' view, than is normally taken by experts." Unfortunately, "ordinary people...today tend to feel utterly powerless." However, they can be effective by supporting movements which "have already started" to combat modern giantism. Examples are local farming and the effort to create technologies which will work for locally based businesses.[8] It is achieved by preferentially favoring the smaller, more local level of organization rather than the larger, as per the quote at the beginning of this chapter. And it requires actively combating the "specific danger inherent in large-scale organization" which is "its natural bias and tendency to favor order at the expense of creative freedom" found in smaller-scale organizations.[9] Elsewhere Schumacher wrote that "huge bureaucracies never achieve anything. They just amble along; the problems don't become smaller, they become bigger and bigger. If we think we can solve things by monster size, we are just mistaken."[10]

In *Small Is Beautiful* Schumacher was primarily concerned with economic organization rather than political organization, although he was quite clear that the concepts applied to the political realm as well as the economic. However, his close friend, colleague and mentor, Leopold Kohr, did analyze the social and political aspects of their philosophy in a book published shortly after *Small Is Beautiful*. In *The Overdeveloped Nations: Diseconomies of Scale*, Kohr takes the widely accepted concept of "economies of scale" and, like Schumacher, turns it around and asks if something can get too big.[11] What is the optimum size for a government?

After extensive analysis, he concludes that the optimum size for a modern state is about 15 million people. "Beyond this point optimum size turns into critical size, with social difficulties now tending to increase faster than the human talent necessary to cope with them, so that further growth can be sustained only at the price of diminishing the services connected with" the critical social functions of ensuring "companionship, prosperity, security, and culture." This "not only begins to entail a distortion of functions, but an insensible change from individualistic to collectivist purposes," such as "social health, power, glory, conquest, empire, sputniks, or anything pleasing to their collectivist ego." Once collectivist purposes prevail there is no limit on the size of the state, "the larger is actually the best; the world state -- the pinnacle of human accomplishment." But then Kohr brings to bear the "small is beautiful" perspective. "Why the farmer in his cottage, the fisherman by the pond, the father playing with his child, the poet admiring nature, the worker enjoying his beer, should require it [the ever expanding state] in their pursuit of happiness is, however, another question."[12]

As states grow ever larger, their problems grow even faster until the only way "the overgrowing political complexes of our time could be spared disintegration under the impact of their increasing growth problems" is to reduce "the share of the citizen's production which could be retained by him to serve his own *summum bonum*, and instead making it available to government..... The new *summum bonum* was therefore no longer that of the citizen but of society as a whole, with the paradoxical result that, the more splendid the social apparatus...the poorer became the individual.... For states are like skyscrapers. The taller they become, the larger becomes the *social* space (occupied by lifts, stairs, etc.) necessary for keeping the structure serviced, and the smaller becomes the *personal* space available for individual purposes."[13] Eventually the functions of government "will increase at a faster rate than the growth of society. Then [they] will now increase also in number, turning previously private activities into spheres of public interest, [until] the requirements of modern monster societies will become such that governmental direction can no longer be restricted to mere *sections* of personal and economic life; it must be extended to every aspect of existence."[14]

To illustrate this "crescendo of claims on the citizen in post-optimum societies" Kohr casts John F. Kennedy's famous saying in a new light, rephrasing it to its real meaning of "ask not what your government can do for you, but what you can do for your government." Kohr asks why this should be so.[15] Why should the state have claim on the individual rather than the other way around? Such a statement would appear ludicrous if made by a leader of a smaller, optimum sized state. Why do we accept it from a bigger state?

The statistics about the growth of the United States government in the last hundred years cited in chapter 1 are certainly consistent with Kohr's hypothesis. From 1913 to 2009 the federal government's share of the nation's economy grew from less than 2% to over 28%.[16] By simple page count, from the 1920s to today the quantity of federal laws and regulations have increased by over 3000%, now equally 33 volumes and 80,700 pages respectively.[17] In the same time period the United States' population only grew threefold. The rates of growth of the federal budget and federal laws and regulations have been, respectively, five times and ten times the rate of population growth. In the 1970s Kohr identified the United States as "second only to China, the countries of the Soviet empire, and Great Britain in her advanced degree of socialization" despite "her capitalist heritage or individualist ideology."[18]

American Giantism

As he was campaigning for President in September 1912, Woodrow Wilson gave a speech in Scranton, Pennsylvania. This speech wonderfully encapsulates the rationale by which the United States has come to have a national government which seemed to Kohr (who, like Schumacher, had fled to Britain from Nazi Germany) to be as pervasive as the most socialistic of the major European countries. In it Wilson forthrightly puts to rest the ghost of Thomas Jefferson in the Democratic Party. Although "we are followers of Jefferson, there is one principle of Jefferson's which no longer can obtain in the practical politics of America. You know that it was Jefferson who said that the best government is that which does as little governing as possible.... But that time has passed. America is not now and cannot in the future be a place for unrestricted individual enterprise."[19] Instead the economy of 1912 was dominated by great companies like US Steel which employed thousands in Scranton and "the treatment of labor by the great corporations is not now what it was in Jefferson's time. Who in this great audience knows his employer? I mean among those who go down into the mines, or go into the mills and factories, and who never see...the president of the corporation.... This dealing of great bodies of men with other great bodies of men is a matter of public scrutiny and should be a matter of public regulation."[20]

In the two decades preceding Wilson's speech, the United States had undergone a rapid process of business consolidation. One historian has noted that "by 1904 one or two giant companies... controlled half the output or more in 78 different industries, from oil and steel and locomotives to biscuits and crackers."[21] These combinations are estimated to have controlled over 40% of the nation's industrial assets. Most were formed by mergers which eliminated thousands of smaller competitors. For example, in 1901 the American Can Company was formed from 120 smaller companies to hold a 75% market share.[22] Although the merger movement had peaked in 1904 after a stock market downturn and several successful antitrust prosecutions by Theodore Roosevelt's administration, the huge new corporations were perceived as dominating the nation.

Here is the essence of the argument for Big Government in America -- it is needed to counteract Big Business. In the one hundred years since the beginning of Woodrow Wilson's presidency, this has been the argument that expanded the share of the US economy consumed by the national government by 15 times, from less than 2% to almost 30%. This has been the argument that expanded the federal workforce at a rate which is a multiple of population growth. This has been the argument that expanded the federal laws from one volume to 33 volumes. This has been the argument for the creation of a national government which exceeds any possible human scale, a government which is most definitely neither small nor beautiful.

So is Wilson right and are Schumacher, Kohr, and Jefferson wrong? Let us examine more closely the core premise behind Wilson's argument for the abandonment of the Jeffersonian vision of small, efficient, and decentralized government. That our economy has many large corporations is indisputable. However, is Jeffersonian "individual enterprise" no longer relevant in our economy? Consider the following US government data:

- Small businesses employ over half of the nation's private work force and provide half of the nation's gross domestic product.[23]

- Specifically, small businesses employ 57% of all private sector employees, including 56% of all women and 67% of all Hispanic workers.[24]

- Since the 1990s, small businesses have created 60 to 80 percent of net new employment. In the 1990-1991 and 2001 recessions firms with fewer than 20 employees were the only ones with positive net job growth, while larger firms were shedding jobs.[25]

- Among the smallest businesses, the self-employed, women and minorities have increased their proportions in the last decade. The number of self-employed Hispanics has more than doubled since 2000. Overall, immigrant entrepreneurs constitute an increasing proportion of those who start their own business.[26]

- In Arizona, California, Florida, Colorado, Texas, Nevada, Idaho, Wyoming, Montana, and Utah around 10% of all employment is with firms less than three years-old.[27]

- Over 40% of all businesses that received at least 15 patents over a recent five-year period were small businesses. These small firms produced significantly more patents per employee than larger firms. Small businesses also often develop more emerging technologies than their larger counterparts.[28]

Even when one looks at larger businesses, a more complex picture emerges. In Wilson's day it seemed that these enormous new monoliths would control the nation's economy for the rest of time. However, today few of them remain. Of the original twelve companies on the Dow Jones Industrial Average, only General Electric is still in existence. Indeed, only half of the companies in the 2009 Dow Jones Industrial Average were on it in 1987. The rest have been added as declining older companies were removed and growing new companies took their place. Nearly 2,000 companies have appeared on the Fortune 500 list since its inception in 1955, which means that most (about 1,500 or 75%) are long gone.[29] They have been replaced by new companies many of which, such as Microsoft or Google, were themselves small businesses not so long ago.

So, what does this have to do with the national government's regulation of the economy? Simply put, everything. Big Government is justified as a response to Big Business. Therefore, federal regulations are written for Big Business. In the last chapter we saw how Big Business usually subverts this regulatory scheme. *However, even if we assume that federal regulations really do impose meaningful restrictions on Big Business, the result is that they impose the same burdens on small businesses as well.* While occasionally small businesses are exempt from some regulations, in general they are subject to the same regulations as corporations hundreds of times their size. Why does this matter? Because it imposes disproportionate burdens on smaller companies. Studies by the U. S. Small Business Administration have repeatedly shown that the cost of federal regulations is significantly higher per employee for small businesses than for larger corporations. Compliance costs for firms with less than 20 employees are 45% to 60% more per employee than for firms with more than 500 employees. Compliance with environmental regulations costs small firms more than four times per employee than for big companies.

In dollar terms, the total difference in compliance costs per employee between big and small businesses is almost $2,400.[30] If there are 20 employees, that's $48,000 more in expenses compared to a big company, and the equivalent of one full-time employee for each small business. And, because these companies are small, it also means that they are locally based, so that is a job lost to the local economy. (And let us not lose sight of the fact that compliance with federal regulations costs all American businesses over $1 trillion annually).[31]

However, that is only the beginning of the disadvantages that federal economic regulations impose on small, local businesses as compared to big corporations. In the last chapter we saw how, from the time that Woodrow Wilson began the modern American regulatory state, big companies used their control of the regulatory agencies to suppress smaller competitors. This continues to the present day. Washington-based investigative reporter Timothy Carney specializes in exposing cases such as these:

- Athletic shoemaker Nike garnered great publicity for its support of the recent Waxman-Markey cap-and-trade climate legislation, even though carbon emissions from its own production operations have steadily increased. However, that legislation does not bother Nike because it has always produced its shoes in Asia, and the legislation only covers the United States. On the other hand it will impose major costs on smaller competitors like New Balance, which follow the admittedly quaint practice of actually manufacturing their products in the United States.[32]

- After giant toy manufacturer Mattel suffered considerable bad publicity for importing toys from China with lead in their paint, it supported legislation regulating such practices. However, it also hired Washington lobbyists which included two former aides to a leading Democratic Senator behind the legislation and the federal commission which enforces it. These assured that there were special exemptions for companies which did in-house testing, exemptions which exactly conformed to in-house testing being done by only one toy company -- Mattel. With input from the Mattel lobbyists, the regulators also allowed testing only of samples, not every product. This increases testing costs for smaller and customized toy manufacturers in the United States compared to off-shore mass producers like Mattel. The net result is that smaller US-based competitors had vastly increased testing costs imposed on them, supposedly designed to combat Mattel's wrong-doing, but which actually effectively exempted Mattel. At the same time Mattel got a federal seal of approval at government expense on the very Chinese-made imports which were the source of the problem in the first place.[33]

- The agribusiness and chemicals giant Monsanto's head of lobbying was a former Clinton administration official who, during his Clinton years, had implemented food safety regulations which imposed costs on smaller producers which were five times the cost per pound of those for big agribusiness producers. At Monsanto he pushed legislation which would regulate genetically modified food. After President Obama brought him back into the Food and Drug Administration from Monsanto, he continued to press for the legislation. Why would Monsanto want genetically-modified food, which Monsanto claims is completely safe, to be subject to federal regulation? Could the fact that such regulations impose vast new costs on smaller biotechnology companies, costs which Monsanto has already absorbed, have anything to do with it? Again, it gives a federal seal of approval at government expense to products which many feel are inherently unsafe. Also, since the legislation covers farms as well as food factories, it discourages farmers from using their own private certification programs to accommodate consumers with preferences for non-Monsanto products such as organically grown food.[34]

Organic farming provides a good case study for how the process works. In 2002 the US Department of Agriculture promulgated regulations dictating what a farm had to do to advertise its products as "organic." The regulations require extensive paperwork and expensive certifications by private inspectors. While the regulations do prohibit use of pesticides and other artificial chemicals, exceptions are made for almost 40 synthetic chemicals. Worse, they say nothing about food being locally grown, the humane treatment of livestock, or the use of sustainable farming practices. Thus, food imported from China can carry the USDA "organic" label whereas food grown just outside of your town is prohibited from doing so by federal regulations.

As a further blow, farmers who use independent certification services to verify that they adhere to the traditional organic farming criteria, such as growing the food locally using sustainable practices while avoiding even the synthetic chemicals allowed by the USDA, are prohibited by the law from claiming adherence to more stringent standards than the government-approved organic producers. Unsurprisingly, these government-approved producers are the big agribusinesses which had major input in preparing these "one-size-fits-all" regulations. In the meantime, the traditional small farmers who founded the organic food movement are now prevented by law from identifying themselves as such, unless they incur major expenses based on the compliance abilities of big agribusiness corporations.[35]

One inspector with long experience observes that these unwavering standards "favor corporate producers who can dominate the marketplace by buying and selling organic products cheaply and en masse. Prohibited from advertising higher ecological performance, smaller 'best practice' farmers will be locked out of the competition. It's unconscionable, a power play by the government."[36] Regardless of what one thinks of organic food, the idea that a small farmer can manage the same paperwork and filing fee obligations as a multinational corporation illustrates the bias of federal regulations in favor of big business.

The examples go on *ad nauseam*. The Congress has enacted a massive law supposedly regulating Wall Street financial institutions which are "too big to fail." Although the Dodd-Frank bill imposes a few minor constraints on the biggest banks, it does nothing to prevent them from continuing to be "too big to fail." Nothing bars their ability to continue to access seemingly unlimited low interest money from the Federal Reserve. No one doubts that these institutions will continue to have a special preferred status that your local community bank will not, that they will be able to go to the government for more bailouts next time they get in trouble.[37] This perception gives these Wall Street financial institutions a significant competitive advantage over local banks. And all this is in legislation which is being promoted as a crackdown on Wall Street.[38] As with organic farming, this law is resulting in massive one-size-fits-all regulations which are being written for, and with the guidance of the lobbyists of, the Wall Street banks.[39] However, these complex regulations will also apply equally to your local community bank, burdening them with the same regulatory regime as banks hundreds of times their size. The resources used to meet these massive new regulatory burdens will, of course, then not be available for loans to local small businesses.[40]

But what does Washington care about small banks, small farmers, any small business? Small businesses do not deploy armies of lobbyists and unleash seas of campaign contributions. The Washington establishment's focus is on the Big Businesses which supply the campaign donations while they are in office, and the high-paying jobs after they leave government. The financial "reform" leaves everything in place, with only minor inconveniences to the big banks.[41] Other than the lawyers and consultants hired to implement the myriad and ineffectual new regulations, every other regular working person loses. In the words of veteran Wall Street reporter Charles Gasparino, Wall Street has figured out "how to maneuver around the bill's various edicts, thus influencing the Big Government it has manipulated" but "the average American worker or the men and women who strive to create businesses on their own to keep the American worker employed.... have no seat at the table when the goodies of Obamanomics are doled out.... Obamanomics...may bode well for the banks, and megacorporations like GE, but it has been an unmitigated disaster for the average American worker."[42]

Of course, this has no relation to the overwhelming edge in campaign contributions from Wall Street that President Obama enjoyed in the 2008 election, as discussed in the last chapter, or the fact that at least 70 former members of Congress and over 50 former senior Congressional aides are working as financial industry lobbyists.[43]

The favorable regulatory treatment that large corporations get, which gives them significant competitive advantages over small and local businesses, is not the only way that the federal government favors Big Business. Big Government also supports Big Business with massive direct aid and subsidies, which are not available to smaller businesses which do not have the big corporations' Washington connections and lobbying operations. In a book with the somewhat despairing name, *Small Is Beautiful, Big Is Subsidized*, the International Society for Ecology and Culture (ISEC) surveys the myriad ways in which Big Business receives preferential support from national governments:[44]

- Our long-distance transportation infrastructure is almost entirely financed by taxes. Without this vast network of government-funded highways, railroads, ports and airports, large corporations could not have transferred the United States' manufacturing base to Asia and still get their products back to the United States for sale to whatever American consumers had not lost their jobs to off-shoring. This free long distance transportation infrastructure is not nearly as essential to locally-based businesses.

- The entire telecommunications industry is based on the taxpayer-funded space and military programs. However, access to this space-based telecommunications infrastructure is almost exclusively reserved to big corporations.

56

- Vast amounts of tax-funded research is made available for free to the big corporations who are better positioned than small corporations to access it.

- The United States military protects access to oil and other valuable commodities at taxpayer expense, but it is major corporations which benefit from the exploitation of these resources.

- The United States government has expended enormous efforts to implement global free trade agreements such as GATT, NAFTA, and the WTO, which authorize international tribunals to override American laws within the United States without regard to our national sovereignty. These almost always benefit multinational corporations while siphoning business away from local companies.

The ISEC study also notes the use of national regulatory schemes by big businesses where "the cost of complying with mounting layers of regulations often becomes so onerous that it can represent a barrier to entry for all but the largest companies.... While many regulations are needed because of *large-scale* production, they burden *small* producers disproportionately." For example, many food safety regulations are needed because agribusinesses and major food manufacturers process their products at huge factory farms and plants, and then ship them long distances. This produces heightened risk of contamination and spoilage. These factors are much less of a risk with locally produced food, but small farmers and local producers are subject to the costs of complying with these "one-size-fits-all" regulations which are needed because of the large-scale producers.[45]

Organic farmer and advocate Joel Salatin begs liberal friends of local community-based organic food to understand that, while federal food safety regulation "may start sincerely, by the time it gets implemented on the ground and has been through the sieve of corporate dinners, it hurts the little guys and helps the big guys." He has written a 326 page book describing the hell he has personally gone through as an organic farmer in dealing with a bureaucratic and regulatory system set up to accommodate massive multinational agribusiness and food processing corporations.[46]

Ralph Nader has also exposed examples of subsidization of big business by big government. These include the grant to major telecommunications corporations under President Bill Clinton at *no charge* of rights to the digital broadcast spectrum, rights which may have worth as much as $70 billion. (This give-away was protested by Bob Dole and John McCain, but they were lone voices.) Another is the licensing to a major pharmaceutical company on a *royalty-free* basis of rights to an important anti-cancer drug developed in government laboratories at taxpayer expense, for which the pharmaceutical company then charged patients the same high prescription drug prices as with the drugs the company had developed itself.[47]

Local businesses are not the only victims of the national regulatory state. Federal regulations also impose tremendous burdens on state and local governments. The National Conference of State Legislatures maintains a database, which is currently 44 pages long, just listing the federal laws which require state and local governments to enforce federal rules, do federal paperwork, and spend their own taxpayer money to comply with federal requirements.[48] The National Conference estimates the cost of compliance with federal mandates in recent years at over $130 billion, none of it paid or reimbursed by the federal government.[49]

In addition to unfunded regulatory mandates, there are numerous cases where federal regulations preempt state regulations, many of which may be more protective. According to the National Conference the "volume of federal legislation that preempts state authority has increased and pressure is mounting for Congress and the White House to support federal usurpation of state authority in a variety of areas such as immigration reform, criminal law, tort reform, driver's license security, and the environment. Federal preemptions impose liabilities on states, they curtail state creativity and state authority, and they often seek uniformity when uniformity is not necessarily the most effective means for resolving issues."[50]

American Localism

Creativity or uniformity. That is the choice we must make. Do we continue with what Kohr called the "American example of increasing national unification and integration" leading to "slowly declining living standards"?[51] Some may protest that our living standards are not "slowly declining." However, even before the current recession average household income for most Americans has been stagnant for decades.[52] Those who consider themselves "liberals" blame this on an economy dominated by big corporations. Those who call themselves "conservatives" blame it on too much government sucking resources out of the economy through taxation.

As we have seen, the two are actually intertwined.[53] Economic factors blamed on Big Business produce a demand for Big Government, which in turn actually facilitates more Big Business, in turn generating more Big Government and so on in an ever-growing cycle. This cycle represses and homogenizes local communities. National and multinational corporations impose a one-size-fits-all economy and culture while their agents in the national government in Washington, D. C., use federal laws to impose a one-size-fits-all regulatory regime on every aspect of daily life to suit the needs of the corporations.

So far we have reviewed the economic aspects of the domination of our nation's life by the multinational corporation dominated national government in Washington. However, there are non-economic costs as well. In the first chapter we gave an example of the ever-expanding powers of the national security state. Intrusive federal regulations, including those relating to an absurdly complicated system of federal taxation, impose other significant constraints on the personal freedom of all Americans. And government measures of stagnant household income do not account for either the costs of environmental degradation or the erosion of family life from the economy and culture generated by this Big Business/Big Government complex. If environmental and social costs were added to the strain on modern families' flat economic positions, we really would show "slowly declining living standards," except that today the decline might not be happening so slowly.

So, what is the alternative? For Kohr, once we could "constitute nations of only sub-critical size, we would neither indulge in group violence nor the building up of firms and markets of such dimensions that they cannot be co-ordinated except by large-scale, complicated and therefore inefficient social planning.... The only method of reducing," these "'monsters of nationalism and mercantilism' whose existence has proved such an obstacle to healthy relationships between men and nations" is "by physical division or...dismantlement."[54] Kohr recognizes that it is impractical to attempt "the actual dismemberment of great powers. It is sufficient if it is applied in the less radical and more acceptable form of devolution and decentralization. In fact, in this mellower version it commands a considerable degree of emotional support even within the great powers themselves.... The carving out of social units of optimum size seems therefore to require hardly more than the strengthening of local autonomies by federalizing the structure of the increasingly centralized great powers along the ancient but still existing boundaries of their component historical regions."[55] Kohr notes that this should be particularly feasible in the United States, since it is already divided into local autonomous regions: the States. "The organizational success of the United States is due to the fact that she is actually a Disunited States."[56]

In *Small Is Still Beautiful*, a recent Schumacher biographer observes that "the progressive erosion of the rights of individual states and the consequent rise of the power of the federal government in Washington...is a classic example of the usurpation of democratic function by the larger institution to the detriment of the democratic functions of the smaller."[57] However, "the principle of small is beautiful must apply to politics as much as to economics. Whereas believers in the politics of scale call for centralization, politics as if people matter demands decentralization. Whereas believers in big is best look towards the evolution of ever larger supra-national political bodies to govern humanity, those who seek the human scale in human affairs call for devolution of power to smaller nations or regions within nations.... to the establishment, or re-establishment, of genuine small-scale local and regional self-government."[58]

Progressive, anti-globalization activist David Korten considers it "to be a near-universal truth that diversity is the foundation of developmental progress in complex systems, and uniformity is the foundation of stagnation and decay.... Our challenge is to create a locally rooted planetary system biased toward the small, the local, the cooperative, the resource-conserving, the long-term, and the needs of everyone." Strong local economies "encourage the rich, flourishing diversity of robust local cultures and generate the variety of experience and learning that is essential to the enrichment of the whole."[59] A key principle in achieving these ends is that "governance authority and responsibility are located in the smallest, most local system unit possible to maximize opportunity for direct, participatory democracy." Such communities are strongest when they have strong social capital, for which locally owned businesses are a key element.[60] However, as we have seen, the national regulatory state is distinctly hostile to small and local business.

At this point you may be having a disconnect. Devolution of power to local governments closer to the people and freeing small business from excessive regulation sounds good, but is that not what supporters of states' rights promote? This is completely contrary to the received wisdom that the federal government is the good guy who protects us from the states' rights people, who are reactionary bad guys. The radical, indeed very radical, historian William Appleman Williams had little patience for such conventional thinking:

61

Each of our states retains a significant sense of identity despite a century of domestic imperialism that has centralized and consolidated power in Washington in the name of efficiency, reform and mission. I have experienced that self-consciousness in Iowa, Texas, Wisconsin and Oregon and have observed it in many other states. That spirit, and the related anger about further encroachments upon self-determination, can be encouraged in the name of democratic Socialist communities just as Georgia and South Carolina built upon it to create a movement for southern independence. Radicals seem forever unable to understand that states' rights can be invoked and honored to create a Socialist community as well as to defend slavery..... That provides a sad but nonetheless revealing example of America's general lack of a true sense of history.[61]

Williams proposed "that we embark upon a sustained effort to organize a social movement dedicated to replacing the American empire with a federation of regional communities...to create alternate institutions that maintain constant pressure on the imperial bureaucracies.... The price of liberty is not so much vigilance as involvement. If you want to rest, vote for a dictator. The crucial arena for such citizen groups is and will remain the states. That is where social movements have to be built."[62]

Even if one's goal is not to build a "socialist community," simple arithmetic argues that States are more democratic than the national government. The 435 members of the national House of Representatives have on average more than 700,000 constituents in each of their districts. (At the beginning of the Republic there were about 30,000 constituents per congressman. Concern was so great that any higher number would result in ineffective representation that the first draft of the Bill of Rights included an amendment fixing the 30,000 constituent per district figure.) In contrast, the more than

7,000 state legislators represent on average just over 50,000 constituents each.[63]

Moreover, for the vast majority of Americans their state capitol is far easier to get to than Washington, D.C. It is undoubtedly true that state governments can be corrupt and influenced by corporate interests just like the national government. However, they are in general far more accessible to dedicated average citizens than the vast national government in Washington and its seemingly limitless bureaucracy. Polls consistently show that Americans trust their state and local governments more than the federal government. Further, in a recent poll 58% said that the federal government is interfering too much in state and local matters.[64]

In the end it is very fundamental. Is power going to be located close to the people or not? Jefferson maintained that "unless the mass retains sufficient control over those entrusted with the powers of their government, these will be perverted to their own oppression, and to the perpetuation of wealth and power in the individuals and families selected for the trust. Whether our Constitution has hit on the exact degree of control necessary is yet under experiment."[65] We have in place the skeleton of a once vigorous decentralized government -- the States. The more power is vested at the state and local level, and away from the national government, the greater the possibilities for real democratic government by the people rather than by multinational corporations and other powerful interests with the resources to manipulate the vast centralized government in Washington, D.C.

Is a decentralization and devolution of power back to the States and local communities from Washington possible? After all, Jefferson also observed that "the natural progress of things is for liberty to yield and government to gain ground."[66] To answer this question we must look at how we came to be subject to this highly centralized concentration of power in the national government, and ask if this is the "degree of control necessary" contemplated by the Constitution.

Chapter 4

Deconstruction and Reconstitution:
How the Constitution Got Unwritten, and How to Fix It

Our peculiar security is in the possession of a written Constitution.
Let us not make it a blank paper by construction.

Thomas Jefferson[1]

The issue of the allocation of power between the national and state governments was there at the beginning. It was one of the main subjects of contention at the Constitutional Convention, and was at the heart of the debates over ratification by the States. And almost as soon as the first administration of George Washington was in place, argument began again over the extent of the powers of this new government. The antagonists were our old friends Mr. Jefferson, serving as the first secretary of state, and Mr. Hamilton, the first secretary of the treasury. The dust-up over Hamilton's *Report on Manufactures*, which was voted down by Congress, was just a prelude to the main bout, the Bank of the United States.

At the end of 1790 Hamilton proposed that Congress charter a national bank which would serve the kind of central banking functions filled by the Bank of England. Hamilton, although a strong American nationalist, admired the British system of government, and was always trying to push the government of the United States as close to the British model as possible. As he had with the *Report on Manufactures*, Jefferson objected. He noted that the tenth amendment reserved all powers to the States which were not on the list of 17 specific powers delegated to the federal Congress in Section 8 of Article I of the Constitution. The tenth amendment states that "the powers not delegated to the United States by the Constitution, nor prohibited by it to the states, are reserved to the states respectively, or to the people." He warned that "to take a single step beyond the

64

boundaries thus specially drawn around the power of Congress, is to take possession of a boundless field of power, no longer susceptible of any definition."[2]

There were, however, two phrases at the beginning and end of Section 8 which were possibly problematic. At the beginning, Congress was authorized to collect taxes "to pay the Debts and provide for the common Defence and general Welfare of the United States." At the end of Section 8 the Congress is authorized "to make all Laws which shall be necessary and proper for carrying into Execution" its powers under the Constitution. Jefferson read these phrases narrowly. He saw the "general welfare" clause not as a separate grant of power "for any purpose they please," but rather just a description of the purpose for which taxes are to be raised. Jefferson defined the "necessary and proper" clause as empowering only those actions which were *essential* for the government to carry out its powers, not merely *convenient*.[3] Jefferson did not see that a bank was essential to carry out any of the specific listed powers.

Unsurprisingly, Hamilton saw matters differently. In his response to Jefferson, he defined "necessary" as "needful, requisite, incidental, useful, or conducive to" carry out the authorized powers of the national government.[4] For Hamilton, the reference to "general welfare" was a limitation only inasmuch as it required that the expenditures not be "for any merely or purely local" purpose. (Even Hamilton would have had a problem with our modern practice of "earmarks"!)[5] In this case Hamilton prevailed, and President Washington signed the bill creating the Bank of the United States.

The dispute continued for decades. After he became President, Jefferson's ally Madison allowed the Bank's charter to expire. However, Jefferson's devotion to strictly limited federal government powers showed some flexibility when he was presented with one of the greatest real estate deals of all time, the Louisiana Purchase. Madison also slipped, if not outright flip-flopped, when he needed to rebuild the nation's economy after the War of 1812, and decided that a national bank could be helpful. Madison did, however, continue to veto expenditures for roads, canals, and so forth because he felt they were not authorized by the Constitution.

In 1819 the Supreme Court under John Marshall used Hamilton's interpretation to decree that the Bank of the United States was constitutional in the case of McCulloch vs. Maryland.[6] (Marshall was always a strong Hamiltonian, even though he was Jefferson's cousin). In it Marshall acknowledges that he was bound by the original text and meaning of the Constitution, but noted that the tenth amendment omits the word "expressly" in referring to the limitation of powers, and the word "absolutely" does not appear before the "necessary and proper" phrase. Marshall justified these rather parsed readings broadening the national government's power by declaring that this was "a Constitution intended to endure for ages to come, and consequently to be adapted to the various crises of human affairs."[7]

Despite the *McCulloch* decision, Andrew Jackson vetoed the renewal of the Bank's charter, declaring that the President, as a branch of the government constitutionally co-equal with the Supreme Court, could make his own determinations as to constitutionality. The States continued to guard their constitutional prerogatives vigorously as well. Much of the conflict leading up to the Civil War came not only from the southern States' fear that the federal government would interfere with slavery, but with the northern States' outrage at the southerners' insistence on using federal power to pursue fugitive slaves into the North. The northern States saw this as violating their states' rights to exercise exclusive police power within their state boundaries.[8]

After the Civil War, a major new element was brought into play. In 1868 the fourteenth amendment to the Constitution was ratified. It is one of the longest amendments, covering many post-Civil War issues. However, at the end of its first section, it states that no State may "deprive any person of life, liberty, or property, without due process of law; nor deny to any person within its jurisdiction the equal protection of the laws." Initially the Supreme Court decreed that that part of the amendment was only intended to apply to the recently freed slaves.[9] However, in the 1880s the Supreme Court changed its mind and decided that corporations were persons within the meaning of the fourteenth amendment and entitled to its protection.[10] Thereafter the Supreme Court began regularly to rule that both state and federal laws restricting economic activity and corporations were unconstitutional.[11] Although one would think that "due process" had to do with assuring that correct legal *procedures* were followed, all kinds of material legal rights of real *substance* were read into the doctrine. As a result it became known by the rather self-contradictory name of "substantive due process."

Even as the Supreme Court went through these stages, all judges still paid obeisance to the principle that the original meaning of the Constitution was fixed, and controlled its judicial interpretation. Even Marshall's broadest statements were seen mainly as rhetorical flourishes, and he always endeavored to show that his decisions were consistent with the original understanding of the Constitution's meaning.[12] However, another view began to emerge in the late 1800s. Although its foremost advocate was Supreme Court Justice Oliver Wendell Holmes, one of this view's most complete presentations was by Woodrow Wilson.

This came in a book on the United States government published in 1908, just four years before his election as President.[13] Wilson begins by criticizing the structure of American constitutional government. Like Hamilton, Wilson was a great admirer of the British system of government, which with its unwritten constitution avoided the risk of becoming "too stiff a garment for the living thing" of government.[14] Unfortunately, creating the American Constitution in 1787 caused the United States government to be "fixed fast...at the stage of constitutional development which England was leaving for forms simpler and more advanced."[15] In this more advanced system power was centralized in Parliament in London, with no interference from the executive (the king) or the courts.

However, in 1787 the British thinkers and the American framers who agreed with them were more concerned with preserving the peoples' liberty from the government than making the branches of government display "quick cooperation [and] ready response to the commands of instinct or intelligence,...Darwinian in structure and in practice." Instead they "sought to balance executive, legislative, and judiciary off against one another by a series of checks and counterpoises" like a machine governed by Newtonian mechanics. "The makers of our federal Constitution followed this scheme...of the theory of checks and balances. The President is balanced off against the Congress, Congress against the President, and each against the courts." This was "meant to limit the operation of each part and allow to no single part of it a dominating force."[16]

Wilson disapproved of this constitutional system of checks and balances. "Government is not a machine, but a living thing.... It is accountable to Darwin, not to Newton.... No living thing can have its organs offset against each other as checks, and live."[17] Fortunately, in Wilson's view, even though the framers were "more interested in providing checks to government than in supplying it with energy," nonetheless "the powers of the federal government have grown, have even grown enormously since the creation of the government; and they have grown for the most part without amendment to the Constitution."[18] Rather the federal government is, "through its courts, in effect made the final judge of its own powers" by vesting in the courts "the statesmanship of control." The Supreme Court has read into the Constitution "an adaptation and an elaboration which would fill its framers of the simple days of 1787 with nothing less than amazement." Admittedly this process is "full of peril...but our courts have stood the test, chiefly because John Marshall presided over their processes during the formative period of our national life."[19]

This "progressive modification and transfer of functions as between the States and federal government" has been undertaken by the courts because the "process of formal amendment of the Constitution was made so difficult...that it has seldom been feasible to use it." Although this "has undoubtedly made the courts more liberal, not to say more lax, in their interpretation than they otherwise would have been," the courts "must sometimes venture upon decisions...which add to the number of things of which the national government must...attempt to control," but without seeking "to find in the phrases of the Constitution remedies for evils which the federal government was never intended to deal with." How is this balance to be achieved since we have dismissed the framers' creaky old Newtonian notion of constitutional checks and balances? Like the government bureaucrats in his article on public administration back in Chapter 2, who would assuredly listen to public opinion even though they were isolated from public accountability, Wilson simply asserts that such "statemanslike initiative" will come from "judges who act with conscience, mindful of their oaths of office..... That the federal courts should have such a conscience is essential to the integrity of our whole national action."[20] Then we can think "less of checks and balances and more of coordinated power,...[and] decrease the number and complexity of the things the voter is called upon to do."[21]

Unlike the wise Professor Wilson, the "framers of the simple days of 1787" naively thought that one could not always count on every judge to act with a conscience, and worse that different men's consciences could come to contradictory conclusions. According to James Madison "as long as the reason of man continues fallible, and he is at liberty to exercise it, different opinions will be formed.... It is vain to say that enlightened statesmen will be able to adjust these clashing interests .... Enlightened statesmen will not always be at the helm. Nor, in many cases, can such an adjustment...prevail over the immediate interest which one party may find in disregarding the rights of another or the good of the whole."[22] In one of his best known passages he observed that "if men were angels, no government would be necessary." However, "in framing a government which is to be administered by men over men, the great difficulty lies in this: you must first enable the government to control

69

the governed; and in the next place oblige it to control itself." To achieve this in the "distribution of the supreme powers of the State," the Constitution's "aim is to divide and arrange the several offices so that each may be a check on the other -- that the private interest of every individual may be a sentinel over the public rights."[23]

We leave to you the question of who was the more realistic judge of human beings and their institutions, the simple-minded eighteenth century Newtonian Mr. Madison or the sophisticated up-to-date Darwinian Professor Wilson. In either case, Wilson was right about one thing. The expansion of national government happens almost entirely by action of the Supreme Court rather than the process of formal amendment provided by the Constitution. And two decades after he wrote his book this expansion ran far beyond what even Professor Wilson might have imagined.[24]

Mr. Roberts nods his head

We must now briefly return to the events of the 1930s, a critical time we reviewed in chapter 2. The economic crisis of the early 1930s contributed to the election as President in 1932 of Franklin D. Roosevelt. Although he was a distant cousin of Theodore Roosevelt and had married Theodore's niece, Franklin had opted to become a Democrat, largely because at the time it looked like Theodore's sons would supply the Republican Party with all the Roosevelts it could absorb. Franklin had served as assistant secretary of the Navy under Wilson and later as Governor of New York, the same career path as his cousin Theodore. However, two events had thrown him off his ambition to follow Theodore's path to the White House. One was a crippling battle with polio in the 1920s, and the other was a failure to find a good war to fight in. Theodore had resigned his position as assistant secretary of the Navy to fight in the war against Spain in 1898, but the First World War did not present the same opportunity to Franklin. However, as one chronicler noted, Franklin was a "world removed from the peace orientation of William Jennings Bryan" and always "thirsted for a good fight."[25]

70

In chapter 2 we saw how the New Deal efforts of his first term focused on establishing government enforced industrial cartels to keep prices high and limit competition from smaller companies. When this failed to solve the Great Depression, Roosevelt turned to a strategy of virulent anti-business rhetoric for the 1936 campaign. (As we saw, this was just rhetoric, since Roosevelt continued to attend to corporate interests in his second term.) A primary focus of his ire was the United States Supreme Court.

During his first term, the Supreme Court had ruled a number of Roosevelt administration measures unconstitutional. Some of these were for violation of economic freedom under the "substantive due process" interpretation of the fourteenth amendment. However, there were other grounds. Schechter Poultry Corp. vs. United States found the National Industrial Recovery Act (which set up the government enforced cartels) unconstitutional because it delegated too much legislative power to the President.[26] In Carter vs. Carter Coal Co., the Court had ruled that another cartel scheme affecting mines operating within one State was not within the reach of federal power under the constitutional authority to "regulate commerce...among the several States."[27] In United States vs. Butler, taxes imposed on farmers to enforce federal limits on agricultural production were found to be unconstitutional infringements on matters reserved to the States under the tenth amendment.[28] However, the case which Roosevelt found most annoying was Humphrey's Executor vs. United States, which ruled that Roosevelt could not fire a Republican member of the Federal Trade Commission prior to the expiration of his term.[29]

Two leading journalists of the time wrote that "those close to him have said that he was most angered by the decision of the comparatively trivial *Humphrey* case." They reported that "perhaps the most immediate of the Court's offenses was its denial of satisfaction to the President's taste for power. The President regards great powers as his prerogative."[30] Those around him urged the

71

introduction of one or more constitutional amendments to authorize the federal government to carry out New Deal programs.[31] Even his most left-leaning advisors, like Rexford Tugwell, urged that he go the route of presenting constitutional amendments to the country. Tugwell told Roosevelt that constitutional amendment was the "forthright and permanent cure," and reported that other Roosevelt advisors "argued strongly for amendment. When it became clear he was turning toward another method, they were...disturbed and disappointed."[32]

Tugwell and other advisors of the Brain Trust were not alone in advocating constitutional amendment as the proper means to address the disagreements between the New Deal and the Supreme Court. The Democratic presidential candidates from both 1924 and 1928, John W. Davis and Al Smith, promoted constitutional amendment.[33] New Deal supporters throughout the country and across the breadth of the Roosevelt coalition enthusiastically called for this solution.[34]

In the 1936 elections, Roosevelt and the Democrats won a great landslide victory. Roosevelt received 61% of the popular vote and carried all but two States. Equally significant, the Democrats held lopsided majorities in both houses of Congress and dominated most of the state legislatures. Surely there were never in American history more propitious circumstances to present amendments to the Constitution to clearly and forthrightly expand the federal government's power, if that was what the country wanted.

However, Roosevelt went to another method. Right after the 1936 election, he proposed a law which would authorize the addition of a new member of the Supreme Court for every member who was over 70 years old. At the time six of the nine Supreme Court justices were at this age, so the law would have allowed Roosevelt to immediately name six new justices to the Court. Very disingenuously, Roosevelt claimed that the reason for the proposed law was just to help make the Court more efficient, rather than to change its ideological make-up to favor the New Deal programs. No one was fooled. Although technically the Constitution allowed the Congress to establish the number of justices on the Supreme Court, the proposal was seen as a simple power play to neuter the last branch of the government Roosevelt did not control. The move evoked opposition even among many Democratic Senators.[35]

Roosevelt dealt with the public's expectation that he was going to propose constitutional amendments by claiming that the amendment process would take too long. Here again he was being completely disingenuous. He enjoyed overwhelming majorities in Congress and most of the States. Only a few years earlier the constitutional amendment repealing Prohibition, a very controversial proposal at the time, had flown through the state ratification process in less than a year after passing Congress.[36] Why did Roosevelt not seek constitutional amendments? Eminent New Deal historian William Leuchtenburg suggests that it was partly because Roosevelt thought it would look like an admission that he was wrong about the constitutionality of the New Deal.[37] Another historian observed that Roosevelt's attitude toward the Constitution was that it was "to be worshiped from afar, but up close it was stumbling block to be circumvented, not a structure to be lived in and remodeled to suit."[38] In Rexford Tugwell's view, Roosevelt may have argued that an amendment "would take too long, but what he meant was that it would not give him what he wanted."[39] Harry Truman probably put it most succinctly when he blamed Roosevelt's insistence on pursuing what came to be called the "court-packing" plan on "that growing ego of his, which notably wasn't too minuscule to start with."[40]

The court-packing plan was eventually defeated, at enormous political cost to Roosevelt. However, he was later to claim that although he had lost the battle he had won the war. The Supreme Court which had found various New Deal measures to be unconstitutional was, like our current Court, a divided Court. A group of four justices, later labeled the "Four Horsemen," firmly believed that the expansion of federal power under the New Deal was unconstitutional. They were usually joined by a fifth justice, Owen Roberts (no relation to the current Chief Justice), and sometimes by the Chief Justice, Charles Evans Hughes.

Shortly after the court-packing law was proposed, the Supreme Court issued a decision upholding a state minimum wage law almost identical to one it had ruled unconstitutional less than a year before.[41] The reversal came because Justice Roberts switched his position. Although he had actually cast his vote before the court-packing plan was proposed, wags competed to claim credit for describing Roberts' vote as "the switch in time that saved nine." However, even at the time he made his switch, he was well aware of the political furor surrounding the Court's decisions.[42]

Later Roberts would acknowledge that the reasoning in this and subsequent decisions where he changed to vote for New Deal programs was "to reach a result never contemplated when the Constitution was adopted, was a subterfuge" carried out to avoid "even more radical changes" in the constitutional structure.[43] Although these decisions "reduce the states to administrative districts rather than coordinate sovereigns" where "not only local business activities but local social and community services may be taken from the states and...assumed by the federal government," the new judicial philosophy required that the Supreme Court yield to "the Congress concerning the necessity and reach of federal power."[44] He admitted that once this power "was conceded, it became difficult for the Court to limit the legislative exercise of that power, however sweeping."[45]

Even New Deal supporters were disturbed by Justice Roberts' change, although they were pleased by the outcome of the cases. "The Constitution ... is today what Justice Roberts says it is," wrote the *New York Times*.[46] Roosevelt advisor and future Supreme Court Justice Felix Frankfurter wrote to Justice Harlan Fiske Stone bemoaning "Roberts's somersault,...everything he now subscribes to he rejected ... What kind of respect for the institution can [now] be aroused in informed and able young minds?" Stone, who generally voted in favor of New Deal programs, replied that it was "a sad

74

chapter in our judicial history."[47] Roosevelt's own Attorney General observed that due to a "change of a judicial mind...the Constitution on Monday, March 29, 1937 does not mean the same thing it meant on Monday, June 1, 1936" and one Democratic Congressman concluded that "Owen Roberts, one single human being, had amended the Constitution of the United States simply by nodding his head instead of shaking it."[48]

The Leviathan State

With the change of one anxious judicial mind, what has been called a "second constitutional revolution" began (the first one being the ratification of the original Constitution in the late 1780s). By the end of his presidency Roosevelt was able to name eight Supreme Court justices. They were to overrule 32 prior Supreme Court decisions, including all restrictions on the expansion of the power of the national government. With a couple of recent minor exceptions, the Supreme Court since then has approved every intrusion of federal power into the rights and liberties of the States and individual Americans. In the words of William Leuchtenburg, "in 1937 the Supreme Court began a revolution in jurisprudence" resulting in "a vast expansion of the power of government in American life" and "legitimated the arrival of the Leviathan State."[49]

In chapter 6 we will begin reviewing specifically how the Supreme Court tore down the constitutional protections against the Leviathan State, and propose language for constitutional amendments to devolve power away from the national government back to the States and the people, as contemplated in the original framework of the Constitution. However, we must first understand why this occurred, why the Supreme Court has been so willing "to reach a result never contemplated when the Constitution was adopted,...a subterfuge" to legitimize the creation of the Leviathan State.

As we saw, there rose in the early twentieth century among intellectuals like Woodrow Wilson a movement to treat the

Constitution as an "organic" document which should "evolve" as times changed. The term "living Constitution" is used. This is wonderfully appealing. After all, who wants a "dead" Constitution? However, let's look behind the rhetoric and see what this really means. No one questions that there may need to be adjustments to the Constitution over time due to changes in society and experience in living with the Constitution. Madison anticipated that there would be "useful alterations...suggested by experience" to the Constitution.[50] However, "in case of experienced inadequacy of these provisions [of the Constitution], an ulterior resort is provided in amendments attainable by an intervention of the States, which may better adapt the Constitution for the purposes of its creation."[51] Neither the Constitution's proponents nor its opponents thought that judges could or should change the meaning of any of its provisions.[52]

In establishing that the Supreme Court could declare laws of Congress unconstitutional in *Marbury*, even John Marshall grounded his argument on the idea that the Constitution's "principles...are deemed fundamental,...supreme, and...permanent." Under the Constitution governmental powers "are defined and limited; and that those limits may not be mistaken or forgotten, the constitution is written." If the legislature "may alter the constitution by an ordinary act...then written constitutions are absurd attempts, on the part of the people, to limit a power in its own nature illimitable." Allowing unlimited governmental power "reduces to nothing what we have deemed the greatest improvement on political institutions -- a written constitution."[53] Later "living Constitution" theorists would cite some of Marshall's broader language, but he always strenuously grounded all of his decisions in the permanent written text of the Constitution.[54]

What Marshall said the Congress could not do, Jefferson feared that the courts would do. This is what he meant by the quote at the beginning of this chapter, "our peculiar security is in the possession of a written Constitution. Let us not make it a blank paper by construction."[55] Both he and Marshall believed that a written

Constitution should fix the government's powers so that it could not weasel its way to greater powers through the kind of gradual, evolutionary expansion possible with the custom-based, unwritten British system.

However, Jefferson knew that in construing the Constitution loosely judges could subvert the protection of its fixed written words by slowly shifting their meaning. He foresaw that they could use the pretense of constructing and elaborating the meaning of the Constitutional language to eventually change its meaning entirely by, as Justice Roberts so bluntly put it, "subterfuge." "Living Constitution" advocates are not usually so blunt, but argue that modification of the Constitution is necessary to adjust to changing social circumstances. While that may sound reasonable in the abstract, the rub comes with the actual application – *who* is doing the modifying? The answer of the "living Constitution" advocates, as we have seen, is a majority of the Supreme Court. So, the nub of the issue is this:

When did the American people authorize five Supreme Court justices to amend their, that is the people's, Constitution?

The answer is, *never.*

The Constitution begins by stating that it was created by "We, the people." It has an amendment procedure which calls for action by super-majorities of the Congress and the States. It is absurd that five unelected judges, serving life terms and accountable to no one, should be able to do what the Constitution requires thousands of members of Congress and state legislatures elected by and answerable to the people to do. As Lincoln warned in his first inaugural address, if "vital questions affecting the whole people [are] to be irrevocably fixed by decisions of the Supreme Court,...the people will have ceased to be their own rulers."[56]

The ridiculous results of such a system were well described by none other than Franklin Roosevelt's assistant Attorney General when testifying before Congress in favor of the court-packing bill. Robert H. Jackson (a future Supreme Court justice and the chief prosecutor at the Nuremberg trials after the Second World War) told Congress that when "the decision of crucial constitutional issues may turn on the death or illness of a single Justice, it would seem that our constitutional progress is governed by a blind fate instead of human reason.... A state of law which depends on the continuance of a single life or upon the assumption that no Justice will change his mind is not a satisfactory basis" for the government (or any other party) to act.[57]

Many who consider themselves progressive in their politics may approve of the expansion in the power and reach of the national government since the 1930s. However, consider the class implications of the "living Constitution" philosophy. Most Americans are uncomfortable talking about social class in the United States. However, progressives recognize the powerful role that class structure plays in our society.[58] As two progressive sociologists have recently written classism, that is discrimination on the basis of social class, "is embedded, or institutionalized, in the routine practices and policies of organizations dominated by privileged class members, such as corporations, government, the mass media, public schools, the criminal justice system, and universities," including the elite law schools and law firms. "It leads to prejudice toward, stereotyping of, and discrimination against members of the non-privileged class." The keepers of this system "actively screen out or marginalize working-class-based values [and] norms."[59] Occasional "rare successes of working-class children within privileged-class-controlled organizations" disguise "the new class society" of "dominant power networks that span the economic, political, and cultural arenas."[60]

Another prominent progressive sociologist has described the Supreme Court as "the most elitist branch of government. Its nine members are not elected and they serve life terms."[61] Yet, the

Supreme Court justices "possess ultimate authority over all the other institutions of government." It "has the authority to void the acts of popularly elected Presidents and Congresses. There is no appeal from their decision about what is the 'supreme law of the land,' except perhaps to undertake the difficult task of amending the Constitution itself. Only the good judgment of the Justices...limits their power."[62]

Elite, class-based control of the top of our legal system is well-illustrated by the current Supreme Court, which even the *New York Times* describes as "heavily tilted toward the Ivy League, the East Coast and work in government and the academy." The *Times* article notes that the background of President Obama's most recent nominee to the Court at the time of this writing was as isolated as the rest of the current justices, which "may tend to limit the justices' collective outlook and cut them off from the real world concerns of ordinary people."[63] With the appointment to the Supreme Court of former Harvard Law School dean Elena Kagan by Harvard Law School alumnus Barack Obama, all of the Supreme Court justices will be products of either Harvard or Yale law schools.[64]

However, the elite class control of the Supreme Court goes much deeper than just the justices themselves, who in the past have had more diverse backgrounds than they do today. To get a case before the Supreme Court requires extensive resources, for the case must first wend its way up through lower courts, a process which takes years and substantial budgets for lawyers. And, unlike a campaign for a constitutional amendment, there is no place for popular (that is, by the people) grassroots support and enthusiasm for a position being advocated before the Supreme Court.

If a case makes it through the gauntlet of the lower courts, to some extent its fate in the Supreme Court then depends on the work of the Supreme Court justices' law clerks.[65] These are generally top graduates of the most elite law schools. Their Supreme Court clerkships almost guarantee their entry into America's ruling elites in the corporate, government and academic realms. They have been accused of slanting their work to influence the justices.[66]

Even if these clerks do not control the justices' decisions on the cases, they almost always write their opinions. These opinions are dense, obscure and abstract, like the law review articles the clerks worked on in law school.[67] This impenetrable style of scholarship was created by the professors at the elite law schools, who enjoy tremendous influence in shaping the work of the Supreme Court, both through their training of the clerks and their domination of the intellectual environment in which the Supreme Court works. Unsurprisingly, the strongest advocates of the "living Constitution" philosophy are to be found among the law school professorate. This idea that the Constitution is a fungible document to be molded, as Jefferson put it, like wax by judicial fiat, gives this elite class of intellectuals enormous prestige and power, power even to change the meaning of the written Constitution as construed by the unelected, democratically unaccountable judges they have trained.[68]

Franklin Roosevelt famously described the Constitution as "a layman's document, not a lawyer's contract."[69] Of course, in saying this he was displaying his usual disingenuousness, for he was more than anyone responsible for giving control over the Constitution to a legal elite which would turn the plain meaning of its provisions upside down and inside out, and make understanding its interpretation by the Supreme Court into an exercise in academic intellectual convolutions deconstructing long, murky, scholastic opinions.[70]

Those who consider themselves "conservatives" have been complaining for decades about activist judges twisting the Constitution's meaning. To those who consider themselves "liberal," progressive historian and Roosevelt biographer James MacGregor Burns warns that although the "idea of the Court as friend to the weak and powerless lingers,...for much of its history the Supreme Court has more often been indifferent to the needs and wants of the great majority of Americans."[71] From the Civil War through the

1930s, the Supreme Court consistently decided in favor of business interests using substantive due process. Progressive public interest attorney Jamin Raskin also maintains that the Supreme Court "has been a force of ferocious political reaction for most of its existence," and argues that that characterizes the current Supreme Court as well.[72]

Under the "living Constitution" philosophy, it only takes the replacement of one justice, or a single justice simply changing his or her mind, to change the Constitution. Whether one agrees or disagrees with the outcomes of particular Supreme Court cases construing the Constitution differently than its original meaning, there always remains this global question: how would the American people respond if they were ever asked this proposition?

It is proposed that an unelected committee of five elite lawyers have the power to amend the Constitution any time that, in their sole opinion, they feel it needs to be updated.

First Principles, Timely Renewed

Algernon Sidney was an English writer, soldier, and anti-monarchical activist who was executed under Charles II in 1683. He was greatly admired by the American founders. In a manuscript on government that he was writing at the time of his execution he declared that "all human constitutions are subject to corruption, and must perish, unless they are timely renewed, and reduced to their first principles."[73] The balance of this book will propose that the American people take back their Constitution through the amendment process provided by the Constitution itself. The goal will be to "renew" the Constitution's original "first" principles by rephrasing important sections of the Constitution to reconstitute what they meant before the original language was distorted by the Supreme Court.

This project does not to pretend that we are back in the world of 1787. Rather the proposed amendments will seek to retain the

Constitution's original underlying principles while restating them in a way that works in our modern world. This will leave out many issues which both "conservatives" and "liberals" may feel should be addressed constitutionally. However, in chapter 5 an amendment to the amending process itself will be suggested to make it more feasible, while preserving the original concept of requiring super-majorities to change the Constitution. In this way the great constitutional issues of our time can be decided the way the framers intended. This is by amendments debated by the people, and enacted by super-majorities of legislators elected by and answerable to the people at both the state and national levels, not by one-vote majorities of the Supreme Court.

Many have argued that the original meaning of the words of the Constitution should control its interpretation.[74] Obviously this view has been vigorously challenged by adherents of the "living Constitution" philosophy.[75] To an extent this debate is beside the point here, since it centers on arguments aimed at influencing the Supreme Court's adjudication of constitutional issues. However, it is somewhat relevant to this book's project of amendment, for it does argue that the original meaning of the Constitution's language is worth restoring. There are several reasons why it is worth going back to "first principles" and reconstituting the original Constitution.

First, chapters 2 and 3 showed that we need desperately to decentralize our government and devolve power back toward the people in the States. A decentralized government with most power lodged at local levels close to the people, and only limited powers vested in the national government at Washington, D.C., was the original arrangement under the Constitution. It is simpler to just re-affirm that original distribution of power inherent in the Constitution rather than try to invent new methods of decentralizing the government and re-empowering the people at the local level.

Second, the Constitution should be a document understandable by the people, not just lawyers. The Constitution was a model of clarity until modern law professors got hold of it through the Supreme Court's submission to the "living Constitution" concept. The proposals that follow attempt to restore the Constitution as a document whose meaning can be plainly understood without a law degree.

Third, the Constitution was intended to control and delimit government power. As both Jefferson and Marshall argued, the fact that it is written is fundamental to this function. Words plainly understood bind. However, this great power is lost if we let the words loose from their original meanings by letting judges interpret them differently, or worse, ignore them or turn their meanings contrary to the original senses of the words. The proposed amendments in the following chapters attempt to frame the restated constitutional provisions tightly enough that law professors and judges can not twist them as they have the original language of the Constitution. The hope is that clear, precise language will restore the barriers against the unlimited power of the national government which were in the original constitutional scheme, but which have been breached and broken down in the last seven decades by federal politicians and judges.

Fourth, the framers intended that the words of the Constitution should be permanently tied to their original meanings.[76] Madison wrote that "the legitimate meaning of the Instrument must be derived from the text itself; or if a key is to be sought elsewhere...in the sense attached to it by the people in their respective [ratifying] State Conventions where it received all the Authority it possesses."[77] It is only by "resorting to the sense in which the Constitution was accepted and ratified by the nation" that there can be any "security for a consistent and stable [and]...faithful exercise of its powers." The meanings of the words must be fixed as of the time they were adopted, otherwise "the shape and attributes of the Government" itself would be subject to the "changeable meanings of the words composing it." Even in his time he feared "that the language of our Constitution is already undergoing interpretations unknown to its

83

founders" which were leading to "a destruction of the States, by transferring their powers into the government of the Union."[78]

The following chapters are by no means comprehensive arguments for the proposed amendments. Each subject can be, and has been, covered by entire books. The chapters can only outline the main arguments so that space can be also devoted to presenting and discussing the specific language of the proposed amendments.

Chapter 5 will first address the high hurdles which currently make the amendment process so difficult. Our Constitution was the first national document of its kind. Subsequent constitutions in both the American states and other countries have recognized that the amendment process can not be too difficult or else there will be either revolution or amendment by subterfuge, as has happened with our Constitution. Many studies have concluded that the United States Constitution is the most difficult constitution in the world to amend.[79] A reform of Article V is proposed making the amendment process more accessible, particularly by re-invigorating the States' ability to initiate amendments and ending Congress' effective monopoly on that critical function. Restoring the States' ability to initiate amendments is essential to restore the original balance between the state and national governments.

Chapter 6 will present a revision of Section 8 of Article I of the Constitution which will endeavor to finally reverse that endless transfer of power from the States and people to the national government. It will instead move power away from the Washington bureaucracy, and the politics dominated by the bureaucracy's own self-perpetuation and the corporate interests which control it, back toward the people in their States. It will also propose additions to the tenth amendment to provide means of enforcing that decentralization of power.

Chapter 7 will seek to redress one of the most significant modern distortions within the federal government, in which the presidency has usurped powers the Constitution intended to be vested in Congress to decide whether the nation goes to war. This proposal will also seek to restore congressional accountability for the massively expensive foreign military commitments which the national government has undertaken beginning with the Franklin Roosevelt presidency.

Chapter 8 will attend to one of the worst perversions of constitutional language by the Supreme Court. This is the imposition on the first amendment's Establishment Clause of the "wall of separation" metaphor, making it a tool to drive faith out of our national public life rather than to protect faith as originally intended.

Chapter 9 will deal with the vaguest language in the Constitution, the language most extensively abused by the courts to insert judges' own personal views into the Constitution. This is the first section of the fourteenth amendment. The proposal will replace it with straight-forward language confirming its original purpose of barring government discrimination on the basis of race. This will also raise one of the most important Supreme Court decisions in our history, Brown vs. Board of Education, to constitutional status. In light of more recent changes in our society, the proposal will also encompass discrimination based on ethnic origins and sex with appropriate accommodations for widely accepted social mores, such as privacy.

Chapter 10 will suggest clarifications for the most disputed language in the Constitution, the second amendment, by again appealing to how it would have been originally understood.

Chapter 11 will end with three proposals which go beyond the original constitutional framework, but which will address the remoteness of our national government from the American people. The first proposal will seek to end the much-abused practice of gerrymandering, which immunizes incumbent members of the House of Representatives from political accountability and breaks up their ties to local communities as they really exist. The second proposal will limit the terms of members of Congress in order to break up the Leviathan State which entrenches politicians in a permanent government answering to corporate interests rather than the electorate. The third proposal will attempt to reduce the arrogance of the federal judiciary by replacing life terms with mandatory retirement as well as fixed terms for justices of the Supreme Court.

Chapter 12 will suggest a new way of looking at why the American people are so frustrated with their national government in Washington. It will also propose an amendment to implement rules of interpretation which will bar judges from imposing their own views on the plain meaning of the constitutional text, and prevent them from imposing foreign laws on the United States. Finally, we will explore the first steps we can undertake to reverse the judicial constructions which have made our Constitution a blank paper.

However, how do we enact these reforms since the current constitutional amendment process is moribund? It has been more than 40 years since the last regular amendment to the Constitution was enacted (the 26th in 1971 slighting lowering the voting age to 18) and almost 100 years since an amendment with major impact (the 19th in 1920 giving all women the vote). Further, even if these reforms are enacted how do we prevent elitist lawyers trained in the "living Constitution" philosophy from using that approach to again make the Constitution into a fungible tool for imposing their social and political views on the rest of the nation? Can we stop their inevitable efforts to figure out new ways to mold our Constitution like wax, to use Jefferson's memorable phrase? The ultimate protection of the people's rights must be the people themselves. And the American people's ultimate power to protect themselves from the Washington elites is their ability to amend the Constitution to correct its abuse by the elites. The next chapter will propose how we can better facilitate that ultimate power and right of the American people, and in the process take back and restore our Constitution.

Chapter 5

Authentic Alterations:
Restoring the People's Voice

> I wish the Constitution which is offered had been made
> more perfect, but ... as a constitutional door is opened
> for amendment hereafter, the adoption of it under the
> present circumstances of the Union, is on my opinion
> desirable.
>
> *George Washington (to Patrick Henry)*[1]

> The basis of our political systems is the right of the
> people to make and to alter their Constitutions of
> Government. But the Constitution which at any time
> exists, 'till changed by an explicit and authentic act of the
> whole People, is sacredly obligatory upon all.
>
> *George Washington (Farewell Address)*[2]

During the Senate proceedings on the nomination of Elena Kagan to
be a justice of the Supreme Court, great efforts were devoted to
trying to ferret out her legal philosophies. Progressive writer Ezra
Klein explained why it was critical that, in Ms. Kagan's own words,
she "reveal what kind of Justice she would make, by disclosing her
views on important legal issues.... We're talking about a lifetime
appointment to a body with vast power and almost unlimited
jurisdiction." Klein noted that the Obama While House was "walking
that view back" and urging Ms. Kagan "to answer questions carefully."
She clearly followed this advice during the hearings. Klein feared
that failure to discover Ms. Kagan's real "views on important legal
issues" will run the risk of repeating the mistakes made in vetting the
nomination of now Chief Justice John G. Roberts, which failed to
avert what Klein considers to be dangerous conservative judicial
activism, such as the Supreme Court's "stunning rejection of limits on

87

corporate spending in the Citizens United case [which] was a wake-up call to the broad authority the court can exercise if it so chooses."[3]

The decisions of the Rehnquist and Roberts courts are showing progressives what conservatives have known since 1937 (and what progressives knew before 1937) -- that the Supreme Court is an undemocratic body which exercises too much control over fundamental constitutional issues in our country.[4] The framers tried to assure in the Constitution that every branch of the government checked and balanced every other branch. Theoretically, the executive and legislative branches check the judiciary by their powers of appointment and confirmation. However, that was before the Supreme Court gave itself the authority to be the final arbiter of the Constitution's meaning. Further, the framers would have been horrified to learn that, under the "living Constitution" philosophy, the Supreme Court has empowered itself to redefine and effectively alter the original meaning of our foundational document.

Frustration with the Court has led one progressive writer to demand that the elected branches of the national government defy the Supreme Court's assumption of sole authority to control the Constitution.[5] Other progressives suggest that the Constitution can be amended by a majority vote of the general population without regard to the Constitution's own procedures.[6] On the other side, some conservatives are reviving the concept of state nullification of federal laws.[7]

Americans of all political views want to know if there is any way to again assert control of a government which is supposed to be theirs, but which seems to attend only to the agendas of the elites. A survey by progressive sociologist Thomas Dye found that 77% of presidential staff and 81% of senior administration officials did *not* think that the American people knew enough to form wise opinions about important issues. In another survey he found that half of policy issues supported by over 60% of the general public were not current policy nor was any effort being made to implement them.[8]

88

Happily the Constitution provides a way to check the Supreme Court's ongoing misinterpretation of the Constitution. This is the right to amend. Of course, originally the framers did not foresee the extent to which the Supreme Court would arrogate to itself the right to change the Constitution; in Jefferson's words, to make of it a blank paper through construction. As Robert Jackson noted, that the fundamental meaning of the Constitution should hang on the health or shifting views of a single justice simply turns our Constitution into a lottery. In the *Federalist* Madison anticipated "that useful alterations will be suggested by experience, could not but be foreseen. It was requisite, therefore, that a mode of introducing them should be provided."[9] As we have seen in previous chapters, the founders thought amendment was the only proper method to change the Constitution. Although they did not foresee that the amendment process would be needed to check an imperial Supreme Court, its availability for that desperately needed purpose shows the amazing resiliency of their careful work. It is as though, like any good system, it had built-in redundancy or back-up.

Unhappily, that back-up system has been too lugubrious for this task. The Supreme Court can act to distort the Constitution by a quick and efficient one-vote majority. The amendment process requires the operation of a vast mechanism. For the framers, amendment was needed to make "useful alterations ... suggested by experience." They did not foresee that it would be needed as a constitutional check on a runaway Supreme Court. Originally, amendment was a sort of mini-constitutional convention. Therefore high hurdles were required for any amendment. One should also keep in mind that this was a first for the entire enterprise of making a national constitution. The English *unwritten* constitution had only been changed by war and revolution. The primary example of *written* fundamental laws were holy writ, like the Ten Commandments, which were by their nature supposed to be unchangeable. The Articles of Confederation which united the States during and immediately after the War for Independence had required unanimity for any revision. The very idea of a peaceful but binding change by less than unanimity was new.

89

Since 1787 all of the States have adopted or revised their constitutions and a hundred plus democratic nations have adopted written constitutions. Political scientist Donald Lutz has made a detailed comparison of amendment procedures in the constitutions of the American States and other democratic nations.[10] He assigned values to each requirement in the amendment process based on the historical frequency of amendment for each. Adding these values gave a measure of the degree of difficulty of amendment.

Professor Lutz concluded that none of the American States make it as difficult to amend their state constitutions as the federal constitution. Only 19 of the fifty States require a two-thirds vote of the state legislature to initiate an amendment, and in 49 the step after proposal by the legislature is approval at a referendum, usually at the next general election. Unsurprisingly, the rate of amendments to state constitutions is .58 per year (even after excluding subject matter peculiar to state concerns) compared to an average of only .13 per year for the federal constitution.[11] Using the same scale to compare the US Constitution to those of other nations, Lutz found that the US Constitution was the second most difficult in the world to amend. The only constitution more difficult to amend when he did his initial study was that of the now defunct nation of Yugoslavia.[12]

Freely and Deliberately Established

"It has been the misfortune ... of other nations that their Governments have not been freely and deliberately established by themselves," wrote Madison, whereas "the boast of ours [is] that such has been its source and that it can be altered by the same authority only which established it." The preamble to the Constitution identifies that authority -- "We, the People." Now that other nations and our own States have freely established their own democratic governments, we should perhaps reflect on their unanimous conclusion that constitutional amendment should not be as difficult as found in our Constitution, a constitution created without the benefit of other models or experience with how

90

constitutional first principles can become corrupted, and require timely renewal. Madison continued "it is a further boast that a regular mode of making proper alterations has been providently inserted in the Constitution itself. It is anxiously to be wished therefore, that no innovations may take place in other modes, one of which would be a constructive assumption of powers never meant to be granted."[13] It now falls to us to correct the national government's massive "constructive assumption of powers never" granted to it by the people, but rather arrogated to it by the Supreme Court.

The corporate, political and academic elites invested in this Leviathan national government are very powerful. To achieve the restoration of the original Madisonian Constitution we must take the example of our fellow democrats in other nations and of our own States, and reduce the old hurdles to the "mode of making proper alterations" to the American Constitution. This is not the first time that reducing the difficulty of constitutional amendment has been raised.[14] Proposals have ranged across the spectrum, from some who thought amendment should be made more difficult to the suggestion that amendment should only require a national referendum.[15] The proposal below seeks to adhere as closely as possible to the original system for amending the Constitution while enabling the American people to use it to take back their right to determine the meaning of their Constitution. Further, it actually revives a critical aspect of the original scheme which has become moribund. First, the current Article V:

> The Congress, whenever two thirds of both Houses shall deem it necessary, shall propose Amendments to this Constitution, or, on the Application of the Legislatures of two thirds of the several States, shall call a Convention for proposing Amendments, which, in either Case, shall be valid to all Intents and Purposes, as Part of this Constitution, when ratified by the Legislatures of three fourths of the several States, or by Conventions in three fourths thereof, as the one or the other Mode of

91

Ratification may be proposed by the Congress; Provided that no Amendment which may be made prior to the Year One thousand eight hundred and eight shall in any Manner affect the first and fourth Clauses in the Ninth Section of the first Article; and that no State, without its Consent, shall be deprived of its equal Suffrage in the Senate.

The first step in amending the amendment process is fairly straight-forward. This is to reduce the super-majority hurdles "one step" by requiring a five-eighths vote in each house of Congress and five eighths of the States to approve an amendment, instead of the current two-thirds of Congress and three fourths of the States. No American State or any other democratic nation requires three-fourths vote to approve anything when amending their constitutions. Professor Lutz estimates that just changing the number of States required to ratify from three fourths to a lower super-majority increases the chances of an amendment being approved threefold.[16] This still tracks the method by which all of our current amendments have been enacted. Both national and state governments still participate in the process and approval by super-majorities is still required.

However, since one of the goals of this reform is to re-empower the people in their States by devolving power away from the over-centralized national government, Congress can no longer be allowed to block proposals limiting federal power. Therefore, the proposal allows the States to initiate an amendment under procedures described below without having to wait for Congress. Congress' approval of an amendment can still count, but it can occur after States have initiated an amendment proposal.

By empowering the States to initiate the constitutional amendment process and ending Congress' monopoly on initiating amendments, we are only fulfilling the framers' original design. Continuing in the *Federalist* number quoted above, Madison wrote that the amendment procedure "equally enables the general and the State governments to originate the amendment of errors, as they may be pointed out by the experience on one side, or on the other."[17] States were supposed to be able to initiate the amendment process.

The procedure set out in Article V to accomplish this is for two-thirds of the States to request "a Convention for proposing Amendments." This probably seemed perfectly normal to the drafters of the Constitution, since they were sitting in just such a convention at the time. However, the boldness of that convention in proposing an entirely new government structure, instead of just adjusting the existing Confederation of States, has raised over every convention proposed since the specter of a "runaway" convention which would open unexpected and unwelcome issues. Some argue that such a convention could be limited as to subject, but scholarly opinion is deeply divided, and offers no reassurance to a state legislator contemplating the invocation of a second constitutional convention.

Numerous other unresolved procedural issues would surround such a convention: how would the delegates be selected, how many would there be, how would they vote, how long could they meet and so forth.[18] These problems were foreseen by James Madison, who strenuously argued against the convention method at the Constitutional Convention, warning that "difficulties might arise as to the form, the quorum, &c which in Constitutional regulations ought to be as much as possible avoided."[19]

There have been several times when calls by States for an amending convention advanced fairly far, but in the end none have ever been convened.[20] All of the amendments which have been enacted have been initiated by the Congress. Unsurprisingly, since 1788 when the Bill of Rights amendments were demanded by the States as a condition of the original ratification of the Constitution, no amendment has ever limited the power of the national government.

In the framers' day the reason a convention was necessary for States to propose amendments was communications. How else were thirteen States going to coordinate and agree on the exact wording of proposals when it took weeks to make one trip between them? However, in our day electronic communications and air travel make the task of coordinating an amendment proposal quite feasible without having to call one single official meeting to work it out. All that is really necessary is that the proposed amendment be uniformly worded. Therefore, the proposed revision allows any five States to initiate a constitutional amendment proposal without having to go through the archaic mechanism of a convention. A proposed amendment's advocates will bear the burden of persuading other States to approve the proposal, and assure that the wording of the proposal is kept consistent among the ratifying States. By requiring that five States act jointly to launch an amendment proposal we reduce the possibility of multiple proposals with the same objective but differing language, and that a single State may clog the "amendment calendar" with perhaps idiosyncratic proposals.

To further empower the States and their people, a second amendment method is proposed which would allow the States to enact an amendment by simply having two thirds of the States approve an identically worded proposition without any involvement by Congress. This is actually not a major change from the current Article V, which provides that amendments can be enacted without congressional approval if they are initiated by a convention called by two thirds of the States and then ratified by three fourths of the States. Since this procedure bypasses consideration by Congress, the proposal also adds a requirement that if an amendment is enacted by two thirds of the States without congressional approval, those States must have a majority of the Nation's population. This will avoid the situation, practically improbable but theoretically possible, where States with less than a majority of the population could enact an amendment. (Canada uses such a requirement in its constitution to balance the interests of preserving provincial autonomy against the fact that its provinces differ significantly in population.)

The proposal will also clarify some procedural matters which have arisen over time as the various constitutional amendments have been enacted. One is how long state amendment ratifications can stay valid without achieving the required number of ratifications to be adopted. In the 20th century, the custom arose of setting a seven-year deadline so that state ratifications can be reasonably simultaneous.[21] This is a good policy since it clears the calendar of amendments which have inadequate support so that other proposals can come forward. This policy is included in the proposal. However, that time limit only applies to amendment proposals initiated by Congress. A longer nine-year limit is proposed for state-initiated amendments since it may take more time to coordinate approval efforts for proposals initiated by the States.

Another unresolved issue is whether an approval can be rescinded. Since the objective of the proposal is to increase popular participation in the amendment process, a State should have the right to withdraw an approval.[22] Explicitly allowing rescissions will also promote deliberation on an amendment, especially if the issue comes up in a subsequent election. The only limit on rescissions is a practical one barring rescission at the last minute before the requisite super-majority is achieved so that approvals and rescissions can be a deliberative process, not one carried out in a rush.

Finally, the proposal also clarifies that a state legislature may refer an amendment proposal to a referendum. The existing Article V provides that in proposing an amendment Congress may designate ratification by either the "Legislatures of three fourths of the several States, or by Conventions in three fourths thereof." Ratification by state conventions rather than state legislatures has only been used once, to approve the twenty-first amendment which repealed Prohibition. It was feared that the amendment would get tied up in the politics of state legislatures where conservative rural legislators had significant influence. By having the amendment ratified by state conventions, it was presented to the voters as a single issue which could not be tied to other unrelated legislative issues. It effectively operated as a referendum since almost all States required candidates to the conventions to declare their position in advance. The conventions merely ratified the popular vote. Indeed, the New Hampshire convention completed its ratification and adjourned in 17 minutes flat.[23] Since the States now use referenda to ratify amendments to their own constitutions, the proposal will also provide that this method can be used in place of the state legislature or ratifying conventions. This will also override an old Supreme Court decision which refused to recognize a state law providing for the submission of a constitutional amendment proposal to a referendum.[24]

Here is the proposed revised Article V in its entirety:

> Section 1: This Constitution may be amended by either: (a) five eighths of both Houses of Congress and five eighths of the States, which approvals by the Congress and the States may occur concurrently, or (b) two thirds of the States with a majority of the nation's population as determined by the most recent Enumeration made pursuant to Article I Section 2 of this Constitution prior to the completion of the procedures set forth in this Section. If the first approval of a proposed amendment is by States, at least five States must approve the proposed amendment within a period of not more than one hundred twenty calendar days. Each State may determine whether actions under this article are to be by its legislature or by referendum.

> Section 2: All approvals of any proposed amendment shall expire if the proposed amendment has not been fully approved (a) for proposed amendments initiated by the Congress seven years after the vote of whichever House of Congress was the first to approve it, or (b) for proposed amendments initiated by States nine years after the first State approval.

Section 3: The operative text of any amendment must be approved with identical wording.

Section 4: Congress and any State may rescind approval of a proposed amendment except during the thirty calendar days prior to the date upon which the proposed amendment is fully approved under Section 1 of this article.

Section 5: An amendment shall be valid to all intents and purposes as part of this Constitution upon completion of the procedures set out in Section 1 of this article unless the amendment itself sets a future effective date. An approval or rescission of an approval of a proposed amendment shall be effective upon the completion of Congress' or a State's procedures for ordinary legislative or ballot actions, or as the legislature or a State's constitution may otherwise provide, except that no executive assent or veto shall apply to any action under this article.

Section 6: Congress' and each State's approvals and rescissions of approvals of proposed amendments must be promptly transmitted to the Speaker of the House of Representatives, who must promptly: (a) publicly post all such actions, (b) transmit them to the Senate and the legislatures of the States, and (c) declare the enactment of an amendment upon fulfillment of the requirements of this article. In the event of any failure to perform an executory action under this article, upon the application of any member of Congress, or with respect to any State any member of that State's legislature, the courts constituted under Article III of this Constitution must decree such action to be effected.

Section 7: No amendment shall deprive any State of its equal suffrage in the Senate without its consent.

(Section 7 is required because the current Article V provides that a State cannot be deprived of its two Senate seats without its consent.)

Although slightly longer than the original Article V, the proposal provides the means for the American people to take ultimate constitutional determinations out of the hands of the Supreme Court, and provides the procedural precision which Mr. Madison told us was desirable in "Constitutional regulations." It is hoped that a more open amendment procedure will be used to adopt the other amendments proposed in this book. However it stands on its own. We are faced with major decisions about the nature of our nation. The "amendment amendment" is not about what those decisions are. It is content-neutral, purely procedural. It is only about assuring that whatever decisions are made come from the level closest to the people, the States, where grassroots input is most effective. Any one who believes in democratic governance, who believes that the American Constitution belongs to the American people rather than the Supreme Court and national elites in Washington, D. C., should support this. With this revised amendment process we may begin a great national discussion as to what our nation should be, a discussion which will then occur where it should – by the people in the public square, not by elitist judges in a courthouse.

Chapter 6

Devolution and Redistribution:
Restoring Power to the People and their States

It is not by the consolidation or concentration of powers,
but by their distribution, that good government is effected.

Thomas Jefferson[1]

The Constitution originally structured the American nation as a
decentralized system. General governmental powers were vested
locally in the States, and only specific, limited powers were allocated
to the national government. If we want to decentralize our national
government and devolve power back to the governments which are
closer to the people, the simplest strategy is to reconstitute the
original distribution of powers. However, there are also certain
practical considerations which must be taken into account in
redistributing power to the States and the people in order for such a
devolution to function under modern circumstances. This devolution
also must learn from the previous abuses of the constitutional text
which have been used to create our current, over-centralized
Leviathan State.

To accomplish this we must look to the primary grant of power to
the national government in the Constitution, Section 8 of Article I.
It is reproduced in its entirety on page 101. As we have seen in the
previous chapters, there are several different parts of Section 8 which
have been misconstrued by the Supreme Court to allow the massive
consolidation of power in the national government which Jefferson
and Madison so feared. Let us take each in turn, and see if there is a
practical way to rephrase them to take power from the national
government in Washington, with its pervasive, intrusive, inflexible,

99

corporate-dominated regulations and bureaucracy, and return it to the American people and their local governments. Let us begin the "Devolution Revolution."

General Welfare

As we have seen, there were disagreements from the very beginning about Clause 1, which authorizes Congress to collect taxes to pay debts and "provide for the common Defence and general Welfare of the United States." In 1798 the John Adams administration had used a war scare to pass laws suppressing civil liberties. The Alien and Sedition Acts made it a crime to falsely or maliciously criticize the national government. Of course, the government claimed the right to decide if the criticism was false or malicious. Jefferson's Republican party criticized the Acts. Although today we would see them as violating the first amendment, at that time the main thrust of the Republican attack was that the federal government had no authority to enact them under the Constitution. In response, the administration deployed the "general welfare" clause.

To this Madison replied that the "true and fair construction of this expression" is that money must go "to some particular measure conducive to the general welfare" and "be within the enumerated authorities vested in Congress." Otherwise the government is "without the limitations formed by a particular enumeration of powers; and consequently the meaning and effect of this particular enumeration is destroyed." This will "consolidate the States into one sovereignty...by extending the sovereignty of the [national government]...to *all cases whatever.*" The "inevitable result of a consolidation of the states into one sovereignty, would be, to transform the republican system of the United States...to enlarge the sphere of discretion allotted to the executive magistrate [and]...an excessive augmentation of the offices, honors and emoluments depending on the executive will."[2] Why enumerate 17 specific powers if the national government could spend money on *anything* it thought to be in the general welfare?

100

Section 8

1. The Congress shall have Power To lay and collect Taxes, Duties, Imposts and Excises, to pay the Debts and provide for the common Defence and general Welfare of the United States; but all Duties, Imposts and Excises shall be uniform throughout the United States;

2: To borrow Money on the credit of the United States;

3: To regulate Commerce with foreign Nations, and among the several States, and with the Indian Tribes;

4: To establish an uniform Rule of Naturalization, and uniform Laws on the subject of Bankruptcies throughout the United States;

5: To coin Money, regulate the Value thereof, and of foreign Coin, and fix the Standard of Weights and Measures;

6: To provide for the Punishment of counterfeiting the Securities and current Coin of the United States;

7: To establish Post Offices and post Roads;

8: To promote the Progress of Science and useful Arts, by securing for limited Times to Authors and Inventors the exclusive Right to their respective Writings and Discoveries;

9: To constitute Tribunals inferior to the supreme Court;

10: To define and punish Piracies and Felonies committed on the high Seas, and Offences against the Law of Nations;

11: To declare War, grant Letters of Marque and Reprisal, and make Rules concerning Captures on Land and Water;

12: To raise and support Armies, but no Appropriation of Money to that Use shall be for a longer Term than two Years;

13: To provide and maintain a Navy;

14: To make Rules for the Government and Regulation of the land and naval Forces;

15: To provide for calling forth the Militia to execute the Laws of the Union, suppress Insurrections and repel Invasions;

16: To provide for organizing, arming, and disciplining, the Militia, and for governing such Part of them as may be employed in the Service of the United States, reserving to the States respectively, the Appointment of the Officers, and the Authority of training the Militia according to the discipline prescribed by Congress;

17: To exercise exclusive Legislation in all Cases whatsoever, over such District (not exceeding ten Miles square) as may, by Cession of particular States, and the Acceptance of Congress, become the Seat of the Government of the United States, and to exercise like Authority over all Places purchased by the Consent of the Legislature of the State in which the Same shall be, for the Erection of Forts, Magazines, Arsenals, dock-Yards, and other needful Buildings;--And

18: To make all Laws which shall be necessary and proper for carrying into Execution the foregoing Powers, and all other Powers vested by this Constitution in the Government of the United States, or in any Department or Officer thereof.

For Madison, this open-ended construction of the phrase would lead to a vast expansion in presidential power and the size of the presidential machinery, the bureaucracy. You may judge the accuracy of his prediction.

As we have seen, debate about the authority of the national government to spend continued at least through the last of the Jeffersonian Democratic Presidents, Grover Cleveland. However, what politician does not like to spend money? Over time, the federal budget steadily increased. Nonetheless, the idea that there might be some limit on federal authority to spend money continued through the 1930s, when a challenge was made to a vast new program of national government taxing and spending called Social Security. After Justice Roberts switched to voting in favor of the New Deal expansion of the national government's powers, the Supreme Court ruled in the case of Helvering vs. Davis that the Social Security program was a valid exercise of the power to tax and spend for the "general welfare," even though it could not conceivably be connected to any one of the 17 enumerated powers.[3] Since then, the Supreme Court has never held any federal taxing or spending to be beyond the authority granted to the national government by the Constitution.

At the same time, in the case of Steward Machine Company vs. Davis, the Supreme Court upheld the new federal unemployment compensation program.[4] The issue there was not whether there could be such a program, but rather whether the national government could tie the States up with rules and regulations as a condition of getting federal funding for the States' unemployment compensation programs. Since then the national government has routinely tied federal funding of the States to elaborate rules and regulations. Many of these are only peripherally related to the purpose of the expenditure, and often impose substantial costs on the States which are not covered by the funding. Examples of such regulations are the requirements that all States raise their minimum drinking age to 21 and impose a 55 mile-per-hour speed limit as a condition of federal highway funding. The first example was upheld by the Supreme

Court in South Dakota vs. Dole despite the special provision in the twenty-first amendment giving States authority over the regulation of alcohol.[5] The second example, of course, is a classic case of how national "one-size-fits-all" regulation fails to take account of local circumstances, such as the time costs of travel in less populated areas. And neither has anything to do with the actual construction of highways. (Fifty-five mile per hour interstates were still built to handle 75 mile per hour traffic.)

To restore something approaching the original federal/state distribution of power, we must take a two-step approach. First, the "general welfare" clause must be removed from Clause 1, and language added which restores the limitation of federal authority only to the powers specifically granted.

Clause 1:   The Congress shall have Power To lay and collect Taxes, Duties, Imposts and Excises, and to pay the Debts of the United States and provide for the common Defence and general Welfare of the United States; **for, and only for, the following purposes;** but all Duties, Imposts and Excises shall be uniform throughout the United States.

Next comes a practical problem. As much as the ideal would be to return to the minimal national government of the founding, we have reached a point where there are federal programs which can not be eliminated overnight. For example, as ill-conceived as it may have been from its beginning, and as doomed to certain insolvency as it now appears to be, virtually all retired and working Americans alive today have been paying into the Social Security program for their entire lives in reliance on commitments that they would receive payments in their old age.[6] It is not feasible to propose a constitutional amendment which would immediately abolish programs like Social Security and Medicare. For now, their problems must be dealt with by Congress. If the amendments proposed in this book can start weaning us from our addiction to federal spending,

103

perhaps fundamental reform of entitlement spending can still be enacted before those programs become insolvent. Eventually, it may even be feasible to enact an amendment which gets the federal government out of the entitlement business entirely. However, this will require a gradual program in several stages over time.

In the meantime, what do we do about the fact that the federal Congress has treated the "general welfare" clause as an authorization to spend on anything Congress wants (as Jefferson warned) since long before the New Deal? Simply deleting it is not politically possible at the present time. One solution would be to leave it and ignore the issue until a time when the other amendments proposed in this book have habituated Americans to a smaller federal government, and then delete it by constitutional amendment. However, have we not gone too long tolerating disrespect of the Constitution's mandates? Can we claim to respect the original constitutional limits on the federal government while ignoring the oldest violation of the principal that it is limited to the enumerated powers?

We therefore propose another approach. It is a compromise, and thus not ideal. Perfectionists will dislike it. However, the program of this book is to do something *now* to restore our Constitution, not to delay until some unforeseeable future time when a majority of Americans become willing to abandon, out of constitutional principle, all of the money taken from them for Social Security. This interim compromise is to take control of the "general welfare" clause by making it one of the enumerated powers of Congress, but with significant restraints and limitations. To do this, after deleting "general welfare" from the prefatory clause, a new Clause 18 would be added to Section 8:

Clause 18:   To make expenditures to promote the general welfare, provided that the criteria for distributing such expenditures make them generally available in fact, any regulation thereunder only applies directly to the specific expenditure, is not applicable to any other expenditure from any source, and shall not be imposed unless its costs are fully funded by the expenditure;

Adding **"the criteria for distributing such expenditures make them generally available in fact"** makes what are called "earmarks" or "pork barrel" unconstitutional. These are federal expenditures which are directed to a specific use. They allow members of Congress to claim that they have benefitted their districts by getting federal projects, when all they are really doing is buying their constituents' votes with their constituents' own tax money. This distorts the budgetary process by giving members of Congress incentives to approve each others' pork barrel projects. Chasing such projects also distracts members of Congress from attending to the really important national issues, which they too often lazily bounce to executive branch bureaucrats. It is also unfair, since it gives preference to districts and States with more powerful Representatives and Senators. This also advantages incumbents since power in Congress comes from seniority. Incumbents use pork barrel earmarks to inhibit voters from voting them out, even after the incumbents have become enmeshed in the world of Washington special interests.

As we have seen, even Hamilton felt that expenditures for the "general welfare" had to be of general, rather than local, application. So, what would be a "generally available" expenditure? According to Hamilton, an expenditure was *"General* and not *local,"* if "its operation is extending in fact, or by possibility, throughout the Union, and not being confined to a particular spot."[7] While avoiding open-ended entitlements like Social Security, which goes to everyone who meets pre-established criteria, general welfare legislation would have to fix priorities for funding based on uniform criteria, such as some measurable need per capita, income levels, or usage.

Thus, for example, instead of being directed to a powerful Senator or Representative's pet projects, transportation funds would be allocated based on a statutory formula that weighed number of persons transported, availability of alternate transportation routes and a neutral civil engineering evaluation of state of repair. Instead of medical research funding being spent based on which disease has the most influential lobbyists and the most high profile celebrity spokespersons, medical research funds would be allocated based on the numbers of victims and severity of the condition. This would move the focus to the health issues of the poor rather than those of the politically connected.[8]

Some members of Congress argue that the elimination of earmarks will just give more power to bureaucrats to allocate government funds. This might be the case if Congress continues its current practice of passing vague, general, poorly thought out laws and then abdicating to the bureaucracy the job of actually defining the law. Thus, another benefit of this provision will be to force Congress to do its job and enact carefully drafted, precise laws that do not give so much discretion and authority to the bureaucracy.

Adding "**any regulation thereunder only applies directly to the specific expenditure, is not applicable to any other expenditure from any source, and shall not be imposed unless its costs are fully funded by the expenditure**" eliminates various practices which Congress uses to control the States through federal funding. The "**only applies directly to the specific expenditure**" language overturns the South Dakota vs. Dole decision and the ends the use of conditions attached to a federal grant which extend beyond the immediate expenditure. For example, highway funding could be regulated to require that funds must actually go to build highways, and that the highways link to the interstate system. Matters unrelated to actual highway construction, such as minimum drinking ages and speed limits, would be beyond federal regulation.

The "**is not applicable to any other expenditure from any source**" requirement further restricts federal control by ending the extension of federal regulations to the entire area of government activity, including those funded by state or local taxes, just because they also receive some federal funds. Thus, there could be no general federal regulation of local or state-funded school systems except with respect to specific activities specifically funded entirely by federal funds. Finally, the language **"shall not be imposed unless its costs are fully funded by the expenditure"** eliminates the practice of unfunded mandates, where regulations are imposed which may apply directly to the expenditure, but the costs of compliance with the regulations have to be born by the entities receiving the funds. For example, if States must test children to receive education funding, the funding has to cover all of the costs of the testing and associated paperwork. This will enable state and local government entities such as school districts to spend their scarce resources on public services rather than complying with federal paperwork and regulations.

The magnitude of such costs on stressed local budgets is substantial. In Ohio, a study estimated that the State would have to spend about $1.5 billion more on education each year to meet the additional accountability requirements of the No Child Left Behind program, even though Ohio only received $634 million from the federal government for those programs. The State of Connecticut sued the federal government in 2005 for allegedly forcing the State to spend millions of its own money on additional NCLB testing.[9]

Other limits might also be included, such as forbidding expenditures under the general welfare clause unless the budget is in balance after fulfilling the 17 original enumerated federal responsibilities.

To regulate Commerce...among the several States

As open-ended as the "general welfare" clause has been, the truly unlimited expansion of the power of the national government has come through the Supreme Court's reinterpretation of the "interstate commerce" clause. The full clause is "to regulate Commerce with foreign Nations, and among the several States, and with the Indian Tribes."

Madison understood the phrase to mean "to regulate trade," and indicated that its meaning "must be sought in the general use of it, in other words in the objects to which the power was generally understood to be applicable when the Phrase was inserted n the Constitution."[10] He indicated that at the time the Constitution was adopted, the term "commerce" was understood to mean "trade," as distinct from the production of goods for trade through manufacturing or agriculture.[11] The phrase "among the several States" meant *between* the States. Even Hamilton, in discussing "commerce," referred to it as the "unrestrained intercourse between the States...by an interchange of their respective productions."[12] Finally, to "regulate" meant to regularize, that is to provide the rules under which something could go forward. It did not mean to prohibit.[13] This is illustrated by contemporaneous uses of the term, such as in the second amendment which speaks of a "well-regulated militia." This meant a well-ordered or well-disciplined militia. It would make no sense to refer to a "well-prohibited militia."

This understanding of the interstate commerce clause was followed by the Supreme Court for 150 years. In Gibbons vs. Ogden, Chief Justice John Marshall did rule that the power to regulate interstate commerce power extended to the regulation of the means of interstate commerce. (In that case it was the first steam-powered ferry service between New Jersey and New York.)[14] With this logical extension, the Court continued to hold to the original meaning of the interstate commerce clause through its decision in Carter vs. Carter Coal Co. in 1936, which found that the interstate commerce clause did not cover a coal mine which operated entirely within one State.[15]

However, with Justice Roberts' switch, the Supreme Court's interpretation of the interstate commerce became much more expansive. Just one year after *Carter*, in NLRB vs. Jones & Laughlin Steel Corporation, a 5-to-4 decision (with Roberts switching to the pro-Roosevelt side as the court-packing crisis raged) the Supreme Court found that labor relations at a steel mill operating only in one

State could be regulated by the national government because of the possible effects on interstate commerce of a labor disruption.[16]

By 1941, with several Roosevelt appointees now on the Court, the case of Wickard vs. Filburn eliminated any restriction on the scope of federal economic regulation under the interstate commerce clause.[17] In that case Filburn, a farmer, had been fined for growing wheat on 12 acres more than he was allowed by federal regulations, even though he only used the extra wheat to feed his own chickens. The Court stated that by growing this extra wheat for his own use he was having a "substantial effect" on interstate commerce because if he had not grown his own wheat he would have had to buy it. Thus he was depressing the price for wheat sold in interstate commerce. One of the most amazing aspects of the *Wickard* decision was that the Court found it unnecessary for Congress to even articulate a rationale for the restriction. As long as "Congress *may* properly have considered that wheat consumed on the farm...would have a substantial effect" on Congress' regulatory scheme it came within interstate commerce.[18] In other words, Congress does not even have to bother with justifying its regulations. The judges will do it for them.

With *Wickard* the Supreme Court ripped a hole in the Constitution big enough for the Leviathan itself to pass through – and it did. It is under this expansive interpretation of the interstate commerce clause that the federal Congress now regulates everything from divorce and child custody to local schools to state drivers' licenses and, most recently, to the entire healthcare system. It is also under this unlimited interstate commerce power that the federal government spies on Americans, provisions enacted by the George W. Bush administration which Barack Obama seems to have forgotten to have repealed. In the words of former Justice Sandra Day O'Connor there are no "meaningful limits on the Commerce Clause...Congress can regulate intrastate activity without check."[19] This interpretation "threatens to sweep all of productive human activity into federal regulatory reach," including activities conducted exclusively in the home for one's own family, if they might be bought instead. "Home care substitutes for daycare. Charades games substitute for movie tickets. Backyard or windowsill gardening substitutes for going to the supermarket. To draw the line wherever private activity affects the demand for market goods is to draw no line at all, and to declare everything economic." The inevitable result is a general "federal police power."[20]

After failing to find any federal regulation unconstitutional for almost 60 years, the Court did finally find a couple of cases where the federal government went beyond even this open-ended interpretation of interstate commerce. One was possession of guns around schools and another was creating a special federal lawsuit for female victims of violence, both areas already covered by state laws.[21] However, even those limitations were cut back in a subsequent case (in which the quotes above from Justice O'Connor were made).[22] The 2012 decision on the Affordable Care Act (Obamacare) did overturn the use of the interstate commerce clause to impose a requirement that individuals buy medical insurance, but that left in place a vast range of other federal regulation of the healthcare system under the Affordable Care Act based on the *Wickard* interpretation of the interstate commerce clause. (And, of course, Chief Justice John Roberts, in an eerie throwback to the earlier Justice Roberts, switched sides to join the Democrat Justices in upholding the requirement that individuals buy medical insurance on the grounds that it was a tax.)

Much more is required if we are to roll back the federal Leviathan State and begin to heal this huge wound inflicted on the Constitution by the Roosevelt Supreme Court. In searching for wording which would reverse this massive federalization of American life, it is always best to go back to the source. What was the original objective of the clause?

On that question, both Madison and Hamilton agreed. In the *Federalist*, Hamilton wrote that a purpose for uniting under the new government created by the proposed Constitution was to prevent a situation where commercial "intercourse would be fettered, interrupted and narrowed by" competitive "rivalships of the parts" of the country.[23] Madison explained that the power to regulate commerce among the States was to provide "relief of the States which import and export through other States from the improper contributions levied on them by the latter...to load the articles of import and export, during the passage through their jurisdiction, with duties which would fall on the makers of the latter and the consumers of the former."[24] Later, Madison wrote that the clause "grew out of the abuse of the power by the importing States in taxing the non-importing, and was intended as a negative and preventative provision against injustice among the States themselves, rather than as a power to be used for the positive purposes of the General Government."[25]

Thus, the purpose of the interstate commerce clause was to empower the national government to prevent States from taking actions which impeded the transfer of goods between States across state lines. The objective was to make of the entire United States a single common market to enhance the common wealth of the whole nation. It was not a grant of authority for the national government to control local economic activity within the States. To get the national government out of local affairs and return control of local matters to the States and the people, it is proposed that the interstate commerce clause be restated to more fully elaborate this underlying objective:

Clause 3:   To regulate Commerce with foreign Nations, **or** ~~and~~ with the Indian Tribes; **or which substantively crosses the borders of** ~~among~~ the several States, **but the latter only so as to directly either (a) promote the passage of persons, goods, services, information, funds, or other economic activity across state borders, or collective bargaining, or (b) prohibit the passage of criminals, criminal activities, and dangerous substances across state borders; and the costs of any such regulation [on the several States] are fully funded by the United States;**

111

With this language the national government will still be able to prevent States from impeding the flow of economic activity from other States, but it will not be able to infringe on economic activity within States. This will free small and local businesses from most federal regulation. They will no longer be subject to burdensome rules developed by and for the big corporations which control the federal regulators in Washington, D. C. This does not mean that local businesses will be able to act however they want. The States will continue to retain their general right to regulate within their borders. In the *Federalist* Madison explained that the "powers delegated by the proposed Constitution to the federal government are few and defined. Those which are to remain in the State governments are numerous and indefinite.... The powers reserved to the several States will extend to all the objects which...concern the lives, liberties and properties of the people, and the internal order, improvement, and prosperity of the State."[26]

Now, anyone with experience in business will know that state and local bureaucrats can be as arrogant, nit-picking, and subject to corrupt influence as their federal counterparts. And there are States where the internal politics are as conducive to a high level of regulation as anything in Washington. Indeed, many big corporations seek out federal regulation precisely in order to override stricter state standards. However, that diversity is the point of federalism. There will be a wide variation in the degree and application of regulation among the States. California will be free to have stricter environmental regulations than Alaska, Massachusetts' minimum wage may be higher than Oklahoma's to account for different costs of living. These regional variations will undoubtedly be maddening to the Washington and academic elites who have been dictating to the entire nation since the New Deal. These elites love to celebrate certain kinds of elite-approved diversity, such as sexual lifestyle. The Devolution Revolution will now test whether the elites can tolerate diversity beyond the approved categories -- that is, regional diversity in the areas that really matter to the American people.

112

Some may be concerned that this proposal will allow major multinational corporations to run free of federal control. However, this is not the case. Once a business crosses state lines it is subject to regulation by Congress consistent with its powers to promote the national common market. As we have seen, corporate influence in Washington considerably mutes the effectiveness of federal regulation in any case. Getting Congress out of the business of regulating small and local businesses will allow it to concentrate on the largest corporate malefactors if the citizenry demands it. (Two proposals discussed in chapter 11 aim to enhancing the American people's ability to regain control of their national government.) Also, some areas of economic activity inherently cross state lines. Therefore federal level regulation could continue in areas such as air travel and broadcasting to prevent airplanes and airwaves from colliding.

The main impact of the proposed revision to the interstate commerce clause will be to free local businesses and governments from the stifling effect of federal regulations made by and for big corporations. No longer will big corporations be able to use federal regulation to snuff out a small new competitor by imposing on little companies the same "one-size-fits-all" federal rules and restrictions created by and for corporations a thousand times larger.

Some comments are in order in two special areas. Current federal environmental laws are based on the open-ended interpretation of the "interstate commerce" power. The proposed revision will limit the federal role in regulating purely local environmental matters. However the "prohibit the passage of...dangerous substances across state borders" language will still authorize large scale environmental protection. In particular waterways almost always cross state lines, so clean water laws to prevent upstream States from polluting downstream States would fall within the federal purview. Moreover, the revision would direct federal environmental protection to larger ecosystem concerns, where a national plan can have a real impact, rather than burdening local governments with elaborate and complex environmental regulations where the impact is only local and limited.

113

Some readers may have also noted the "promote...collective bargaining" language. Certainly the modern American labor union, with its featherbedding, often unrealistic wage, benefit and work rule demands, undemocratic leadership, political activities contrary to the views of its members, mismanagement of pension funds, and outright corruption, has hardly fulfilled its responsibilities to promote the interests of American working people. Unions would like to attribute their steadily declining memberships to corporate anti-union activities, but it is an insult to American working people to think that they are not aware of the substantial internal failings of labor unions. That said, the ability of workers to organize to deal with corporate management deserves protection.

The reason for this was explained by none other than Adam Smith, the first great philosopher of the free enterprise system. In his great work, *An Inquiry Into the Nature and Causes of the Wealth of Nations*, Smith notes that as between employers and employees it is not "difficult to foresee which of the two parties must...have the advantage in the dispute and force the other into a compliance with their terms.... In all such disputes the masters can hold out much longer ... Many workmen could not subsist a week, few could subsist a month, and scarce any a year without employment."[27] Thus, writes Smith, when government "regulation...is in favour of the workmen, it is always just and equitable; but it is sometimes otherwise when in favour of the masters."[28] Contrary to modern interpretations of Smith's economics, he saw no problem in the possibility that this might increase labor costs. In Smith's view "the liberal reward of labour...increases the industry of the common people.... Where wages are high...we shall always find the workmen more active, diligent and expeditious than where they are low."[29]

Smith's principal proof of this was the British North American colonies, where high wages accompanied a rapidly growing economy. Famously, *The Wealth of Nations* was first published in 1776. In *The Wealth of Nations*, which of course was written before the colonies had

114

declared independence, Smith urged that the colonists' demands be accommodated. After the War of Independence began, he wrote a memorandum to the British government advising that the attempted military repression of the American Revolution would be fruitless and counter-productive.[30] Jefferson and Madison were great fans of *The Wealth of Nations*, which Jefferson considered "the best book extant...in political economy."[31] Admittedly our current labor laws and labor relations are seriously flawed. However, the federal government should be able to pass laws giving employees a fair chance to offset the inherent bargaining advantages of large employers.

Aside from the issue of economic fairness, there is also a practical political expedient. Labor union members are as fed up with our over-centralized, domineering and corporate-dominated national government as all other working Americans. This amendment to the interstate commerce clause is about taking power away from the corporate and academic elites and Washington politicians and bureaucrats and pushing it back down to the States and the people. Assuring that collective bargaining rights are preserved under the Constitution will enable these working Americans to freely join the campaign for the Devolution Revolution without the distraction of elitist union leaders alleging that the proposal is anti-labor.

With regard to federal funding of the costs of regulations, some may argue that allowing private individuals and companies and local governments to claim reimbursement for regulatory costs may open a Pandora's box of lawsuits. One way to obviate such claims is to limit the right to recover regulatory costs to the States. Hence the bracketed language "on the several states." A counter-argument in favor of making the recovery of regulatory costs a general right is that it will give Congress a strong inducement not to regulate. This is an issue which may require further analysis to resolve.

Reserved to the states respectively, or to the people

Unfortunately, all of these steps to restore the Constitution's original allocation of power between the States and the federal government are of little use if they remain words on a page. After all, the original words were already there, and yet were egregiously misconstrued by the Supreme Court with the collusion of the other branches of the national government. This what Jefferson meant in the quote at the beginning of chapter 4 – a written constitution is no more than blank paper if judges do not respect the meaning of the words on that paper, and worse write their own views and biases on to the constitutional paper. To believers in the original Constitution, one of the most frustrating aspects of this process is that, not only is the Constitution's language quite straight-forward but, in addition, the tenth amendment clearly provides that the "powers not delegated to the United States by the Constitution, nor prohibited by it to the states, are reserved to the states respectively, or to the people."

Since the New Deal the Supreme Court has largely treated this constitutional provision as a nullity. This is not surprising since the tenth amendment was intended to affirm the original federalist arrangement in which the national government was one of limited defined powers, and the State were the depositories of general governmental power. Obviously, that arrangement did not fit into the New Deal program of nationalizing all problems, with the national government given general power to enforce universal, nation-wide, "one-size-fits-all" dictates.

However, there are two revisions which could return legal vitality to the tenth amendment and enable it to serve as an enforcement mechanism for the Devolution Revolution. The first would be to take up the point made by Chief Justice Marshall in Gibbons vs. Ogden, where he used the absence of the word "expressly" to push for a concept of federal power not strictly limited to the specific enumerated powers. In the proposed revision of the first clause of Section 8 of Article I we added the words "**for, and only for, the**

116

following purposes" to clarify that we were returning to a national government of specific limited powers. This could be reinforced by adding Chief Justice Marshall's missing word to the tenth amendment.[32]

> The powers not **expressly** delegated to the United States
> by the Constitution, nor prohibited by it to the states,
> are reserved to the states respectively, or to the people.

We are still left with the issue of how to enforce this reversal of powers on a national government staffed by people raised in the mythology of the benevolent New Deal, people whose entire careers have been devoted to the Leviathan State. A great part of this difficulty comes from the nature of American litigation. Section 2 of Article III of the Constitution authorizes the courts only to hear "Cases." This means that there must be a real dispute in order to commence a lawsuit. As a general rule, this is good since it works to keep the courts focused on real life instead of abstract controversies.

However, it presents a major difficulty when it comes to deciding fundamental constitutional controversies. First, some specific person or entity must show some actual damage to themselves. This actual damage gives them what is called "standing" to bring a lawsuit. Next, the lawsuit has to start in lower courts, undergo the whole trial process, and then go through various levels of appeal before it can come before the Supreme Court. Even then, the Supreme Court is not obligated to hear every case which is appealed to it and, in fact, actually only accepts a small percentage of the appeals it receives. This whole process takes years and substantial amounts of money before a constitutional claim has a chance of being heard by the highest court. This was vividly illustrated by the two years required for the States' challenges to the Affordable Care Act to reach the Supreme Court, during which time neither supporters nor opponents knew how to handle the Act's numerous mandates. Finally, any decision is submitted based on the facts of the actual case. Again, as a general rule this is a good policy. However, in the case of critical

117

constitutional issues, this rule can make a judgment affecting fundamental constitutional rights turn on the often idiosyncratic and peculiar facts of whatever case in which it first happens to come up.

Americans are justifiably proud of their Constitution as being the first and most enduring of its kind in the world. However, being first does not always make one the best. As other democratic countries have followed the United States' example and adopted written constitutions, there has been a realization that it is important that fundamental questions about the meaning of the basic constitutional law of the nation be resolved quickly and clearly. Waiting for a lawsuit with perhaps odd facts to work its way through the court system can make for dangerous uncertainty and delay in implementing the basic rights of the nation.

Therefore, many democratic nations have implemented in their modern constitutions the institution of the "constitutional court." This is a high level court which only hears disputes about basic constitutional issues. It does not wait for a lawsuit to come along which raises the issue. Instead various institutional parties, such as the states or provinces or members of the national legislature, can bring the issue directly to the constitutional court, which rules on the overall issue without being tied to facts peculiar to a particular case.[33]

Such a procedure is proposed to enforce the proper constitutional limits on our national government. Rather than set up a separate special court, it is proposed that the existing Supreme Court serve this function. After raging for five chapters about how the Supreme Court has distorted the meaning of the Constitution, it may be surprising that this proposal vests this new procedure in the national Supreme Court. However, there are good reasons for this allocation of responsibility. First, the Supreme Court is already there in the Constitution, and still enjoys a degree of historical dignity. Second, it has been deciding on the meaning of the Constitution since Marbury vs. Madison, so it has been effectively acting as our 'constitutional court' anyway, just without efficient procedures. Third, it is hoped

118

that the language of the amendments proposed in this book are drawn with sufficient precision to foreclose the most abusive interpretative methods used by the Court in the past. Finally, to assure this, in Chapter 12 we will propose a constitutional amendment which will require the use of original textual meanings in constitutional interpretation.

This proposal is a major innovation in our original constitutional arrangement. To be conservative in implementing it, for now it is to be used only to enforce the newly restored limits on the powers of the national government. Thus, it is appropriate to place it in the tenth amendment. If it proves a useful procedure, future amendments could expand its scope. However, for now it is most needed to give the States a mechanism to enforce that amendment's limitation on the powers of the national government. Therefore, the current text of the amendment (with "expressly" added) would become Section 1 and a new Section 2 would be added reading:

> **Section 2. Without limitation to Section 1 of this Amendment, any state may require a declaratory judgment from the Supreme Court as to the violation of this Constitution by any act of Congress or any regulation or action of the executive as soon as such act takes effect under Section 7 of Article 1 of this Constitution or such executive regulation or action becomes effective. The Supreme Court shall exercise original jurisdiction over such causes, except that it may designate a Master or inferior Court to discover factual matters relating to the cause, but it shall not be bound by any such findings.**

Under this proposal, as soon as an act of Congress became law (Section 7 of Article I governs when a law becomes effective) a State could bring a lawsuit before the Supreme Court challenging its constitutionality. Since the Congress has abdicated much of its law-

119

making responsibility to federal regulatory agencies in the executive branch, executive regulations and actions are included as well. "Standing" for these actions would be limited to the States. If there was general standing for anyone to bring a lawsuit under this procedure the Supreme Court would be bombarded with challenges to everything Congress did. Limiting the right to bring these suits to the States assures that the procedure will be used responsibly only when there is a genuine constitutional question. This will also restore the States as defenders of their citizens' rights against the national government, as contemplated by the founders.

Allowing the case to be put before the Court as soon as the law or the regulation goes into effect avoids the delay of having a test case work its way over years through the court system. However, since there will not be any factual record established at a trial, the proposal provides a method for the Supreme Court to answer any relevant factual questions. The appointment of special masters by the courts to investigate factual matters is a well-established procedure. The Supreme Court could also order a trial-like procedure in a lower federal court. This would permit the use of the adversary system, where advocates for the different points of view could cross-examine evidence presented. However, the Supreme Court would retain the final responsibility for the determination of the case. This is why the language "it shall not be bound by any such findings" is needed.

A final issue with this proposal is "logrolling, " where members of Congress vote for each others' special interest legislation. States may hesitate to challenge other States' special interest provisions in order to preserve their own special interest pork. Also, some may object to the use of State resources to challenge the constitutionality of provisions on principle where the State making the challenge may not have an immediate interest in the unconstitutional legislation or regulation. Therefore, States should be compensated for their costs in such cases by adding a new Section 3 to the tenth amendment:

Section 3. Upon any successful action under Section 2 of this article, the state or states prosecuting the action shall be reimbursed by the United States treasury in an amount equal to three times the reasonable costs of prosecuting the action.

Finally, since we have seen that the Supreme Court has too often colluded in the unconstitutional expansion of federal power, an additional mechanism is needed to permit the states to reverse intrusive federal laws and regulations:

Section 4. Without limitation to Section 1 of this Amendment, five eighths of the states may rescind any act of Congress or any regulation or action of the executive within one year of the time such act takes effect under Section 7 of Article 1 of this Constitution or such executive regulation or action becomes effective.[34]

These procedures could revitalize the States' original roles as guardians of the limits on the national government's powers, as protectors of the rights of their citizens from federal encroachments. However, as noted above, the expansion of federal power is not limited to the Congress. Woodrow Wilson and Franklin Roosevelt began aggressively expanded presidential power within the federal government as well as the power of the federal government in general. The next chapter will address the most egregious of these manifestations of what liberals began calling the "imperial presidency" during the times of Lyndon Johnson and Richard Nixon, but which very much continues with us to today.

Chapter 7

Declarations and Encroachments: Restoring Peace

In Union, all the parts...will avoid the necessity of those overgrown military establishments, which, under any form of government, are inauspicious to liberty, and which are to be regarded as particularly hostile to Republican Liberty.... It is important, likewise, that the habits of thinking in a free country should inspire caution, in those intrusted with its administration, to confine themselves within their respective constitutional spheres, avoiding in the exercise of the powers of one department to encroach upon another. The spirit of encroachment tends to consolidate the powers of all the departments in one, and thus to create, whatever the form of government, a real despotism.... If, in the opinion of the people, the distribution or modification of the constitutional powers be in any particular wrong, let it be corrected by an amendment in the way, which the constitution designates. But let there be no change by usurpation; for, though this, in one instance, may be the instrument of good, it is the customary weapon by which free governments are destroyed.

George Washington[1]

In chapter 6 we suggested ways to reverse the encroachment of the federal government on the States, and return power to the people in their local state governments. Encroachment by the federal government into the domains of the States is not the only constitutional imbalance which has led to the rise of the Leviathan State in the 20th century. The massive growth of the federal government which began under Franklin Roosevelt is not limited to the domestic domain. Prior to Roosevelt's presidency, the United

122

States did not maintain a very large military during peacetime. However, beginning with Franklin Roosevelt's presidency a large part of the growth of the federal government has come from maintaining a substantial permanent military. Since the end of the Second World War, the United States has spent almost twelve and a half trillion dollars on national defense.[2] And that figure is in absolute dollars. Adjusted for inflation to current dollars that figure would be many times higher. In this time, the United States has engaged in dozens of overseas military operations, ranging from Korea and Vietnam to the two Gulf wars, the operations in Afghanistan and the air strikes in Libya. Currently there are approximately 300,000 US military personnel posted at over 700 US military facilities outside the United States.[3] Most significantly, since the end of the Second World War these numerous overseas military operations have resulted in over 87,000 Americans dying in combat.[4]

Whether or not all of these foreign military involvements were necessary or justifiable is not within the ambit of this book. However, an element common to all of these does implicate the Constitution's original balance of governmental powers. None of these combat deaths, operations or bases in foreign lands has come in a declared war. The last time the United States officially declared war was on December 11, 1941 (against Nazi Germany). Article 8 of Section 1 of the Constitution includes among the enumerated powers of the Congress:

Clause 11:   To declare War, grant Letters of Marque and Reprisal, and make Rules concerning Captures on Land and Water;

Five more clauses give Congress the authority to make regulations for the armed forces and the state militias (today the National Guard) when called into federal service. Then Clause 1 of Section 2 of Article II makes the President "Commander in Chief of the Army and Navy of the United States, and of the Militia of the several States, when called into the actual Service of the United States." In the

123

Federalist, Hamilton explained how the congressional and presidential functions related. Although the title of "commander-in-chief" might make the President's authority "nominally the same with that of the king of Great Britain" it would be "in substance much inferior to it. It would amount to nothing more than the supreme command and direction of the military and naval forces, as first General and admiral of the Confederacy; while that of the British king extends to the *declaring* of war and to the *raising* and *regulation* of fleets and armies, -- all which, by the Constitution under consideration, would appertain to the legislature."[5]

As with so many of our basic constitutional issues, a dispute over the proper balance of presidential and congressional authority arose at the very beginning, and the antagonists again were Messrs. Hamilton, Jefferson, and Madison. The United States' first foreign policy crisis was maneuvering through the global conflict between Britain and France. Of course, the United States had used that conflict to its advantage by allying with France against Britain during the War for Independence. However, by the beginning of Washington's second term the need to avoid getting squashed between the two warring superpowers of the day had led him to issue a decree stating that the United States would henceforth be neutral in the conflict despite its wartime alliance with France. During the summer of 1793, Hamilton wrote a series of newspaper articles under the pen name "Pacificus" arguing that while the "Legislature can alone declare war...it belongs to the 'Executive Power' to do whatever else the laws of Nations...enjoin in the intercourse of the UStates with Foreign Powers."[6]

Hamilton was not contradicting what he wrote in the *Federalist*, because this was a case of the President keeping the country *out* of a war, not starting one. Nonetheless he acknowledged the "Executive in the exercise of its constitutional powers, may establish an antecedent state of things which ought to weigh in the legislative decisions." This results in a "*concurrent* authority" between the two branches where "though treaties can only be made by the president and Senate, their activity may be continued or suspended by the President alone."[7]

As Secretary of State, Jefferson had concurred in the neutrality decision. Also, it was ratified afterwards by Congress, a point which Washington emphasized in his Farewell Address.[8] Nonetheless, Jefferson was horrified at the expansive vision of executive authority Hamilton had set forth. At Jefferson's urging, Madison wrote a series of newspaper replies under the pen name "Helvidius."[9] Jefferson and Madison saw that allowing the President such broad power of independent action would result in the President getting the nation into situations where war would be unavoidable, despite everything the Constitution (and Hamilton) said about the Congress' exclusive right to declare war. Madison wrote that "in no part of the Constitution is more wisdom to be found than in the clause which confides the question of war or peace to the legislature, and not to the executive department." For Madison, there had to be "rigid adherence" to the "fundamental doctrine of the constitution, that the power to declare war, including the power of judging the causes of war, is fully and exclusively vested in the legislature; that the executive has no right in any case to decide the question, whether there is or is not cause for declaring war."

Madison's approach was always to construct government with a realistic appraisal of human nature in mind.[10] The Constitution had to contemplate not Presidents "such as nature may offer as the prodigy of many centuries, but such as may be expected in the ordinary successions" to the presidency. For such ordinary men "the trust and temptation would be too great for any one man.... War is in fact the true nurse of executive aggrandizement. In war, a physical force is to be created; and it is the executive will which is to direct it. In war, the public treasuries are to be unlocked; and it is the executive hand which is to dispense them. In war, the honours and emoluments of office are to be multiplied, and it is the executive patronage under which they are to be enjoyed. It is in war, finally, that laurels are to be gathered, and it is the executive brow that they

125

are to encircle. The strongest passions and most dangerous weaknesses of the human breast; ambition, avarice, vanity, and honourable or venial love of fame, are all in conspiracy against the desire and duty of peace."[11]

The founders had already suffered under a king who had the sole authority to commit his country to war, and were determined that the President of the new American Republic would not have such power. Therefore, according to Madison, "those who are to *conduct a war* can not in the nature of things, be proper of safe judges, whether *a war ought* to be *commenced, continued,* or *concluded.* They are barred from the latter function by a great principle in free government, analogous to that which separate...the power of executing from the power of enacting laws."[12] In other words, it was a basic part of the constitutional set-up of the separation of powers that the President had absolutely no authority to initiate any military activity. He only carried out those military operations previously authorized by the Congress. The only exception to this would be if the actual territory of the United States was invaded, when the President could act to repel the invasion.

As Presidents, Jefferson and Madison adhered to these principles. When American ships in the Mediterranean Sea were threatened from North Africa, Jefferson sent the young American Navy to protect them. Although he did not ask for a declaration of war, he did get congressional approval for the expedition. (It was during this expedition that the Marines saw their first foreign action on "the shores of Tripoli.") Madison sought the United States' first formal declaration of war when he launched the War of 1812 against Britain in response to its constant depredations against American ships.

Despite these early precedents, most of the Presidents since Franklin Roosevelt have acted in violation of this carefully framed constitutional balance of powers.[13] This includes Roosevelt himself, who acted surreptitiously to circumvent the United States' neutrality laws in actively aiding Great Britain in the two years before Pearl

Harbor.[14] Those who believe that the United States' foreign military actions since then have been ill-advised at best, and imperialistic aggression at worst, would readily agree that this presidential usurpation of Congress' exclusive right to commit the United States to war is a key element in producing these military misadventures.[15]

However, even if one generally supports the foreign conflicts in which we have been so frequently embroiled during the last seven decades, consider how these engagements have been conducted. Since they have been launched by presidential action, often covertly, without a full debate in Congress, they have usually been fought "on the cheap." Uncertain of congressional support, the Presidents have hesitated to commit the country's full resources to the military missions. Avoiding a congressional debate also allows the President to avoid sacrificing his domestic agenda, even if it means shortchanging the military action. For example, Lyndon Johnson did not want the Vietnam conflict to divert resources from his domestic Great Society programs, and George W. Bush did not want to reverse his recently enacted tax cuts when he launched the invasion of Iraq. Therefore, these and other modern conflicts were financed with deficit spending and, far worse, American military personnel are sent into harm's way without all of the nation's resources behind them.

If the Presidents had followed the Constitution and requested congressional approval in advance, is it possible that the nation would have been more unified in support, and seen to it that our soldiers, sailors, and airmen had the backing they deserve? I must interject here that this is not an abstract issue for me, for as I write this I have a nephew and a cousin on active duty in combat zones overseas.

Of course, Congress is not without blame here. Too often it has acquiesced in this presidential usurpation of its constitutional responsibilities.[16] Congress has granted Presidents vague, open-ended authorizations such as the "Gulf of Tonkin" resolution which was the sole authority for the longest war in our history, or the authorization which was given to George W. Bush to carry out actions in Iraq and

Afghanistan which now threaten to run on longer than the Vietnam conflict. In 1973, a War Powers Resolution was enacted over Richard Nixon's veto, which requires presidential consultation with Congress and an approval within sixty days of beginning a foreign military operation.[17] However, both this law and other laws seem to have all been largely ineffectual in curbing the prerogative that the Presidents have assumed of commencing wars on their own authority.[18] The courts have also declined to challenge this usurpation.[19] We have reached a point where presidential war power authority is viewed so expansively that it has been argued that even the weak War Powers Resolution is an unconstitutional congressional usurpation of the President's authority![20]

Our strategy in this project has been to attempt to restate constitutional provisions with a view to restoring their original meaning. In considering how one might restore the constitutional balance of power in this critical area, Madison's comments on the subject in the *Federalist* offer a possibility. He noted that "a standing force...is a dangerous, at the same time as it may be necessary, provision.... A wise nation...will exert all its prudence in diminishing both the necessity and the danger of resorting to [a standing army] which may be inauspicious to its liberties. The clearest marks of this prudence are stamped on the proposed Constitution."[21] He then points to this clause authorizing Congress:

Clause 12:   To raise and support Armies, but no Appropriation of Money to that Use shall be for a longer Term than two Years;

The dangers of a large permanent military establishment, he argues, should be mitigated if their funding has to be renewed by Congress every two years. Presidents have claimed that congressional funding of their foreign military ventures after the fact is the equivalent of the congressional pre-approval required by the Constitution. Fearful of cutting off funds for the troops after the President has already gotten them into harm's way, Congress has usually gone along with this rationale.   Any proposal to restore the original constitutional allocation of responsibility must thus address the Congress' failures as well as the Presidents' usurpations.

In doing this, we have to take into account aspects of modern warfare which may differ from that of the 1700s. Many modern wars are "fuzzy." They are small or unconventional actions, where there is not a clear and distinct action by conventional armed forces to mark the start of the conflict.[22] Also, wisdom sometimes dictates limiting the scope of a conflict where the other side has allies with whom we do not want to wage war, such as China during the Korean and Vietnamese conflicts. Another aspect of the post-Second World War security situation is the permanent or long-term posting of US armed forces overseas. This both drains our national treasury, and makes it more likely that US forces will get into some armed conflict without a formal commencement of hostilities.[23]

These circumstances have led proponents of presidential war power to argue that the President has sufficient constitutional authority to engage in armed conflict in these circumstances without any congressional approval at all.[24] However, as we have seen, this is absolutely contrary to the framers' goal of limiting the executive's ability to commit US forces to armed conflicts without legislative approval. So, how can we restore this constitutional balance in modern circumstances? The point where congressional control over US foreign military activities must be re-established is in making the initial decision to send US armed forces overseas, before the facts start to get fuzzy. That is the point where there is still an opportunity for deliberation. Once US forces have been posted abroad, the exigencies of modern warfare can require faster action than Congress can provide. However, to avoid open-ended commitments, there also must be regular review, just as the Constitution provides for military appropriations. To achieve all of this, it is proposed that Clause 11 be amended as follows:

Clause 11:   To declare War, grant Letters of Marque and Reprisal, ~~and~~ make Rules concerning Captures on Land and Water, **and approve any placement of the United States' armed forces outside the United States or its territories, but no such approval shall be for a term longer than two years [unless provided by a treaty approved in accordance with the second clause of Section 2 of Article II of this Constitution].**

This proposal would require that the Congress re-approve every overseas deployment of US military personnel biannually, and to do so separately from the appropriations process, which can unfortunately get bogged down any many extraneous considerations such as pork barrel projects.[25] As an absolute rule applying to any foreign deployment, it would leave Presidents with no more wiggle room to put US armed forces personnel in harm's way and then run back to Congress with a situation where to deny approval means abandoning US troops in combat.

Another advantage of this proposal is that it will also force Congress to regularly account for our sprawling worldwide deployment of forces. Many of the United States' overseas military commitments were made in times past when our budgets were in balance, our technology unrivaled, and before our manufacturing capabilities had been outsourced overseas. Would it not be wise to review these obligations now that we are in an era of endless budget deficits running into the unforeseeable future?[26] Many of history's greatest powers have fallen not because they were defeated in war, but simply because their military reach became over-extended, and irretrievably sapped their national resources.[27]

In order to force both the President and the Congress to comply with their constitutional responsibilities and limits, my view is that there should be no exceptions. This would make US "allies" realize that they can not take for granted the defense shield provided by

130

American taxpayers with their precious tax dollars and American service personnel with their precious lives, while these "allies" cut their defense budgets and use any excuse to avoid assisting the United States in maintaining international security. However, some may feel that international security requires that the United States be bound by formal treaty commitments. The bracketed language, "**unless provided by a treaty approved in accordance with the second clause of Section 2 of Article II of this Constitution,**" allows an exception where a formal treaty has been approved by a two-thirds vote of the Senate. You may decide whether that is necessary.

To make it absolutely clear that the President's war-making powers are completely subject to congressional authorization, a corresponding amendment to the first phrase of Clause 1 of Section 2 of Article II should be made:

Clause 1:   The President shall be Commander in Chief of the Army and Navy of the United States, and of the Militia of the several States, when called into the actual Service of the United States**, all subject to authorization by the Congress under Section 8 of Article I,**....

With these amendments the constitutional balance of power between the President and Congress may be restored so that Presidents are no longer able to commit America's fighting men and women to foreign postings and possible combat without the full approval and support of the national legislature and the American people who speak through them.[28] Of course, if the American people and Congress fail to speak, it may not make any difference.[29] The Constitution is about creating structures to facilitate the operation of the will of the American people through their Republic. Constitutional structures can not force the people to exercise this civil morality. It can, however, support or impede what the founders considered to be the source of what they called the "republican virtue" of the people. We will address this next.

131

Chapter 8

Disestablishments and Foundations:
Restoring Virtue

Of all the dispositions and habits, which lead to political prosperity, Religion and Morality are indispensable supports. In vain would that man claim the tribute of Patriotism, who should labor to subvert these great pillars of human happiness, these firmest props of the duties of Men and Citizens. The mere Politician, equally with the pious man, ought to respect and to cherish them. A volume could not trace all their connexions with private and public felicity.... Let us with caution indulge the supposition, that morality can be maintained without religion. Whatever may be conceded to the influence of refined education on minds of peculiar structure, reason and experience both forbid us to expect, that national morality can prevail in exclusion of religious principle. It is substantially true, that virtue or morality is a necessary spring of popular government. The rule, indeed, extends with more or less force to every species of free government. Who, that is a sincere friend to it, can look with indifference upon attempts to shake the foundation of the fabric?

George Washington[1]

We now pick up the history we left off in chapter 6. It is the late 1940s. The Second World War is over, having created the economic mobilization that the New Deal had promised but failed to produce. The Supreme Court is now composed of New Deal Democrats appointed by Franklin Roosevelt and Harry Truman.[2] Since these Justices had forsworn any oversight of the new, vastly expanded national government, some wondered if the Court would have anything to do. The next two chapters will describe how, through the creative distortion of history and application of the "living Constitution" philosophy, this New Deal Democrat Supreme Court assured that it and its successors would have plenty of business.

The main story is told in the next chapter. However, first we will look specifically at one of the most reaching of these developments. It is 1947, and a case has come before the Court called Everson vs. Board of Education.[3] Arch Everson had brought a lawsuit against his local public school board in New Jersey to stop it from reimbursing families for the costs of bus transportation of students to Catholic parochial schools, a program that also covered public school children. Among many arguments he made was that this violated the first amendment to the Constitution which provides that "Congress shall make no law respecting an establishment of religion." Now this presents a couple of immediate questions. First, the school buses were being provided by the school board of Ewing Township New Jersey, not the United States Congress. Second, what exactly is "an establishment of religion," and what does it have to do with driving little Catholic children to school? Today the answers to these questions impact every school, courthouse, workplace, park, and government in America and, to many, threaten George Washington's "foundation of the fabric" of American free government. To many others these answers stand as a bulwark against pernicious religious control of that same free government. In either case, they represent one of the most persistent sources of division in our public felicity.

We will begin with the 1940s Roosevelt/Truman Court's answers to these questions. The first was that, although the words of the first amendment clearly specify a prohibition only against action by the national Congress, those provisions were now applicable to the Ewing Township New Jersey school board because they were made binding on the States by the first section of the fourteenth amendment. This provides that "no state shall...deprive any person of life, liberty, or property, without due process of law; nor deny to any person within its jurisdiction the equal protection of the laws." This is called the "incorporation" of the Bill of Rights through the fourteenth amendment. This first question will be the focus of the next chapter, although we will discuss its applicability to this part of the first amendment later in this chapter. But now we focus on the answer to the second question, what is "an establishment of religion?"

Writing for the Court, Justice Hugo L. Black declared that the establishment prohibited by the first amendment meant that "neither a state nor the Federal Government can set up a church. Neither can pass laws which aid one religion, aid all religions, or prefer one religion over another ... No tax in any amount, large or small, can be levied to support any religious activities or institutions, whatever they may be called, or whatever form which they may adopt to teach or practice religion.... In the words of Jefferson, the clause against establishment of religion by law was intended to erect "a wall of separation between Church and State."[4] Earlier in the opinion, Justice Black described the movement toward religious freedom in the United States, and said that it had "reached its dramatic climax in Virginia in 1785-86 when the Virginia legislative body was about to renew Virginia's tax levy for the support of the established church. Thomas Jefferson and James Madison led the fight against this tax."[5] It was because Jefferson was so central to this struggle, in Justice Black's view, that he made Jefferson's description of the first amendment, the "wall of separation between Church and State," the central concept in his opinion.

That metaphor, the "wall of separation between Church and State," has become so common that many Americans think that that is the actual wording of the first amendment. Since Justice Black based his decision on a presentation of the supposed history of the first amendment, we will begin with that history. Of course, historical facts are often disputed, so we will begin with the most basic facts used by Justice Black. First of all, Thomas Jefferson had nothing to do with either the Virginia religious freedom law of 1786, the Constitutional Convention of 1787, or the First Congress of 1789 which drafted the Bill of Rights. He was in France serving as the United States' ambassador throughout this entire period. He did

134

correspond with Madison, but the subject of religious freedom was barely mentioned in their correspondence. Second, the "wall of separation" phrase does not come from any official record of the Constitutional Convention, the First Congress which wrote the Bill of Rights or any of the states' ratifications of the Bill of Rights. It comes from a private letter Jefferson wrote when he was President to a group of Connecticut Baptists in 1802, more than a decade after the first amendment was approved by the Congress and the States. Third, although Virginia was the largest State at the time the first amendment was approved, there were twelve other States, all of which had their own histories of dealing with the issue of religious freedom.[6] No historian would consider Virginia's action in any way a "dramatic climax" or especially influential when it came to drafting the first amendment. The other States had their own views, and were in no way intimidated by Virginia's example from pressing them in the First Congress.

Justice Black's "history" consisted of a single State's experience several years before the Bill of Rights, a quote from many years after the Bill of Rights from a man who had nothing to do with their drafting or enactment, and no mention at all of the actual congressional or state actions which produced the first amendment.

With this many basic factual problems, it may not be surprising that Justice Black's *Everson* decision suffers from more fundamental historical problems. Let us begin with the actual wording of the first amendment. "An establishment" of religion was a well understood concept at the time the first amendment was drafted. It was government sponsorship and support of a particular religious faith.[7] The early Americans knew very well what it was because most of the colonies had established churches. In the southern colonies this had been the Church of England. Nonetheless they had a fair degree of religious diversity, and with some struggle had disestablished the Church of England (which in America now called itself the Protestant Episcopal Church) during and after the War of Independence. However, in most of New England the established church was the

135

Congregationalists, the religion of the original Puritan colonists. The Congregationalist clergy continued to enjoy state support and preference after Independence. Government support of particular churches continued in parts of New York as well.[8] One historian concludes that "Americans both before and after the Revolution thought of establishment as an exclusive government preference for one religion."[9] This had been the accepted meaning of "religious establishment" in the English language for centuries by the time it was inserted in the first amendment.[10]

What "establishment" did *not* mean, at least to most Americans at the time of the founding, was government relations with religion (or at least Protestantism) generally, as long as there was no preferred status given to a particular denomination.[11] The views expressed by George Washington in the quote from his Farewell Address at the beginning of this chapter express the general American consensus of the time.[12] That government should preferentially support a particular religious faith was losing favor (by the 1830s even Massachusetts ended its state support for the Congregationalist church), but support for and acknowledgment of religion in general was considered essential to good social order.[13]

This understanding of the meaning of "establishment" can be seen in the wording of the official Bill of Rights proposals submitted to the First Congress by Virginia and New York. Virginia urged language providing that "no particular religious sect or society ought to be favoured or established, by law, in preference to others," and New York that "no religious sect or society ought to be favored or established by law in preference to others."[14] Note that they were identical except for Virginia's addition of "particular." Other States' proposals ran along similar lines. The record of the debates in the House of Representatives show Madison saying that the purpose of the amendment was to assure that Congress "not establish *a* religion and enforce the legal observation of it by law."[15] In the negotiations between the Senate and the House of Representatives the reference to "*a* religion" became a bar to "*an* establishment of religion" in the

136

final language.[16]   Either way, taken together with the commonly accepted meaning of what constituted "religious establishment," the first amendment clearly is barring a governmental preference for a particular religion, not religion in general.[17]

That general non-preferential government support of religion was not intended to fall under the first amendment can be seen from the conduct of the very First Congress which produced it. Shortly after approving the Bill of Rights the First Congress voted to pay for congressional chaplains, required federal judges to declare "so help me God" at the end of their oaths of office, reenacted the law governing the admission of new States which required that public schools be set up to promote "religion, morality and knowledge," and passed a resolution calling for a national day of thanksgiving and prayer "to acknowledge the providence of Almighty God."[18] Full of religious language, it was gladly issued by President George Washington, whose views on the necessity of a religious foundation for public morality were re-iterated in his Farewell Address as quoted at the beginning of the chapter.

The Wall of Separation

No where in any records of the First Congress' or the States' approval of the first amendment does the term "separation" appear.[19] So, where does it come from? As we noted, a number of States continued to have official established state churches after the first amendment was passed forbidding Congress from creating a "national" established church.[20] One of these was Connecticut, and it is here that Thomas Jefferson finally historically enters this story. Historians endlessly debate Jefferson's religiosity, but one can safely say that, whatever it was, it was at least somewhat unconventional for his time.[21] When he ran for President against John Adams in 1800, Adams' Federalist party accused Jefferson of lacking religion, a serious charge in an era when most Americans believed that religion was a critical underpinning for a free society. Jefferson's views on the relation of religion to government were also unconventional. When he declined to issue thanksgiving proclamations, unlike his predecessors Washington and Adams, this seemed to confirm the charges of irreligion.

As one might expect, the established churches of New England were politically opposed to Jefferson. After he had been in office for a year, a letter from an association of Baptist churches based in Danbury, Connecticut offered Jefferson an opportunity to score some political points on his Federalist opponents. It was in his short reply to the Connecticut Baptists that he said that the first amendment was to build a "wall of separation between Church and State."[22]

There are several points to note about this now famous letter. First is that its fame is of modern vintage. No one other than a few scholars would even know of it were it not for Justice Hugo Black's *Everson* opinion. In 1802 it was reprinted in a few newspapers as a partisan political piece, and then forgotten.[23]

Second, it was ignored by its addressees. The Baptists believed deeply that their faith should apply to all aspects of their lives, and the idea that the political sphere should be separated from the well-spring of all goodness would not have sat well with their views. They just wanted to be free from having to pay taxes to support the ministers of the Connecticut Congregational Church. However, like most Americans, they believed that religious faith should infuse the public sphere.[24]

Third, Jefferson may not have disagreed with this point of view as entirely as modern scholars would have us believe.[25] The Sunday after sending his letter to the Connecticut Baptists, Jefferson began attending the interdenominational church services which were held in the Capitol building, and attended them almost every Sunday for the rest of his presidency.[26] (The use of the Capitol for regular religious services is also another example of the early view that non-preferential government support of religion did not violate the first

138

amendment.) And even though he would not mandate days of thanksgiving, he certainly showed no hesitation in invoking divinity in his political rhetoric.[27] An example is his first inaugural address, where he described the United States as "enlightened by a benign religion, professed, indeed, and practiced in various forms, yet all of them inculcating honesty, truth, temperance, gratitude, and the love of man; acknowledging and adoring an overruling Providence, which by all its dispensations proves that it delights in the happiness of man here and his greater happiness hereafter."[28] While with Madison he was among the most adamant in opposing traditional religious establishments, he also rejected his political enemies' accusations that he wanted a "government without religion."[29]

So if Jefferson introduced the term but did not really hold rigid strict separationist views, where did the *Everson* decision come from? The answer does not lie in the historical origins or original meaning of the first amendment. The authors of the first amendment would have firmly rejected Justice Black's contention that the first amendment prohibition on "an establishment of religion" meant that government could not "aid all religions," or that government could not "support any religious activities or institutions, whatever they may be called." The true origins of the ideology of strict separation between religion and government came later, and are not nearly as stirring to recount as the fictional history concocted by Hugo Black in 1947.

Most of the first European immigrants to British North America were Protestants. They were of many different Protestant professions. The English were either Anglicans or Puritan dissenters, the Scots and Scots-Irish were usually Presbyterian, the Dutch were Reformed, the Germans and Swedes were Lutheran. And new Protestant tendencies had arisen from the Great Awakening of the first half of the 1700s, the Methodists and Baptists. The need for these disparate Protestants to get along in the new nation was a powerful impetus for the elimination of established churches and the passage of laws assuring religious freedom.

139

Historically there was one thing that united all Protestants. That was opposition to Roman Catholicism. That, after all, was what they were protesting. Thus, as the United States moved into the 1800s there was broad concern when new immigrants were increasingly Catholic. Most disturbing were the Irish, who began to come in huge numbers after the potato famines of the 1840s. It was charged that not only did Catholics' loyalty to the papacy interfere with complete loyalty to the United States, but it also prevented Catholics from developing the independent spirit needed for citizens of a free republic. (It is important to distinguish this conflict from present-day immigration controversies. Since there were no immigration laws, these immigrants were all in the United States legally.) It was in the context of this virulent anti-Catholicism that separation talk first began to take hold.[30]

It was hoped that the public schools, which were heavily influenced by the Protestant churches which had founded them, would convert Catholic immigrant children to the true paths of Protestant republicanism. In response Catholics set up their own schools.[31] Concern grew that the increasing numbers of Catholic voters would secure public funding for their schools like that offered to the Protestant-oriented public schools. In 1875, a constitutional amendment forbidding government support for sectarian schools sponsored by Congressman James G. Blaine failed passing Congress by only two votes. However, "Blaine amendments" were made to many state constitutions. Anti-Catholicism continued to be politically potent. It was something which could unite northern and southern Protestants who were looking for common ground to heal the divisions of the Civil War.

Of course, this approach only opened new divisions. These divisions were exploited by both respectable and not so respectable parties. In the 1920s the Ku Klux Klan rose to nation-wide prominence outside of its southern base on a campaign which was as much or more anti-Catholic as it was anti-black. Incongruous as it may seem to us today,

140

the Ku Klux Klan and similar groups were staunch advocates of the "separation of church and state," and Klan members took oaths to sustain it. These, and more innocent Protestants, saw this separation only in terms of preventing Catholic influence in politics. Their own sense of Americanism was so tied into the Protestant identity of the country that they did not heed the small groups of true secularists, such as the National Liberal League, which sought to use separation to eliminate any religious influence in public life.[32]

Americans do not like to recall this aspect of our history, but this virulent anti-Catholicism was a powerful and ugly force in America for a majority of that history. And it was this force that drove the rhetoric that held the "separation of church and state" to be an aspect of true Americanism. Eventually the rhetoric grew so widespread that one could almost ignore that it was a code for anti-Catholicism. However, time and again, the underlying reality broke through. An example was the sensational 1921 trial in Mobile, Alabama of a preacher who had murdered, in cold blood, a Catholic priest who had married the preacher's daughter to her Puerto Rican boyfriend. The Klan arranged to have a bright young lawyer defend the preacher. The lawyer used veiled Klan rhetoric and even gave the jury a Klan hand signal. When the Puerto Rican son-in-law was brought in to testify, the lawyer had the shades drawn so he would appear dark-skinned. The jury acquitted the preacher of the priest's murder, despite overwhelming evidence against him.

Following this successful service to the Klan, the lawyer rose rapidly in the ranks of both the Klan and Alabama politics. Eventually, with the Klan's strong support, he was elected to the United States Senate. There, like many other southern Democrats, he staunchly supported the New Deal, as long as it left out southern blacks, which it mostly did.[33] He was rewarded by becoming Franklin Roosevelt's first nominee to the Supreme Court. That lawyer was Hugo L. Black.[34]

The discovery of his Klan past caused considerable controversy right after he got on to the Supreme Court. He gave a radio speech where he claimed his Klan involvement was minimal. However, he also used veiled Klan language in his broadcast. Democrats defended Black's address as adequately responding to concerns. Many blacks were not convinced. Others were convinced. After the broadcast, a great celebratory burning cross appeared over the Mountain Lakes dam in New Jersey.[35] Ten years later Arch Everson, who was a member of a fraternal order which shared the Klan's deep anti-Catholicism, began his lawsuit against the school board in nearby Ewing Township. Sometimes Justice Black seemed to be trying to overcome his Klan background in his Supreme Court decisions. However, even his own son allowed that Black and the Klan still always "had one thing in common. He suspected the Catholic Church.... He thought the popes and bishops had too much power and property."[36]

Although the Catholic Church was technically not the defendant in the *Everson* case, that Supreme Court decision clearly presented a culmination of a century of anti-Catholic agitation under the guise of the separation of church and state.[37] Hugo Black was certainly not the only anti-Catholic in America in the 1940s.[38] Some readers may recall that even in 1960, John F. Kennedy's Catholic religion was a major issue in his presidential campaign. However, litigation over the first amendment's prohibition on establishment of religion then took a turn that sincere Protestants now regret as much as any Catholic. The next year, in the case of McCollum vs. Board of Education, the plaintiff was an atheist objecting to a program in which religion teachers came into a high school to give voluntary religion classes at the school.[39] Justice Black carried his *Everson* opinion forward to ban this voluntary arrangement. This opened a deluge of litigation by atheists which continues to this day. As a result:

- A teacher cannot read a Bible in school, even outside of class.[40]
- A college instructor can not mention his religious views in class, even when he makes it clear that they are personal opinions not part of the required subject matter.[41]

- A student was forbidden to present her beliefs about homosexuality on a school panel and told that her religious beliefs were the equivalent of racism.[42]
- A student may not pray aloud over lunch in school.[43]
- A cemetery planter in the shape of a cross is forbidden because it might cause "emotional distress" to non-Christian visitors.[44]
- A law providing for a moment of silence at the beginning of the school day is unconstitutional because the legislator who introduced it might have had a religious motive.[45]
- Illinois public employees cannot have a paid holiday on Good Friday.[46]
- City seals cannot contain religious subjects, even if they are historically significant.[47]
- A Nativity can not appear on public property unless it is accompanied by secular symbols like Santa Claus' reindeer.[48]
- An anti-drug counselor was banned from presenting a non-religious anti-drug message because he was also a minister.[49]
- Students may not offer voluntary prayers at voluntary school assemblies where they are otherwise free to speak on any other topic.[50]

The examples continue ad nauseam:[51]

- A high school student was forbidden to write about the life of Jesus for a school assignment.
- School officials removed a kindergartner's picture of Jesus from a display of items for which the children were grateful.
- Coaches are not allowed to participate in their teams' pre-game prayers.
- Brochures about summer Bible camp were banned in school even when those for other summer camps were allowed.
- Even Christmas trees have been banned from public property as religious symbols.
- Religious items were confiscated from gift bags children brought for a holiday party.

- A school girl was rebuked by the principal for wearing a necklace with a cross.

The Supreme Court's establishment jurisprudence imposes a double standard where even the slightest emotional dismay can justify the prohibition of religious speech, whereas other forms of free speech are protected even if many find them offensive.[52] Thus a clergyman can not give a short prayer at a school graduation for fear of exposing unwilling non-believers to a minute of religion, yet parents are forced to have their children use textbooks for an entire school year even though the parents feel the textbooks denigrate and conflict with their religious beliefs (and reasonable alternative textbooks are available).[53]

Another example of the double standard is the special standing granted to plaintiffs in cases alleging violations of the prohibition on religious establishment. In chapter 6 we discussed the concept of "standing," which requires that you be able to show some specific damage to yourself in order to start a lawsuit. Normally, simply being a taxpayer does not give you standing to object to government spending which does not otherwise affect you in any way. However, in the case of Flast vs. Cohen, the Supreme Court ruled that an atheist objecting to some indirect government assistance to parochial schools had standing to sue even though he had no relation to the issue other than his status as a taxpayer.[54] This special taxpayer standing status has not been granted to any other class of plaintiffs.

Even if you are not offended by these examples of the use of the establishment clause of the first amendment to repress religious exercise and belief (which is supposed to be protected by the other half of the religion clauses of the first amendment -- "Congress shall make no law respecting an establishment of religion, *or prohibiting the free exercise thereof*") there is another significant issue of legal justice raised by the Supreme Court's post-*Everson* jurisprudence. Simply put, it makes no sense. Even if you find the "wall of separation" to

144

be a lovely metaphor, poetry does not help when a judge is trying to sort through the nitty-gritty of real-life facts. In Lemon vs. Kurtzman the Supreme Court tried to lay out an elaborate formula for deciding what constituted an impermissible "establishment" of religion.[55] The Court proposed three tests which were that "the statute must have a secular legislative purpose; second, its principal or primary effect must be one that neither advances nor inhibits religion...[and] finally, the statute must not foster 'an excessive government entanglement with religion.'"[56] Failure of any one of these three tests could render a government action unconstitutional.

What separates the rule of law from the rule of men is that the law should allow people to reasonably predict what conduct falls under the legal rules, independent of human dictates. The *Lemon* criteria and every other test used in first amendment establishment cases utterly fail this critical test. Instead, religion decisions turn on indeterminate judicial predilections. Even pro-separation scholars acknowledge how ridiculous establishment clause jurisprudence has become. Professor Leonard Levy writes that the distinctions that Supreme Court Justices make in religion cases "would glaze the minds of medieval scholastics," and that the use of the tests "lends the appearance of objectivity to a judicial opinion, but no evidence shows that a test influences a member of the Court to reach a decision that he would not have reached without the test. And, Justices using the same test often arrive at contradictory results."[57]

For example, Levy notes the case of Aguilar vs. Felton, where the Supreme Court ruled that it was unconstitutional to send remedial education specialists from the public school system to parochial schools for special needs students.[58] In that situation the *Lemon* criteria create a "Catch-22" where the public schools must monitor the special needs classes to assure that they are not "advancing religion," but by doing so become "entangled" with the parochial schools' religious mission.[59] Levy concludes that the "Supreme Court has been inexcusably inconsistent in its interpretation of the establishment clause."[60]

145

Within a period of only a few years the Supreme Court ruled that legislatures may have chaplains paid by the State but may not place privately funded nativity displays in a courthouse foyer.[61] What is the status of religion in the workplace? Only a few years apart, the Court ruled that religious employers may discriminate in favor of their followers, but that a religious person is not entitled to be excused from work on their religious holy days.[62] That inconsistency continues, as illustrated by two recent cases challenging the placement of copies of the Ten Commandments on public grounds. In 5-to-4 decisions rendered the same day, the Court ruled that one on the grounds of the Texas State Capitol was permissable while another in a Kentucky courthouse was not. The differences turned on such minutiae that it would be impossible to predict the outcome of any future "Ten Commandments" case.[63]

Pro-separationist Jeffrey Rosen lambasted the wildly inconsistent jurisprudence of the *Lemon* criteria in an article in the *New Republic*. After noting the contradictory situation created by the *Aguilar* case, he writes that the "Court's efforts to apply the Lemon test are even more absurd. Under *Lemon* bus trips from home to religious school are constitutional, but bus trips from religious schools to local museums are unconstitutional. (The latter, but not the former, bring government too close to religion, according to the Court.) Standardized tests are OK, but teacher-prepared tests are not. Government can provide parochial schools with books but not maps, provoking Senator Daniel Patrick Moynihan's quip, 'What about atlases?' The Court has invoked *Lemon* to strike down a nativity scene surrounded by poinsettias and to uphold a nativity scene surrounded by elephants, teddy bears, Santa's workshop and a talking wishing well. This is the Court's idea of equal time for atheists; practitioners call it the 'three plastic animals' rule."[64]

More recently some Supreme Court Justices have expressed doubts about the *Lemon* criteria. However, the proposed replacements, such as "endorsement" or "neutrality," are just as vague and subjective as

146

the *Lemon* tests, still calling for judgments as to whether something is "too religious" or determining the "mental state" of legislators.[65] And none of these alternatives have commanded a majority of the Court, leaving the *Lemon* tests as the controlling law.[66]

First amendment establishment clause jurisprudence faces an even more fundamental challenge. The preponderance of historical evidence shows that most of the founders favored a close relationship between government and religion.[67] Many defended the States' existing established churches, and those who objected only opposed a preferred status for a particular religion, not government acknowledgment of religion in general. As scholars have finally studied the actual history of the Bill of Rights, as distinct from Hugo Black's invented history, many have concluded that the prohibition on establishment in the first amendment can best be understood as a political compromise between these two viewpoints. The second phrase banning laws which prohibit the free exercise of religion was the primary religious freedom clause. In contrast, the anti-establishment clause was not about religious freedom at all. Instead it was a states' rights provision, banning Congress from creating a national church which would compete with the States' existing established churches. According to Yale law professor Akhil Amar the "original establishment clause ... is not anti-establishment but pro-states' rights; it ... simply calls for the issue to be decided locally."[68]

This interpretation offers a way out of the argument about what constitutes "an establishment of religion." However, it presents a major new difficulty. If the entire point of the establishment prohibition was to bar the federal government from interfering with the States on religious matters, then it is meaningless, even a logical contradiction, to then apply it to the States under the *Everson* case and its progeny. Even if incorporation of other parts of the Bill of Rights against the States through the fourteenth amendment is valid, it makes no sense to incorporate the establishment clause of the first amendment if its explicit purpose was only to keep the national government out of the States' religious affairs.[69]

Of Pillars, Principles and Preferences

So, is there any way to sort out the mess the Supreme Court has made of the first amendment's prohibition against "an establishment of religion"? The only party which gains anything from the mess is the American Civil Liberties Union, which collects fees from defendants in its establishment clause lawsuits pursuant to the Civil Rights Attorneys Fee Awards Act of 1976. The ACLU will only disclose that these fees are "of a substantial amount."[70] One author has identified over $4 million collected by the ACLU from the taxpayers in specific cases where the ACLU sued state and local governments in establishment clause cases.[71] This is why the ACLU ignores the pleas of pro-separationists like Leonard Levy that "suits brought by the ACLU to have courts hold unconstitutional every cooperative relationship between government and religion can damage the cause of separation by making it look over-rigid and ridiculous." Levy continues to note that "one of the principal arguments of separationists against certain practices that breach the wall of separation...is that those practices are divisive and stimulate conflict among people of differing faiths. Some silly suits, such as those seeking to have declared unconstitutional the words 'under God' in the pledge of allegiance or in the money the motto 'In God We Trust' have the same deleterious effects."[72]

Here Levy echoes the argument of Justice Arthur Goldberg, concurring in Abington School District vs. Schempp, that "both the required and the permissible accommodations between state and church frame the relation as one free of hostility or favor and productive of religious and political harmony." Justice Goldberg stressed that "untutored devotion to the concept of neutrality can lead to invocation or approval of results which partake not simply of that noninterference and noninvolvement with the religious which the Constitution commands, but of a brooding and pervasive devotion to the secular and a passive, or even active, hostility to the religious. Such results are not only not compelled by the

Constitution, but, it seems to me, are prohibited by it. Neither government nor this Court can or should ignore the significance of the fact that a vast portion of our people believe in and worship God and that many of our legal, political and personal values derive historically from religious teachings. Government must inevitably take cognizance of the existence of religion and, indeed, under certain circumstances the First Amendment may require that it do so."[73]

It is now clear that the *Everson*-based jurisprudence advocated by separationists like Justice Goldberg and Professor Levy has produced the very result they thought it would prevent. The wall of separation has produced divisions, conflicts, hostility and anything but political harmony. The metaphor itself can help us to understand why this is inevitable under Hugo Black's *Everson* interpretation. The metaphor of the wall implies that there can be an absolute and sharp division between the worlds of government and of religion. However, that is not reality. Religion and government exist in the same world. Even in *Lemon* Chief Justice Burger's majority opinion admitted that "judicial caveats against entanglement must recognize that the line of separation, far from being a 'wall,' is a blurred, indistinct, and variable barrier depending on all the circumstances of a particular relationship."[74] Over half a century of court cases since *Everson* have failed to produce any clear guidance in this area which would comport with the requirements of the rule of law. They have only proven that real life is entirely too "blurred, indistinct and variable" to make any strict separation of government and religion workable.

Not only is the wall of separation infeasible, but it has leant itself to the very "secular and passive, or even active, hostility to the religious" that Justice Goldberg feared. The ACLU and other anti-religious groups have used the *Everson* wall of separation doctrine to push courts to rule that only the complete absence of religion from the public sphere complies with the first amendment.

Here we must take account of the changes in our country since 1802. When Thomas Jefferson wrote his little letter to the Connecticut

Baptists, the national government was minuscule compared to today, and even the state governments were much smaller. Education and other social services were almost entirely private, not government, responsibilities. In our time government fills a vast space that was private in the founders' day. How can government and religion avoid each other in our modern complex, interrelated society and economy?

Furthermore, this is not a stationary wall. It moves. As we have seen, government is always expanding its reach. Therefore, if religion and government must be absolutely separated by an impregnable wall, then as government expands, religion must contract. Since separationist activists are also almost always on the political left, the *Everson* wall of separation gives them a double benefit. As they work to increase the government's role in society, they can also decrease the role of religion.[75] Is it shocking that those for whom religious faith is vital resist this court-mandated secularization of America?

The solution here is the same as in previous chapters. We must go back to the original understanding, to recognize, as Washington said, that no patriot would "labor to subvert these great pillars of human happiness, these firmest props of the duties of Men and Citizens.... Let us with caution indulge the supposition, that morality can be maintained without religion.... reason and experience both forbid us to expect, that national morality can prevail in exclusion of religious principle." The first amendment must be amended to make it clear that what is prohibited is government giving preference to a particular religion, not religion in general.

However, in doing so we also have to take account of our modern America. One sharp distinction between our America and that of the founding is the status of religious belief. Although the United States remains far more religious than other economically developed countries, recent polls still show 16% of Americans as without any religious affiliation, including 4% who identify themselves as atheist or agnostic and another 6% who describe themselves as "secular." And a quarter of Americans aged 18 to 29 indicate that they have no religious affiliation.[76] These secular Americans maintain that their lack of religion does not make them any less ethical than the religious. If we are to do a better job of bringing Americans together than the separationists, we must take account of Americans who have no religion as well as the wide diversity of those who profess a religious faith. To achieve this the first amendment could be revised to read:

> Congress shall make no law **preferring a religion or irreligion** ~~respecting an establishment of religion~~, or prohibiting the free exercise thereof; or abridging the freedom of speech, or of the press; or the right of the people peaceably to assemble, and to petition the government for a redress of grievances.

This addition of "irreligion" does two things. First, it gives constitutional recognition to the 10% of Americans who strive to lead ethical and moral lives without benefit (or, in their view, hindrance) of religion, and gives them the benefit of the "free exercise" clause which follows in the first amendment. Second, it makes clear that secularism is no longer the "default" setting for government involvement with religion. Simply purging religion from the public sphere will no longer satisfy the first amendment since that would constitute "preferring...irreligion."

Instead, all viewpoints will be presented. If Christians want to use public spaces for displays celebrating the birth of their founder, then the atheists are entitled to display their point of view as well, perhaps honoring David Hume's birthday or if, against historical evidence, they insist on counting him amongst their numbers, Thomas Jefferson's (it is April 13). If a professor can advocate Marxism, then another can do the same for Thomism, the religious philosophy of another Thomas. Let the schoolchildren write their essays on what Jesus, Moses, or Mohammed mean to them. And let the schoolchildren learn openly and without embarrassment who these world-changing men were.

It was a bizarre notion that suppressing the religious presence in the public sphere was necessary to promote harmony. In what other field do we believe that suppressing speech is the best course for a free republic? No, the American way is for all to be heard. Read the rest of the words of this first charter of our freedoms – free exercise of religion, freedom of speech, press, assembly, and petition. That is the American way, to let all viewpoints be heard rather than using the power of the courts and their misinterpretation of the Constitution to stifle voices disapproved by an elite minority.

Obviously, there will still be questions. Technically the revised amendment would now allow government financial support for religion, which many, including myself, would find objectionable as a matter of legislative policy. However, we would have Madison's solution if that were to happen. In the *Federalist* No. 10 he observed that America's very size would keep her both free and stable because the "multiplicity of sects" would counteract against any one becoming dominant. For example, if some large religion would be so unwise as to push through government salaries for clergy, they would see their folly as soon as the Wiccans, Scientologists, and Satanists showed up to collect their checks. As Madison and Jefferson foresaw, it is America's religious diversity which both protects religious freedom and promotes America's religiosity in general. We are a far more religious nation than other economically advanced countries.[77] This revised first amendment will allow us to celebrate that faithfulness in all its varieties, and the republican virtue it sustains.

This restored and revised first amendment can heal the divisions which the doctrine of the "wall of separation," with its virulent anti-Catholic origins and current day exploitation by anti-religious secularists, has opened. Now we must turn to another part of the Constitution where the Supreme Court has run seriously off track. Restoring this next section of our founding document will not only put the Constitution back on track and in the hands of the American people, but also solidly build into the Constitution the cure to our nation's greatest error, our legacy of African-American slavery.

Chapter 9

The Four Word Constitution: Restoring Clarity

To avoid an arbitrary discretion in the courts, it is indispensable that they should be bound down by strict rules and precedents, which serve to define and point out their duty in every particular case that comes before them.

Alexander Hamilton[1]

In the last chapter we saw the Roosevelt/Truman New Deal Supreme Court seize a major new arena of power by its historically inaccurate and constitutionally suspect application of the first amendment's prohibition on religious establishment to the States. We will now look at how it came about that the Supreme Court rewrote the Constitution to vastly expand its power in this and so many other arenas. To do so, we leave the Constitution of the founders and the framers; the world of Washington and Hamilton, of Jefferson and Madison, of the Father of our Country and the Father of our Constitution. We leave names we know so well from streets and cities, counties and colleges, monuments and the pictures on the money in our purses and wallets.

Instead we are now in 1866, and meet a new set of framers whose names would test the most devout buff of historical trivia. These framers are the Republicans of the Thirty-ninth Congress, the Congress elected in 1864. The Civil War is over and Abraham Lincoln is dead. The generals, Lee and Grant, Johnston and Sherman, have ended the war in good order, even with a start toward reconciliation. However, now the politicians have taken over. Andrew Johnson, a Tennessee Democrat who remained loyal to the

153

Union, has succeeded Lincoln, who had made him Vice President as a gesture of reconciliation toward the South. Johnson and his fellow southern whites want a speedy readmission to the Union of the states of the late Confederacy. Northern Republicans fear that this will simply return the nation to the condition it was in before the war.[2]

The original Constitution of 1787 had acknowledged obliquely the existence of slavery, using euphemisms like persons "held to Service or Labour" or referring to the "Importation of such Persons as any of the States now existing shall think proper to admit." Even before the Civil War was over Lincoln had begun the process of initiating an amendment to the Constitution abolishing slavery. This thirteenth amendment was ratified in 1865. (The struggle to pass it in the House of Representatives was recently dramatically portrayed in the Steven Spielberg movie *Lincoln*.)

However, the fact that southern blacks were no longer slaves did not automatically mean that they possessed the right to vote or other civil rights. Even in the North, free blacks often did not enjoy full legal equality. For example, they might be barred from juries, and did not have the right to vote in many States. In the southern States far more drastic legal conditions were being imposed on the newly freed blacks. These included limiting their ability to travel, requiring them to enter into labor contract, and other legal restrictions that came close to imitating slavery.[3]

In response, in 1866 Congress passed the Civil Rights Act over President Johnson's veto. It provided that all "persons within the jurisdiction of the United States shall have the same right in every State and Territory to make and enforce contracts, to sue, be parties, give evidence, and to the full and equal benefit of all laws and proceedings for the security of persons and property as is enjoyed by white citizens." (This pioneering law is still on the books today.[4]) However, the Republicans feared that a future Congress might change the law. Others, such as Representative John Bingham of Ohio, were concerned that it did not have a solid basis in the

154

Constitution, and that a future Supreme Court would find it unconstitutional. Therefore, they proposed another amendment to the Constitution.

The great champion of the black freedmen was Representative Thaddeus Stevens.[5] (Previously obscure, Stevens has recently become better known through his portrayal by the actor Tommy Lee Jones in the movie *Lincoln*.) A bachelor with a foot seriously deformed from birth, he was 74 years old in 1866, and had been a champion of the cause of abolition from long before the war. He had constantly pressed Lincoln to move faster, toward the Emancipation Proclamation, the enlistment of blacks in the Union army, and the grant of full civil rights to African-Americans. His district was in southern Pennsylvania. He had lived in the town of Gettysburg for many years, and had a part interest in an iron foundry there. He was so hated in the South that in 1863, when the Army of Northern Virginia invaded the North, Confederates had made a special point of razing Stevens' foundry (although Robert E. Lee had issued orders that civilian property not be deliberately damaged). Stevens turned down a special fund which was raised to compensate him, insisting instead that the money go to the relief of the now unemployed foundry workers. More than a generation before William Jennings Bryan, Stevens had been given the accolade of the "Commoner."

Stevens thought the thirteenth amendment was adequate authority for the Civil Rights Act (which he had sponsored), but was disappointed that it did not go the full distance in granting blacks the vote and full equality. Therefore he proposed language for what would be the fourteenth amendment which declared that "all laws, state and national, shall operate impartially and equally on all persons without regard to race or color."[6]

Stevens' proposals ran into the great original sin of America. Northern whites were no more inclined to treat blacks as equals than southerners. Politically, a clear and straightforward declaration of full

155

legal equality for African-Americans was not going to pass.[7] Still Stevens tried again, introducing a tighter version drafted by Robert Dale Owen, the American son of the famous British reformer. It stated that "no discrimination shall be made by any state, nor by the United States, as to the civil rights of persons because of race, color or previous condition of servitude." Another section specifically provided an 1876 deadline for full African-American suffrage.[8] Still Stevens could not persuade his colleagues to forthrightly acknowledge the rights of their black fellow Americans.

Enter Congressman Bingham, who had also been proposing language for the amendment. He was a type we would recognize today. A politician given to expansive and sometimes incoherent flights of rhetoric, he was described by the legendary constitutional scholar Alexander Bickel as "a man not normally distinguished for precision of thought and statement."[9] Bingham would be right at home in our age of birthers and truthers, for he went to his grave swearing that he, and only he, knew the real truth behind the conspiracy to assassinate Abraham Lincoln.[10] Bingham tended to sweeping generalities and, after many iterations, it was Bingham's approach which prevailed over Stevens' forthright declarations of full equality. It is from Bingham that we get this language now in the first section of the fourteenth amendment:

> No state shall make or enforce any law which shall
> abridge the privileges or immunities of citizens of the
> United States; nor shall any state deprive any person
> of life, liberty, or property, without due process of
> law; nor deny to any person within its jurisdiction the
> equal protection of the laws.

Now these are fine-sounding words. Representative George Boutwell of Massachusetts said of Bingham's passion for this language that "its euphony and indefiniteness of meaning were a charm to him."[11] The nub is in Boutwell's incisive observation of its "indefiniteness of meaning." This vague and general language could mean different things to different people.[12] For some, it meant only the rights referred to in the Civil Rights Act, which was going through Congress at the same time as the amendment. The purposes of the new amendment were to assure that Congress had authority under the Constitution to pass the Civil Rights Act, and to write its principal provisions into the Constitution so that a future Congress could not repeal them.[13] Bingham and the amendment's sponsor in the Senate, Jacob Howard, sometimes said that the amendment comprised the Bill of Rights, but no one focused on this. Others mentioned only particular rights, some in the Bill of Rights and some not. In the words of one historian, these comments "were made casually, without systematic development. The due process clause slipped into subordinate, almost forgotten, position, being commonly read and frequently discussed as if it were a part of the equal protection requirement."[14]

If anyone in the Thirty-ninth Congress had been inclined to give closer consideration to these grand phrases, they quickly would have found themselves in a mess of questions. Did "due process" mean simply that regular judicial procedures were followed? This was the traditional sense of the term. As Hamilton explained long before, "the words 'due process' have a precise technical import, and are only applicable to the process and proceedings of courts of justice; they can never be referred to an act of the legislature."[15] Did "due process" require a certain level of procedure or did the term incorporate some substantive rights such as would normally be enacted by the legislature, not the courts? If it did the latter, what were these rights, and how would you decide what they were? "Equal protection" is no clearer. Is the emphasis on the "equal" or on the "protection"? Does it mean only that whatever protection is supplied has to be supplied equally, or does it impose a positive obligation to supply some kind of protection? If the latter, the same questions arise as with substantive due process -- what protection is required and how do you determine what it is?[16]

If you look at the full text of the fourteenth amendment in the Appendix, you can see why the members of Congress paid so little attention to the first section. The fourteenth amendment is the longest of all of the amendments. Sections 2, 3, and 4 deal with major issues of the post-Civil War Reconstruction – how will Congress be apportioned now that blacks counted as full people rather than three-fifths, what was the citizenship status of former Confederates, was the United States liable for the Confederacy's war debts? These issues were the focus of the Thirty-ninth Congress. Section 1 was just "surplusage."[17] No one really cared about its "indefiniteness of meaning." In fact, that was its virtue to these politicians. Its vague language sounded good, indeed euphonious, but did not mandate equality for blacks. It left in place segregation and the denial of political rights such as jury service and the suffrage to blacks.[18] Indeed, it did not even mention them. That it could mean so many different things made it easy to campaign on, and getting re-elected in 1866 was the first priority for these Republicans.[19]

A shilly-shally bungling thing

Stevens was bitterly disappointed in the version of the fourteenth amendment which was finally enacted. He called it "an offspring of cowardice" and a "shilly-shally bungling thing."[20] While recognizing that this was all that was possible as a practical political matter, he nonetheless eloquently declared his sentiments. "In my youth, in my manhood, in my old age, I had fondly dreamed that when any fortunate chance should have...released us from obligations the most tyrannical that ever man imposed,...that the intelligent, pure and just men of this Republic...would have so remodeled our institutions as to have freed them from every vestige of human oppression.... In short, that no distinction would be made in this purified Republic but what arose from merit and conduct. This bright dream has vanished."[21] For most readers, Stevens' words will call to mind another speech about a dream which was delivered almost a century later. Stevens died in 1868, shortly after leading the effort to impeach Andrew Johnson, and was buried in an obscure spot because he refused to be interred in a cemetery which was segregated by race, as most were.[22] Although technically blacks would gain the right to vote with the fifteenth amendment in 1870, that 20th century speech about a dream reminds us of the continuing challenge to realize that dream, the dream of Thaddeus Stevens and of a preacher named King.

The consequences of using Bingham's vague verbiage rather than Stevens' clear and explicit words became almost immediately apparent in one of the first significant Supreme Court cases under the fourteenth amendment. In 1873 the Supreme Court heard the *Slaughter-House* cases. Here, white-owned New Orleans slaughterhouses sued the city for forcing them into a single facility whose owners were politically connected.[23] The Supreme Court rejected their challenge, partly on the grounds that the fourteenth amendment was supposed to be used to protect the newly-freed slaves, not white businessmen. However, the Court also ruled that the "privileges and immunities" clause of the fourteenth amendment only applied to the rights of United States citizenship rather than state citizenship. This arcane distinction essentially vitiated that part of the fourteenth amendment, and still holds to this day.

We should note here a critical point about the fourteenth amendment. Whatever its meaning was, it placed restrictions on the States in the federal Constitution. Its main purpose was to empower Congress to pass laws like the Civil Rights Act to enforce those restrictions. The framers of the fourteenth amendment saw Congress, not the courts, as the active agent.[24] This is provided for in Section 5 of the fourteenth amendment. However, it also meant that the federal courts could hear cases under the fourteenth amendment, and that is how the Supreme Court becomes the primary actor in the rest of the story of that "surplus" first section of the fourteenth amendment.

Perhaps as important as the majority ruling in the *Slaughter-House* cases was a dissent by Justice Stephen Field. He argued that the open-ended wording of the fourteenth amendment should be applied

159

to restrict economic regulations by local governments. Field saw such regulations as interference with personal freedom and property rights, and often motivated by political influence more than the public interest.[25] Over the next two decades, more Justices came around to Field's views. One critical step was the decision in the 1880s that corporations were entitled to the protections of the fourteenth amendment.[26] With this, the Court abandoned the view from the *Slaughter-House* cases that the purpose of the fourteenth amendment was to protect the rights of African-Americans. Soon thereafter the Court ruled that the fourteenth amendment limited the States in their ability to set railroad rates, even though everyone agreed railroads were generally subject to regulation as "subject to a pubic interest."[27] Although the traditional understanding was that "due process," as Hamilton stated, was about court procedure, not substantive issues handled by the legislature, the Supreme Court now declared that "due process" granted substantial rights. Thus was born what has been called "substantive due process," a concept as odd as its name.

With the arrival of substantive due process, it was open season on state economic regulations. In Allgeyer vs. Louisiana the Supreme Court specifically ruled that the fourteenth amendment guaranteed "freedom of contract" by overruling a state law restricting purchases of out-of-state insurance.[28] In one of the most famous cases of this era, Lochner vs. New York, the Court overruled a statute limiting the working hours of bakers to sixty hours a week because it interfered with their freedom to contract whatever hours they wanted.[29] Although "freedom of contract" does not appear in the Constitution, the Court reasoned that the statute "interferes with the right of contract between employer and employees.... The general right to make a contract in relation to his business is part of the liberty of the individual protected by the Fourteenth Amendment of the Federal Constitution."[30] In Coppage vs. Kansas the Court overruled a statue which prohibited railroads from forbidding their employees to join unions, because it limited employees' freedom to agree to such clauses in their employment contracts.[31] The Court overruled a

160

similar federal law in Adair vs. United States.[32] Over one hundred statutes were overturned by the Supreme Court until 1937 when, with Justice Owen Roberts' "switch in time," the Court abruptly swung to the opposite extreme and ended all oversight of government economic regulation.

The "equal protection" clause fared no better. In the 1896 case of Plessy vs. Ferguson the Supreme Court ruled that segregated railcars did not violate equal protection under the fourteenth amendment.[33] The Court opined that the "assumption that the enforced separation of the two races stamps the colored race with a badge of inferiority...is...solely because the colored race chooses to put that construction on it."[34] Cases approving the widespread practice of segregating schools were cited by the Court in defense of its position. *Plessy* was finally overruled in 1954 in the famous case of Brown vs. Board of Education, which held that segregated schools violated the fourteenth amendment's equal protection requirement.[35]

Although the result in *Brown* is now widely heralded as a great breakthrough, it has always rested on an uneasy foundation. The continuation of segregation in schools and elsewhere after 1866 made it clear that the original authors of the fourteenth amendment did not intend to outlaw segregation, an intention made very obvious when they adopted Bingham's vague generalities over Stevens' unambiguous declarations.[36] However, at least the rights of African-Americans were the subject of the debate behind the fourteenth amendment. Instead of focusing on finally realizing the equal place of African-Americans in America, after *Brown* the Supreme Court embarked on a spree of judicial legislating, expanding the reach of the equal protection clause to groups and situations which not one of the fourteenth amendment's framers or ratifiers would ever have considered as falling within its scope.[37] There are no clear criteria as to how a group gets to be covered under the fourteenth amendment, other than that enough Supreme Court justices think it should be. And even then there are different levels of scrutiny as to whether a legal distinction relating to the group is invalid.

For example, in Craig vs. Boren (which ruled that Oklahoma could not have a higher legal drinking age for men than for women) a highly divided Court decided that sex discrimination was subject to more stringent review than just any old law, but maybe not as strict as for race discrimination.[38] Even feminists agreed with then Justice William Rehnquist's charge that the Court's standard of review that such a law "'must serve important governmental objectives and must be substantially related to the achievement of those objectives' apparently comes out of thin air. The Equal Protection Clause contains no such language, and...the phrases used are so diaphanous and elastic as to invite subjective judicial preferences or prejudices relating to particular types of legislation, masquerading as judgments whether such legislation is directed at 'important' objectives or, whether the relationship to those objectives is 'substantial' enough."[39]

Although it was not obvious at the time, this embarkation on a new jurisprudence of subjective judicial preferences and prejudices was foreshadowed in the 1938 case of United States vs. Carolene Products Co., a year after Justice Roberts' switch to supporting the New Deal.[40] In it the Supreme Court upheld a blatantly special interest inspired prohibition on the sale of a dairy product which competed with certain large food manufacturers. In conformance with the new pattern, the Court deferred to Congress even though the justification for this law in the congressional record was negligible.[41] However, in a footnote to the opinion, Justice Harlan Fiske Stone commented that "more searching judicial inquiry" may be needed where "discrete and insular minorities" were involved.[42] Of course, nothing in the Constitution says that property rights or the rights of "non-insular" citizens are less worthy of judicial protection, but from this obscure footnote a major judicial industry was to be born, an industry founded every bit as much on "substantive due process" as the economic rights' decisions.[43]

This loading of judicial preferences and prejudices into the two little words "equal protection" is rivaled by what has happened to the words "due process." Here we meet again Justice Hugo L. Black. Based upon the expansive statements of Congressman Bingham and Senator Howard, Black decided that the two words "due process" subsumed the first eight amendments of the Bill of Rights and applied them to the States. This is called "incorporating" the Bill of Rights into the fourteenth amendment.[44]

In the last chapter we saw what happened when he did with this with the first amendment's establishment clause in the *Everson* case. Scholars quickly showed that Black's reading of the history about the assumption of the entire Bill of Rights into the two words "due process" was as off-base as his reading of the history of the establishment clause in the first amendment.[45] Even if a few members of Congress made a few statements to this effect, it certainly was not the understanding of most of their colleagues, or of the States which ratified the fourteenth amendment.[46] Decades later a law professor dredged up a few more instances of historical support for Black's view, and he has been refuted in turn.[47] This book is not the place to go into this argument. The point is that there is an argument, an argument which fills hundreds, indeed thousands, of pages about what the two words "due process" mean.

Black's colleague Felix Frankfurter had no tolerance for this, and he and Black had it out in dueling opinions in the case of Adamson vs. California.[48] For Justice Frankfurter it "would be extraordinarily strange for a Constitution to convey such specific commands in such a roundabout and inexplicit way" as to read the entire first eight amendments of the Bill of Rights into the Constitution through the two words "due process"[49] It was suggested that there be "merely a selective incorporation of the first eight amendments into the fourteenth amendment. Some are in and some are out, but we are left in the dark as to which are in and which are out. If the basis of selection is merely that those provisions...are incorporated which commend themselves to individual judges as indispensable to the dignity and happiness of a free man, we are thrown back to a merely subjective test."[50]

Selective incorporation is in fact the road the Court has taken. Interestingly, the provisions of the Bill of Rights which have been applied against the States through the fourteenth amendment tend to be matters which law professors and judges find important, whereas less intellectually fashionable provisions, such as a non-secularist reading of the establishment clause (as we saw in the last chapter) or the second amendment's right to bear arms (as we will see in the next chapter), have not been incorporated into "due process." (Although the second amendment was recently incorporated in the McDonald vs. Chicago case, it was by a narrow 5-to-4 vote, and many justices, legal academics and gun control advocates want to overturn it as soon as they can get another vote in their favor on the Court.)

However, the Supreme Court has stuffed more than just the approximately two hundred fifty words of the Bill of Rights into the two words "due process." Beyond the selective incorporation of the Bill of Rights, there is another line of cases where the Supreme Court has written an entirely new doctrine into the Constitution through the "due process" clause of the fourteenth amendment.[51] Instead of a right to "freedom of contract" which is not found in the Constitution, these cases are founded on a right to "privacy" which is also not found in the Constitution.

In a challenge to an unused, dormant Connecticut law against distributing contraceptives, Justice William O. Douglas quite disingenuously declared in Griswold vs. Connecticut that the Court does "not sit as a super-legislature to determine the wisdom, need and propriety of laws that touch economic problems, business affairs or social conditions."[52] Douglas acknowledges that the issues in the case "implicate the Due Process Clause of the Fourteenth Amendment" and the *Lochner* case.[53] This was anathema to an old New Dealer like Douglas. However, he then goes ahead and does exactly that with an argument that is far more amorphous than Justice Stephen Field ever used. Acting exactly like a "super-legislator" whose decisions cannot reversed by a vote of the people, Douglas found, somehow, "that specific guarantees in the Bill of Rights have penumbras, formed by emanations from those guarantees that help give them life and substance" to create "zones of privacy."[54]

This was too much even for Hugo Black, who dissented. He correctly saw this as the same old substantive due process reasoning which Franklin Roosevelt had appointed him and Douglas to the Court to overcome. "The Due Process Clause with an 'arbitrary and capricious' or 'shocking to the conscience' formula was liberally used by this Court to strike down economic legislation in the early decades of this century.... That formula...is no less dangerous when used to enforce the Court's views about personal rights than those about economic rights. I had thought we had laid that formula...to rest once and for all." Instead "such a loose, flexible, uncontrolled standard...will amount to a great unconstitutional shift of power to the courts which...will...jeopardize the separation of powers the Framers set up and...take away much of the power of States to govern themselves which the Constitution plainly intended them to have."[55] Echoing Jefferson without quoting him, Black protested that "one of the most effective ways of diluting or expanding a constitutionally guaranteed right is to substitute for the crucial word or words....another word or words.... 'Privacy' is a broad, abstract, and ambiguous concept which can easily be shrunken in meaning but which can also ... easily be interpreted as a constitutional ban against many things."[56]

Black was not the only liberal to be disturbed by this new development. Columbia law school professor and ACLU director Louis Lusky agreed that this was just the same old discredited doctrine of "substantive due process...under a different banner bearing the watchword privacy" which "cannot be justified on the basis of an expressed mandate from the Constitutors [his term for the framers of the fourteenth amendment], and the Court has tendered no other persuasive justification." If the Court continues to pursue this course, Professor Lusky foresaw "a conflict of cataclysmic proportions between judicial review and self-government."[57]

Krytocracy vs. Democracy

In our times it is usually people considered "conservative" who inveigh against judicial decisions which go beyond the "strict rules" of the law to exercise an "arbitrary discretion" in writing their own preferences and prejudices into the Constitution. However, even progressives who like many post-1937 Supreme Court decisions recognize deep problems with this expansive exercise of judicial power.

First, as one progressive public interest attorney has observed, the Supreme Court "has been a force of ferocious political reaction for most of its existence,"and he sees the current Supreme Court headed in that direction.[58] Not all of the economic substantive due process decisions have been overruled, and are still available.[59] And even for those that have been, as long as the overall doctrine that due process embodies substantive rights is alive and well, economic substantive due process, or some variation on it, can make a comeback under the fourteenth amendment any time five justices of the Supreme Court so choose.[60] And as for the "equal protection" clause, that it gave George W. Bush the presidency in 2000 shows that even the most progressive-sounding language can be turned in any direction if it is vague enough.[61]

Second, beyond the risk that loose language can be easily turned in unwanted directions by an ideological Supreme Court, there is a more profound question. A large number of the Supreme Court's fourteenth amendment decisions have been directly contrary to the will of a majority of Americans. Anyone who values democracy must ask how legitimate progressive policies are if they are consistently imposed by an unelected elitist institution without any majoritarian accountability. Indeed, since *Brown* progressives have often seemed to prefer to use the courts to achieve their policies. As one progressive scholar argues, implementation of new rights through a "lavish and expensive" reading of the fourteenth amendment "could have come from Congress, but in fact they have mostly come from

166

the courts." Therefore she looks to the courts to "lead much further, to protect the rights of groups never even discussed by the Reconstruction Congress."[62] Another looks to the courts to police the levels of police protection provided in communities under the equal protection clause.[63] The courts already run the schools and prisons, why not police departments too?[64]

But why stop with having the courts run the police department? Prominent progressive law professor and former Obama administration official Cass Sunstein has recently argued that the courts should incorporate into the fourteenth amendment Franklin Roosevelt's "second bill of rights." This would force all state and local governments by judicial edict to supply everyone with a host of economic benefits such as housing, medical care, employment, clothing and even recreation.[65] These may be good policies for the legislature to adopt. The legislature is elected by the people. Its actions can be revised and repealed and, most importantly, the legislature itself can be voted out if the people disapprove of it. No such checks exist on courts imposing policies under the supposed constitutional mandate of the fourteenth amendment's two two-word clauses. Of course, that could be their very appeal. Policies dictated by the courts are not subject to the difficult compromises and persuasion required for legislative action.

Progressives' enthusiasm for court-mandated policy implementation raises a legitimate question about their true commitment to democratic governance. One progressive legal scholar has observed that contemporary progressive legal "theorists offer little more than a veiled apologia for rule by a liberal oligarchy. Since that oligarchy itself can no longer draw on a healthy tradition of rational enquiry, its decisions are, and will increasingly be, as hoc responses to political pressure and personal preferences."[66] How can you claim to represent the real interests of the people when you look to the court clerk's office rather than the polling booth to carry forward your goals? At what point have we replaced democracy, rule by the *demos* (the people), with krytocracy, rule by the *kriteis* (the judges)?

Another dissent in the *Griswold* case was written by Justice Potter Stewart. He was well known for cutting through to the nub of matters, such as his famous reaction to the Court's tortured efforts to define obscenity when he commented that "I know it when I see it."[67] First he noted that with "all deference, I can find no such general right of privacy in the Bill of Rights, in any other part of the Constitution, or in any case before decided by this Court."[68] He then went on to note that, having been made aware that the obscure law was still on the books, the Connecticut legislature was in the process of repealing it when the Supreme Court cut short the legislative proceedings with its *Griswold* decision. Rather than having the Supreme Court create new constitutional law out of thin air, "the people of Connecticut can freely exercise their true Ninth and Tenth Amendment rights to persuade their elected representatives to repeal" antiquated laws. Justice Stewart concluded that "that is the constitutional way to take a law off the books."[69] And, of course, the constitutional way to revise the Constitution is by amendment.

As early as 1955 Justice Felix Frankfurter observed that fourteenth amendment cases were the most numerous before the Court, and that certainly has continued to be true today.[70] This is because the Supreme Court has written entirely new bodies of law into the two two-word phrases "due process" and "equal protection" in the first section of the fourteenth amendment. The Supreme Court has used these four words to override the rest of the Constitution, with its careful limitation of the powers of the national government (of which the Supreme Court is a part) vis-a-vis the States, and its explicit reservation of powers to the States and the people in the ninth and tenth amendments. In championing the first eight Bill of Rights amendments Hugo Black blithely ignored these last two amendments, and the Supreme Court continues to ignore them to this day.

The program of this book is to rephrase the Constitution by amendment to restore its original meaning and structure. But how do you rephrase four words which have been so misconstrued and

168

abused? The only solution is to completely delete the offending words. But then what goes in their place? Here again the answer comes from the beginning. America is certainly far from resolving its sad natal conflict over race. However, as much as remains to be done, there can be no doubt that we have made real progress since 1866.

Now is the time to do what should have been done in the beginning. For Thaddeus Sevens the fourteenth amendment was only "one step, a mincing step, in the line of reform."[71] Now is the time to rewrite the fourteenth amendment the way it should have been written in the first place, the way Thaddeus Stevens wanted to write it. Now is the time to finally specifically prohibit discrimination on the basis of race in our Constitution.[72] Now is the time to finally confirm the holding of Brown vs. Board of Education by constitutional amendment, by the united voice of the American people.

A few issues do present themselves. First of all, "race" is a difficult term. It drives biologists crazy. For them it is social construct without any genetic equivalent.[73] At the genetic level humankind has far more diversity than simply different skin pigmentations. Indeed, there can be far more genetic difference between different groups of Africans, even within one village, than between Africans and the rest of humankind.[74] To truly catch all possibilities, we should include "ethnic origin" to fully encompass the hard-to-define concepts of "race" and "color."

Another issue is an area where the Supreme Court's expansion beyond the intent of the fourteenth amendment's framers did capture a fundamental majority shift in American society. This is discrimination on the basis of sex. To enact Thaddeus Stevens' version of the fourteenth amendment, we will need to include sex discrimination in our new fourteenth amendment.

In 1923, fresh from the final achievement of full suffrage for women with the 1920 ratification of the nineteenth amendment, some women's rights activists proposed another constitutional amendment. As finally drafted some years later, it stated that "equality of rights under the law shall not be denied or abridged by the United States or by any state on account of sex." It languished for decades, primarily because it would have overturned special legal protections for women for which the progressive movement had long labored. For example, the law upheld in West Coast Hotel Co. vs. Parrish, the case in which Justice Owen Roberts made his famous switch, was a minimum wage law applicable only to female workers.[75] Opponents of the amendment included such eminent champions of women's rights as Eleanor Roosevelt.[76]

In 1972 it was finally passed by Congress and quickly ratified by many States. However, it then began to encounter significant opposition. Congress had originally set a seven-year deadline for its ratification. This deadline was extended to 1982, but in the end it still failed of ratification. In addition to falling short of the necessary number of state ratifications, several States rescinded previous ratifications. The validity of these rescissions was disputed, but the issue became moot when the amendment expired with the passing of the 1982 deadline.[77]

Some readers will recall the bitter disputes which surrounded the efforts to ratify the Equal Rights Amendment (ERA) in the 1970s and early 1980s. We certainly do not want to get caught up in those disputes here. Recuperation of the fourteenth amendment is too important. Some of the issues raised in the ERA debate are now moot as well since, whether constitutionally proper or not, the Supreme Court has treated sex discrimination as unconstitutional since the 1970s.[78] Indeed, much of the impetus for the ERA was sapped by these Supreme Court decisions, another example of Supreme Court activism cutting short the democratic resolution of political issues by the people.[79]

However, there were some questions which still resonate for many Americans. The ERA proper contained no exceptions, so ERA proponents had to resort to either minimizing these questions, or claiming that were covered by other constitutional protections. This latter argument ignored the risk posed by the general rule of legal interpretation that a later enactment supersedes a prior enactment.[80] While this rule would certainly be used sparingly on constitutional language, we do want to minimize any openings for judicial creativity. Therefore, we must include some explicit exceptions in our new fourteenth amendment.

The first is physical differences. There are many cases where law must account for simple physical facts. Funding for ovarian cancer research is only going to benefit women, and funding for testicular cancer research is only going to benefit men. Laws regulating sperm donation can only apply to men, and those regulating surrogacy can only apply to women. However, the most important issue covered by this exception is the crime of rape. Despite a few sensational accounts of older women committing statutory rape by seducing teenage boys, overwhelmingly the perpetrators of rape are men and the victims are women. Penetration is a traditional element of the crime of rape, and that is based on a physical difference. A normal person might find it mind-boggling that equality would make rape unconstitutional, but unfortunately we have seen how clever lawyers can be in making outlandish arguments, and how willing courts have been to accept them. There must be no constitutional shadow on the prosecution of this heinous crime.

The next category is privacy. Opponents of the ERA raised the specter of court-mandated unisex bathrooms, to which proponents pointed to the *Griswold* privacy doctrine.[81] However, not only are these substantive due process privacy rulings constitutionally suspect, but those rulings have not explicitly run to the kind of privacy concerns raised by the ERA. That line of cases has run instead to other subjects, like abortion and homosexual relations.[82] "Privacy" as understood under the Supreme Court's fourteenth amendment cases is about promoting sexual intercourse, not sexual modesty. An explicit privacy exception is necessary to assure that laws requiring single-sex privacy in public accommodations are not endangered.

171

One of the most contentious objections to the ERA was that it would mandate the military conscription of women.[83] In the 1970s, most ERA proponents had recently come out of the 1960s anti-war and anti-draft movements. Their response was to belittle that concern with general anti-war, anti-draft statements (sons should not have to go to war either) or to treat the issue as a question of equal employment opportunity.[84] However, combat is not an employment opportunity and most Americans are not prepared to see their drafted daughters come home in body bags. The status of gender in the military must be left to Congress under its Article I Section 8 powers to regulate the armed forces.

One issue current today which was not much discussed in the 1970s arises as a result of one of feminism's great political successes. Title IX of the federal educational funding laws requires equal athletic opportunities for women. This has led to a veritable explosion of female athletics. However, there is no popular support for integrated sports teams. Few would want to see some obnoxious boys winning a court-mandated right to play on girls' teams. Further, without an athletics exception, it is entirely conceivable that the Olympics or other sex segregated international sports competitions could not be held in the United States, since these events unfortunately usually receive extensive taxpayer support, which subjects them to constitutional requirements as government operations.

Another issue which was raised in the 1970s and has become even more topical is the status of same-sex orientation. At that time most ERA proponents, including its sponsors in Congress, stated that the ERA would not mandate same-sex marriages as long as the prohibition applied equally to gay and lesbian unions.[85] Until very recently many progressive politicians, such as Barack Obama and Hillary Clinton, opposed same-sex marriage, and many progressives argued that a Supreme Court fiat dictating nation-wide gay marriage would be very damaging to the acceptance of gays.[86] However, in 2015 the Supreme Court nonetheless imposed same-sex marriage on all of the States by a narrow 5-to-4 vote in the case of Obergefell v.

172

Hodges. For constitutionalists the *Obergefell* decision is simply the latest example of the Supreme Court abusing its power to write five justices' personal social and political views into the Constitution. However, even those who support marriage equality should be concerned by this decision. How secure is a right which depends on a 5-to-4 vote in what Justice Jackson called a judicial lottery? It will be far better if the constitutional status of homosexual orientation is democratically and definitively resolved by amendment, not by the swing vote of one aged Supreme Court justice. For drafting purposes homosexual orientation is excluded from the revision in order to be consistent with the law in place for 226 years. However, if the people take control of their Constitution again through the new amendment process proposed in chapter 5, the way is open to adding homosexual orientation when and if the people reach that point of view.

The last category of exception is the internal government of religions. Many world religions mandate an all-male clergy. This is not only the case for Roman Catholicism, but also for the Eastern Orthodox, many orthodox Protestants and Jews, Moslems, and traditional forms of eastern religions such as Buddhism and Shinto. ERA proponents argued that these practices would be exempt under the first amendment. However, in light of the hostility to religion evidenced by the courts as described in the last chapter, an explicit exception is also needed here.

There remains one more item. The first sentence of the first section of the fourteenth amendment says that "all persons born or naturalized in the United States, and subject to the jurisdiction thereof, are citizens of the United States and of the state wherein they reside." This clause was added at the last minute in 1866 to assure that American-born freed slaves would be recognized as citizens. That is no longer an issue. There is considerable controversy over the interpretation of this language now that this sentence only serves to promote the birthright citizenship of "anchor babies," delivered by mothers present in the United States illegally to try to gain leverage to get legal status for the foreign-born members of the family.[87]

Deleting this sentence will empower Congress to deal with this practice under its original authority to "establish an uniform Rule of Naturalization" under the fourth clause of Article I Section 8.

As the most recent and carefully scrutinized text, we will use the ERA language as the template for our proposed new Section 1:

> Section 1. Equality of rights under the law shall not be denied or abridged by the United States or by any state on account of race, ethnic origin or sex. This article shall not prohibit laws or regulations taking account of sex which relate to physical differences, privacy, athletic competition or the military. This article shall not apply to homosexual orientation, transgenderness, or the internal government of any religion.

One last area of concern with the ERA was the status of domestic relations and family law. Often these laws have been rewritten in gender-neutral language and there is no indication that either the Supreme Court's rulings or state ERAs have resulted in any material disadvantage to divorcees or mothers. Nonetheless, there is a federalism concern with Section 5 which authorizes Congress to enforce the provisions of the fourteenth amendment. After all this work to free the States from the control of the federal courts, it would be counter-productive to federalize major areas of law which traditionally have been under state control. ERA proponents emphasized that the ERA would not "alter the basic constitutional structure" in areas of traditional state responsibility such as "domestic relations, property and criminal law."[88] Therefore, we must add an exception to exclude these traditional areas of state competence.

> Section 5. The Congress shall have power to enforce, by appropriate legislation, the provisions of this article, **except with regard to laws taking account of sex regarding family, domestic relations, property rights or criminal laws**.

174

Sex discrimination in criminal, property, domestic relations, and family laws would be prohibited, and those prohibitions could be enforced in federal courts. However, the federal Congress could not override state legislative provisions to enforce and interpret those prohibitions. Thus, for example, the federal Congress could not use the fourteenth amendment to impose a nation-wide divorce law.

Every clause and word

The fourteenth amendment is the longest in the Constitution. This is because, in addition to the important but hopelessly vague first section, it is loaded down with three other sections dealing with post-Civil War business. Section 2 contains a voting rights remedy which has never been used, Section 3 deals with the ineligibility for office of former Confederates, and Section 4 assured that if former Confederates did return to Congress that they could not vote to renege on the North's war debts or to pay those of the South. One might dismiss these sections as dead historical curiosities. However, there is a maxim of judicial interpretation that it is the court's "duty to give effect, if possible, to every clause and word of a statute."[89]

This maxim applies even more to a constitution. So, what happens when constitutional provisions are no longer relevant? Courts, lawyers and law professors try to come up with new meanings for the outmoded language. This is exactly what happened to Section 4's provision that the "validity of the public debt of the United States, authorized by law, including debts incurred for the payment of pensions and bounties for services in suppressing insurrection or rebellion, shall not be questioned." In 2011, during the battle over raising the debt ceiling, former President Clinton and many Democratic pundits argued that this section authorized the President to borrow money without congressional authorization to pay the federal government's debts.[90]

Invented in the midst of a heated partisan fight, this horrific idea would destroy the constitutional balance and separation of powers. The Constitution gives Congress the exclusive authority to borrow money (Article I, Section 8, clause 2), and to allow the President to usurp this authority would lead to an unconstitutional expansion of executive power beyond even that which has been exercised in the name of war. The foundation of the Anglo-American tradition of representative government is that the legislature, not the executive, holds the "power of the purse." If the executive, be it President or king, can raise money on his own authority by borrowing it, the legislature loses its most ancient and powerful check on executive tyranny. As Harvard law professor Laurence Tribe wrote in the *New York Times*, if a president can "usurp the congressional power to borrow, what would stop him from taking over ... other powers, as well" such as Congress' "powers to impose taxes, to coin money, or to sell federal property?"[91] Even the proposal's leading academic advocates admitted that it would be unconstitutional and, to his credit, President Obama did not use it.[92]

Although it did not happen this time, the political precedent has been established for exploiting the inoperative sections of the fourteenth amendment for dangerous distortions of the Constitution. If we are to amend the fourteenth amendment to restore its original purpose, this is an excellent opportunity to also delete Sections 2, 3 and 4. The Civil War is now well behind us, and we should eliminate the possibility of future misuses of this obsolete constitutional language. (The current Section 5, as revised, would then become Section 2.)

With these refinements to the fourteenth amendment, the Supreme Court's massive imposition of its power on the States would end, an imposition as intrusive in its way as the Congress' abuse of the interstate commerce clause. Its jurisdiction would be restricted to discrimination on the basis of race, ethnic origin, or sex with the exceptions just noted.

However, there remains one last question. Most Americans now assume that the Bill of Rights limits all government action against them. Although all state constitutions contain protections as broad, and often broader, than the Bill of Rights, we are used to looking to the federal Constitution to protect us from all levels of government. On the other hand, we are trying to correct the cooption of so much power by the national government from the States, to restore a bit of the old balance between the national and the state governments which are closer to the people. The deletion of the hopelessly vague and massively abused "due process" clause will eliminate the old basis for federal courts to apply the Bill of Rights against the States. To assure Americans that they are still fully protected by the Bill of Rights, but at the same time restore to the States the powers which the Supreme Court has stolen from them, the following new Section 6 (which would become Section 3 if the current Sections 2, 3 and 4 are removed) can be added to the fourteenth amendment:

> Section [3][6]. Without limitation to any other powers prohibited to the states by the Constitution, no state shall deny or abridge the rights set forth in the first, second, third, fourth, fifth, sixth, and eighth amendments to the Constitution, as amended from time to time. The several states shall have exclusive jurisdiction as to the interpretation and enforcement of this Section within each respective state. No state shall be bound in such interpretation or enforcement by any prior decisions of the courts of the United States.

(The seventh amendment is omitted because it deals with technical provisions for civil trials, most of which the Supreme Court has not applied to the States.) With this provision, the Supreme Court's long quest to insert itself into the States' and the people's affairs will largely end. It will be out of the law enforcement business, it will be out of the nativity creche and school prayer business, and it ill be out of the business of telling States what they can and can not do to protect their citizens from abuses by big business. Never again will the Supreme Court protect corporations by overturning States' reasonable regulations. The federal courts would be limited to cases involving the three categories covered by the new first section and federal laws.

It is still critical that the anti-establishment clause of the first amendment be clarified as discussed in chapter 8. We do not want the state courts to perpetuate the same abuses as the Supreme Court. And there is one other provision of the Bill of Rights which requires clarification before enforcement of the Bill of Rights is passed to the States by a revised fourteenth amendment.

Chapter 10

Arms and Freedoms:
Restoring Security

All power is inherent in the people;... it is their right and duty to be at all times armed; they are entitled to freedom of person, freedom of religion, freedom of property, and freedom of the press.

Thomas Jefferson[1]

In our times, few provisions of the Constitution have been as controversial as the second amendment. It provides that a "well regulated militia, being necessary to the security of a free state, the right of the people to keep and bear arms, shall not be infringed." The interpretation of this brief clause has called into play the approaches we have seen in previous chapters. However, with the second amendment they make a curious dosey-doe, which has split the Supreme Court along with the rest of the country.

First the history. In contrast to the common practice on continental Europe, English armies relied on armed commoners, particularly their famous archers. From earliest times, English laws had encouraged maintenance of, and skill with, the longbow amongst the yeomanry. It was of such common soldiers that Shakespeare's Henry V speaks in his famous discourse on the eve of the battle of Agincourt:

> We few, we happy few, we band of brothers;
> For he to-day that sheds his blood with me
> Shall be my brother; be he ne'er so vile,
> This day shall gentle his condition.[2]

Of course, these armed and militarily trained subjects could also be a threat to a monarch, and various English kings sought to restrict this right over the centuries. When these efforts to expand royal power were repulsed, the monarchy was forced to affirm this right to arms in such landmark documents of English liberty as the Magna Carta of 1215 and the English Declaration of Rights of 1689.[3] The English martyr for liberty Algernon Sidney (from whom the title of this book is taken) wrote that in a popular government "the body of the people is the publick defence, and every man is arm'd and disciplin'd."[4]

Thus, in 1768 when the first confrontation occurred between the British colonists in Massachusetts and the British royal government, it centered on British efforts to station regular troops in the colony and to disarm the colonial militia. The American colonists saw themselves standing in a long tradition of English rights in resisting this intrusion. While the crisis of 1768 was defused, a few years later the grievances of the American colonies led to open breach with the British empire. Although the regular army developed under General George Washington was essential to the American victory, the local militias also played an important role, particularly in the early stages of the conflict. It is not an exaggeration that the minuteman of the militia is the iconic symbol of American independence.[5]

The militia at the founding of the Republic was an institution the likes of which we are too unfamiliar today. Militia statutes in every State required all able-bodied adult men to equip themselves with appropriate arms and be available for service. Drills were obligatory, but also served as civic events for socializing and politicking. In a society without professional law enforcement, and frequently located far from any other aid in the event of attack by Native Americans or hostile European powers, militia service was a fundamental civic duty. The experience of the Revolution also embedded in the American mind the ideal of the local militia as a defense against governmental tyranny. Thus, when the new Constitution of 1787 proposed that a stronger national government be formed, many Americans were leery. What would prevent this national government from turning into another imperial power like Britain with a large standing army to oppress the States and their people? The first response to this was in the Constitution proper. As we saw in chapter 7, Article I Section 8 gives the Congress, not the monarch-like President, exclusive power to declare war and make the laws and regulations for the armed forces. Then the second amendment was added in the Bill of Rights to assure that the national government would not interfere with the state militias or try to disarm the men who served in them.

Unfortunately, in the decades following the founding the traditional universal militia fell on hard times. The increasing sophistication of warfare and the press of other opportunities in daily life made it hard for the universal militias to remain "well-regulated," meaning well trained. By the time of the Civil War, they had been largely superseded by what were called "select" militia. These were all-volunteer groups of men who were willing to devote time to regular military training. It was regiments of this volunteer select militia which filled both the Union and Confederate armies in the Civil War. These were the units usually known by the name of their State and a numerical designation, many of which have become legendary, such as the all black 54th Massachusetts or the Irish-American Fighting 69th New York. These select militia are the direct precursors of our modern National Guard. The old universal militia is largely forgotten, although popular culture preserves a faint memory of the spirit of the older militias in the western film, when the sheriff deputizes the men of a frontier town to form a posse to chase the bad guys.

It is at this point that the history intersects two paths of constitutional interpretation. In the first, the right to keep and bear arms is tied to service in the state militia. After all, what place does a private individual right to bear arms have in a republic? The militia was completely a creature of the States, which the founders saw as the reliable democratic protector of the people's interests. Surely a democratically elected state legislature would not oppress the people. As the old universal militias disappeared, the value of individual ownership of weapons to society was displaced by fears of individual violence, fears which politicians used to introduce restrictions on private ownership of arms.[6] The need for gun control seemed especially compelling as the 20th century brought the rise of organized crime and widely publicized criminal activities, such as Chicago's notorious 1929 St. Valentine's Day massacre.

Previously gun control had been a state matter. These State and local laws did not raise any issue under the second amendment because the Supreme Court had affirmed that it did not apply to the States.[7] However, after the St. Valentine's Day massacre, a federal law requiring the registration and taxation of certain forms of firearms was passed. A prosecution for unregistered possession of a sawed-off shotgun under this federal statute brought the second amendment before the Supreme Court. The defendants in U.S. vs. Miller had been represented by a public defender who was unable to travel to Washington. Thus, only the government's case was presented to the Supreme Court. The Court ruled that the second amendment was not violated because a sawed-off shotgun was not a military weapon and thus unrelated to maintaining a militia.[8]

With *Miller* appearing to open the way to federal firearms control, and the older cases leaving the States unrestricted by the second amendment, gun control laws proliferated. Pro-gun control law professors triumphantly produced second amendment histories tying the right to keep and bear arms exclusively to the now-defunct universal state militias. Its meaning was limited to the circumstances of its original adoption, and there could be no larger right which evolved as those circumstances changed. The functions of the old militias were now filled by the professional armed forces and local police. The second amendment was seen as outmoded and obsolete, effectively repealed by time.[9]

Composed of the Body of the People

Pro-gun control legal scholarship presents the odd spectacle of "living Constitution" law professors, who otherwise have little use for the original meaning of the Constitution, advocating the narrowest, most restrictive possible originalist reading of the second amendment. To their credit, a few legal scholars of the "living Constitution" school have acknowledged that, to be consistent, their philosophy requires a less crabbed reading of the second amendment. One observed he could not "help but suspect that the best explanation for the absence of the Second Amendment from the legal consciousness of the elite bar, including that component found in the legal academy, is derived from a mixture of sheer opposition to the idea of private ownership of guns and the perhaps subconscious fear that altogether plausible, perhaps even 'winning,' interpretations of the Second Amendment would present real hurdles to those of us supporting prohibitory regulation.... The [Second] Amendment may be profoundly embarrassing to many who both support such regulation and view themselves as committed to zealous adherence to the Bill of Rights."[10]

This analysis starts with the language of the second amendment itself. The Constitution distinguishes between the "states" and the "people," as in the wording of the tenth amendment reserving rights not delegated to the federal government "to the states respectively, or to the people."[11] If the sole purpose of the amendment was to prevent federal interference with state militias it would have been easy enough to write the "Congress shall have no power to prohibit state militias."[12] However, instead we have "the right of the people to keep and bear arms shall not be infringed." For the pro-gun control scholars the prefatory clause about the well-regulated militia consumes the rest of the amendment. But could the second part of the amendment be the core, and the prefatory clause surplusage? Most of the rights protected by the Bill of Rights are rights of individuals, not the States. Can we not read the right to keep and bear arms as a general right of the people in their individual capacities, and that it is because that individual right is protected that the State is able to call its armed citizens to the militia for its defense?[13] Beyond that, the notion that the people had to be armed to defend themselves against tyrannical government was very much a part of American political rhetoric at the time of the founding. The

183

American revolutionaries would have been keenly sensitive that, to paraphrase the bumper sticker, "if guns are outlawed, only the government will have guns."[14]

The original versions of the second amendment support this alternate reading. In Madison's original proposal the clauses were reversed, reading that the "right of the people to keep and bear arms shall not be infringed; a well armed, and well regulated militia being the best security of a free country; but no person religiously scrupulous of bearing arms shall be compelled to render military service in person."[15] Here the right of the people was the primary clause. The special committee on amendments revised the wording to "a well regulated militia, composed of the body of the people, being the best security of a free state, the right of the people to keep and bear arms shall not be infringed; but no person religiously scrupulous shall be compelled to bear arms."[16] Although the phrases were now flipped, the phrase defining the militias as being "composed of the body of the people" made it even clearer that the right to keep and bear arms was a right of the entire population, and not just those who happened to be serving in the militia. No one in the First Congress seemed to have a problem with that definition. Debate instead largely focused on the last clause on conscientious objectors, which was ultimately dropped. The Senate then condensed the language to what we have today. There are no records as to why it dropped the phrase "composed of the body of the people," but it was probably to avoid the redundancy of using the "people" twice in the same sentence.[17]

This "republican" interpretation of the second amendment, that the right of the people to keep and bear arms was a right essential to preserve liberty even against their own national government, was used by Madison in arguing why there was no need to fear the army of the new federal government. Any standing army of those days would be unlikely to be able to marshal more than "twenty-five or thirty thousand men. To these would be opposed a militia of near half a million citizens with arms in their hands, officered by men chosen from among themselves, fighting for their common liberties .... Those

184

who are best acquainted with the last successful resistance of this country against the British arms" would know how doubtful it was that such a citizen force "could ever be conquered" by regular troops, unlike "the military establishments in the several kingdoms of Europe" where "the governments are afraid to trust the people with arms."[18] Hamilton concurred in this view, arguing in a court case that "never can tyranny be introduced into this country by arms.... An army can never do it. For ages it can never be attempted. The spirit of the country with arms in their hands, and disciplined as a militia, would render it impossible."[19]

Of course, the right to bear arms is subject to abuse. However, in this it is no different than other rights under the Bill of Rights, like free speech. The solution is not a total ban, but the policing of the abuses.[20] Some progressive scholars have even compared the National Rifle Association's defense of the second amendment to the American Civil Liberties Union's defense of the first amendment.[21] This shifting view of the second amendment finally landed in the Supreme Court in 2008 with the case of District of Columbia v. Heller.[22] In the *Heller* case the Supreme Court decided by a 5-to-4 vote that the second amendment prohibited the District of Columbia government from banning Mr. Heller from having a handgun in his home. In its opinion by Justice Scalia, the Court adopted the view that the second amendment does secure an individual right to bear arms separate from militia-like service. However, Justice Scalia also wrote that "nothing in our opinion should be taken to cast doubt on longstanding prohibitions on the possession of firearms by felons and the mentally ill, or laws forbidding the carrying of firearms in sensitive places such as schools and government buildings, or laws imposing conditions on the commercial sale of arms."[23] This sentence has been relied on by lower federal courts to uphold every gun restriction so far challenged using the *Heller* precedent.[24]

This interpretation of the second amendment was subsequently applied against the States by incorporation through the fourteenth amendment in the case of McDonald vs. Chicago.[25] As confused as the history of the fourteenth amendment is, it is quite clear that one of the rights the Thirty-ninth Congress wanted to assure to the freedmen was the right to bear arms for self-defense.[26] During 1866, when the fourteenth amendment was being passed in Congress, there were vicious riots in which not just white civilians but armed police had massacred unarmed blacks. Forty-six were killed in Memphis and 34 in New Orleans.[27] Thaddeus Stevens certainly saw the general right to arms as fundamental since to "disarm a community...you rob them of the means of defending life. Take away their weapons of defense and you take away the inalienable right of defending liberty."[28]

Like *Heller*, the *McDonald* case was decided by another 5-to-4 vote, with five different opinions totaling over 200 pages in length. There can be no doubt that the controversy will continue. Gun control supporters will strive to narrow the impact of *Heller* and *McDonald* and, with a change of Court personnel, perhaps some day overturn them. Gun rights advocates will seek to expand them, and battles will rage over what extent of gun control regulation is permissible. Everyone will continue to disagree about the place of guns in our society and the proper interpretation of the second amendment.[29]

There is another solution, at least as to the meaning of the second amendment. No matter which side one is on, it is a simple statement of fact that there is extensive disagreement about the meaning of the current text. Why not amend it? Why not restate it in a way which will at least clarify the basic issue of whether it or not it protects a fundamental individual right to keep and bear arms, and what the extent of that right is. Here are some possibilities:

> The second article of amendment to the Constitution of the United States is hereby repealed.

If gun control advocates really believe that the second amendment died with the old universal militia, then let them lead the battle to have it repealed outright, rather than asking the courts to do it by subterfuge.[30] The Constitution should not be cluttered with invalid

186

provisions. If simply deleting the amendment seems too harsh, it could be restated to express the restricted understanding of its meaning:

> Congress shall make no law infringing upon the right of the several States to maintain a State National Guard or militia.

For advocates of an absolute individual right to keep and use arms, it should suffice to simply delete the prefatory clause. However, if they want to keep the structure of the old amendment but with the broader understanding of its purpose, the amendment might be restated with a prefatory clause which expresses that understanding:

> A populace skilled in the use of firearms being necessary to the defense of life, liberty, property, and the nation, the right of the people to keep and bear arms shall not be infringed.

A middle ground which makes the right to keep and bear arms real but subject to some reasonable regulation would delete the confusing prefatory clause and then read:

> The right of the people to keep and bear arms shall not be infringed, except for regulations restricting possession by persons convicted of a felony, or individually found by due process to be a threat to public or personal safety, or to assure public safety in the use of arms.

This would secure to law-abiding citizens a right to own and possess firearms, but would allow public safety controls over their use and who could use them.

Regardless of your views on the issue of gun rights and gun controls, the central issue is: who decides? Should five unelected judges decide, or a super-majority of the American people? The subtitle of this chapter is "Restoring Security." For many, security will come from eliminating guns. For many others it comes by assuring that citizens can defend themselves with their own weapons. Either way, the place of firearms in our society is a fundamentally important issue. It should be decided by the people, not the judges. An amended second amendment is the way to achieve that.

Chapter 11

Judges and Gerrymanders:
Restoring Balance

The House of Representatives is so constituted as to support in
the members an habitual recollection of their dependence on
the people. Before the sentiments impressed on their minds by
the mode of their elevation can be effaced by the exercise of
power, they will be compelled to anticipate the moment when
their power is to cease, when their exercise of it is to be
reviewed, and when they must descend to the level from which
they were raised; there forever to remain unless a faithful
discharge of their trust shall have established their title to a
renewal of it.

James Madison[1]

I am not unaware that the Judiciary career has not
corresponded with what was anticipated.... And latterly the
Court, by some of its decisions, still more by extrajudicial
reasonings & dicta, has manifested a propensity to enlarge the
general authority in derogation of the local, and to amplify its
own jurisdiction, which has justly incurred the public censure....
 If no remedy of the abuse be practicable under the forms of
the Constitution, I should prefer a resort to the Nation for an
amendment of the Tribunal itself.

James Madison (to Thomas Jefferson)[2]

Up to this point we have looked at amendments designed to repair
the damage done to the Constitution by the Supreme Court and
Congress, amendments which attempt to restore as much as
practicable the original meaning and framework of our fundamental
law. We seek to do this not out of some blind reverence for the past,

189

but rather because the system developed by the original framers offers a proven solution to our present excessively centralized national government. However, as we have seen, they certainly anticipated that there would need to be, in Madison's words, "useful alterations...suggested by experience" to the Constitution.[3] In this chapter we will propose three alterations which experience suggests will make the overall constitutional framework conceived by the framers work the way they intended. Two relate to how the national legislature is elected. The third introduces more effective checks on a federal judiciary which has clearly exceeded the role the framers originally contemplated for it. All seek to restore the original concepts of checks and balances which were at the heart of the framers' Constitution.

An habitual recollection of their dependence on the people

In the original constitutional framework, the House of Representatives was supposed to represent the direct popular interest. Voters for Representatives were to be the same as those for "the most numerous Branch of the State Legislature."[4] Furthermore, their districts were to be "apportioned among the several States...according to their respective Numbers," assuring that every voter would be equally represented in that House[5] The Senate was supposed to be a more indirect body, elected by the state legislatures essentially to serve as the States' "ambassadors" to the national government. That was changed with the seventeenth amendment, which provided for the direct election of Senators. While arguments can be made for the repeal of that amendment and the restoration of the original allocation of electoral power to the States, that step lies beyond the program of this book, which is to try to fix changes to the Constitution which have been made illegitimately outside of the official Article V amendment process.

The most important method of assuring that the House of Representatives was responsive to the direct popular will is the requirement that they face re-election every two years. Madison was

190

referring to this requirement in the quote above. He felt that frequent elections would constantly remind members of the House of Representatives of their "dependence on the people." However, facing an election is not a very effective check on a member of Congress if they are not "compelled to anticipate the moment when their power is to cease, when their exercise of it is to be reviewed, and when they must descend to the level from which they were raised...unless a faithful discharge of their trust shall have established their title to a renewal of it." If their re-election is not in question, Representatives lose their incentive to see to the "faithful discharge of their trust."

Unfortunately, this has been increasingly the case. In the Thirty-ninth Congress elected in 1864 there were only three members who had served more than six consecutive terms. In modern Congresses that number approaches two hundred.[6] An even better indication of the declining competitiveness of congressional elections is the number of incumbents who seek re-election and are defeated. As recently as the 1940s, the percentages of successful incumbents ranged only in seventies and eighties.[7] Now incumbents are almost never defeated. In the 2002 elections, only four incumbents lost to challengers.[8] In 2004, there were only five incumbents defeated.[9] With the Democratic gains in the 2006 and 2008 elections these figures increased, but even then 95% of incumbents were re-elected. Further, four out of five of incumbents were re-elected by over 20% of the vote even though a party shift was occurring. In 2010 when the Republicans took back control of the House, two thirds of incumbents still had victory margins of over 20%. Subsequent elections have trended back to the norm, with only 13 House incumbents defeated in the 2014 congressional elections.[10]

A number of reasons are suggested for this decrease in competition in House races, but there is broad agreement that one of the major, if not the major, reasons is the practice known as "gerrymandering." This practice was first identified and named in 1812 when new districts were drawn in Massachusetts following the 1810 census. The

Jeffersonian party created a district from the outer edges of Essex county which concentrated supporters of the opposition Federalist party into only one district. A map of the new district reminded one journalist of the sinuous shape of a salamander. The pro-Jeffersonian party governor of Massachusetts, Elbridge Gerry, approved the plan. It was said that he did so with some reluctance. Perhaps he would have been more active in resisting the proposal if he had known that he was going to be remembered in American history for the name which the Federalist newspapers attached to the scheme. By combining his name with the salamander image, they created the word *gerrymander*. Even worse it is mispronounced as well, since gerrymander uses a soft '*j*' whereas Governor Gerry pronounced his name with a hard '*g*.' He probably deserves better. He was a signer of the Declaration of Independence and active participant in the Constitutional Convention (although he was one of the three delegates who stayed through the entire convention but refused to sign the Constitution because of the absence of a bill of rights). He was also elected Vice President in 1812 for James Madison's second term, and died while serving in that office.

At least Governor Gerry's district resembled something which occurs in nature. No creature could survive with the shapes of today's gerrymandered congressional districts, which remind one of the worst abstract art, if not simply senseless doodles. Unfortunately, they are not senseless. Although gerrymandering has gone on for most of the nation's history, it achieved new levels in the 1970s with the advent of sophisticated computer programs. These permit politicians to finely slice and dice their States in order to maximize the re-election prospects of incumbents of the party controlling the redistricting. This increase in precision gerrymandering has corresponded with the marked decrease in the competitiveness of congressional races.

This decreased competitiveness has a number of ill effects. Voter apathy increases when there is no real contest. It also promotes partisan polarization since Representatives do not have to appeal to a variety of voters.[11] Representatives become entrenched in the special

192

interest dominated political culture of Washington described in chapter 2 when they do not have to worry about facing serious competition for re-election. Worse, with their strangely-shaped, stretched-out districts they no longer represent cohesive communities. A city may be represented by two or more Representatives who are also looking after pieces of towns in faraway parts of the State. If we are going to devolve power away from Washington back to the American people in their local communities, so those communities can again become the center of government, then the members of Congress must represent these whole communities, not bits and pieces spit out by a computer program.

Many opponents of the ill effects of gerrymandering propose instead proportional representation. This is where legislative seats are allocated based on the percentage of the vote a political party receives, regardless of how many local districts it carries.[12] Proportional representation, which is used in many countries, has a number of drawbacks which can be seen wherever it has been used. It encourages political fragmentation, which then necessitates the formation of weak and fractious coalition governments. It also leads parties to concentrate on their ideological base rather than trying to develop a broader consensus, which is also one of the drawbacks of extreme gerrymandering.

It also has drawbacks peculiar to the American constitutional tradition. The founders saw "faction" as a great evil. Although we have made our peace with the place of political parties in our politics, a system which makes political faction the central operating element in elections would be an even further betrayal of the founders' vision. More critically, proportional representation makes legislators answerable to the party leaders rather than the people. Since legislators represent national parties rather than local districts, it works against pushing power back to the people in their local communities since no legislator is responsible to the voters in a particular locale. You get elected based on how high on the party list the party leadership places you, not whether you have served your constituents. Further, since party leadership is always based in the capital city, this increases the centralization of government power. This runs directly contrary to the need for decentralization discussed in chapter 3.

The real solution is a constitutional amendment outlawing gerrymandering. How does one do that? He key is to make congressional districts as compact as possible. Unfortunately, this can become very complicated, for there are many ways of calculating compactness. We do not help move the Constitution away from being a "lawyer's contract" back to being a "layman's document" if we turn it into something only a mathematician can understand. Therefore, we must use the most basic formula possible. This is the "sum-of-the-perimeters" method.[13]

If you recall your geometry from school, a perimeter is the boundary of any shape. The shorter a shape's perimeter, the more compact it is. The most compact shape is a circle, but if you are dividing a shape up into the most compact possible subunits, rectangles (four-sided shapes) generally produce the greatest level of compactness. However, congressional districts within a State are also supposed to have equal populations. Simply dividing a State into rectangles will not work, because populations are always spread out unevenly over a State. Therefore, we need a way of measuring the compactness of different configurations of districts of equal populations. We can do this by adding up all of the lengths of the perimeters (boundaries) of the districts. The smaller this total, the more compact the districts.

There are factors other than partisan gerrymandering which could make a slightly less compact set of districts defensible. Maybe you have to draw a crooked line to keep an entire city or county in one district, or want to assure that a minority group is well-represented in a district.[14] And frankly, since this proposal does have to be enacted by politicians, maybe we must allow them a *little* wiggle room for their games. Therefore the proposal will be framed in terms of what is referred to in the law as a "safe harbor." This is a limit below which

194

the legislature retains its traditional discretion in setting district boundaries. Having such a safe harbor limit also avoids the possibility of nuisance court cases where someone produces a map with perimeters two yards shorter than the adopted boundaries. The proposal presented below allows a five percent variation, but that figure could be higher or lower. Any limit will be a vast improvement on the current monstrosities which pass as congressional districts.

Water presents a problem with the sum-of-the-perimeters method, since meandering rivers and coastlines are often sensible boundaries but lengthen the perimeters as they follow their natural courses. This can be solved by providing that the length of boundaries following water are measured as a straight line between the points where the district boundary connects to the water boundary.

Theoretically, districts are supposed to be as equal in population as possible. However, they are also required to be based on the data collected by the U.S. Census, which generally has a margin of error of one percent more or less, and often greater for some minorities.[15] Of course, this uncertainty and variability did not stop the Supreme Court from imposing itself on the process, and making a mess of it as might be expected. In 1964 the Court ruled that congressional districts had to be equal in population.[16] Later cases disallowed the desire to keep a community together in one district, or even to make the districts as compact as possible, as bases for small variations in population.[17] Finally the Court decreed by a 5-to-4 vote that it would not even allow variations which were less than the Census' admitted margin of error.[18] In another confusing ruling, trying to maximize minority representation in compliance with a law of Congress and pressure from the Department of Justice was said to be permissible to some extent, but not too much.[19] Lawsuits have been argued over population variations as small as 72 and 19 persons.[20]

In 1986 the Court also appeared to rule in a 3-way decision that "equal protection" challenges could be made even to districts of equal numbers if they were too bizarrely gerrymandered.[21] However, the

195

Court could never agree on one standard for judging that. In a more recent multiple opinion decision the Court has backed away, for now, from trying to police partisan gerrymandering.[22]

However, that has not stopped the Court from promulgating an utterly confusing morass of decisions on the redistricting of state legislatures. Initially, it first decreed that the fourteenth amendment's equal protection clause required that they be apportioned on a "one man, one vote" basis.[23] Eventually the Court decided that the Constitution allowed a "nine-tenths to eleven-tenths person, one vote" test.[24] Even with that, you do not want to know the convoluted arguments behind what may be and what may not be allowed in state redistricting.[25]

As with the shape of districts, it is proposed that we remove the federal courts, with their indefinite standards and internal squabbling, from the business of redistricting and simply establish a population "safe harbor" to go with the sum-of-perimeters safe harbor standard. As long as the districts established by the democratically elected state legislatures meet these two "safe harbor" standards, they can not be challenged in federal court. The logical standard for the population "safe harbor" would be the Census' one percent margin of error. While this may allow greater variation than some rigid, abstract "one-person, one-vote" standard, it is actually more realistic. As noted, the Census count is not perfect and, even if it was perfect when made, over the decade between censuses the normal mobility characteristic of American society makes the Census numbers obsolete.

Other democratic countries allow far greater variations in the populations of election districts. In Canada it can be as much as 25%, and in Australia and New Zealand it is 10% and 5% respectively. In the United Kingdom, England has 20% fewer seats in Parliament in proportion to its population than Scotland and Wales. France and Japan have variations between their most populous and least populous election districts on an order of three-to-one.[26]

Although it impacts the allocation of seats in the House of Representatives according to Article I Section 2, this proposal will probably work best as a free-standing amendment rather than a revision of the existing text of the Constitution.

Because the proposals in this book focus on the federal government, the proposed amendment does not apply the anti-gerrymandering standard to state legislative districts. However, the bracketed Section 4 below does address the issue of the population of state electoral districts by implementing the "nine-tenths to eleven-tenths person, one vote" test as a safe harbor. This will remove the federal courts from another area where they have intruded on local democratic government. (Note that the revision of the fourteenth amendment proposed in chapter 9 would remove the basis for the court's interference with the redistricting of state legislatures.) And if a State's people want to stop the gerrymandering of state as well as federal electoral districts, the anti-gerrymandering language proposed below could serve as a model to be adopted by each State into its own constitution. Here is the proposed amendment:

> Section 1. In any State entitled to more than one seat in the House of Representatives, the sum of the lengths of all of the boundaries of the districts for such seats shall not be more than five percent longer than the shortest possible distances for such boundaries consistent with Section 2 of this article. For purposes of this article, boundaries which follow any body of water or a state line shall be measured as a straight line between the two points where the other boundaries intersect the boundary which follows a body of water or state line.

> Section 2. The populations of all districts referred to in Section 1 shall not differ by more than one percent from each other based upon the Enumeration made pursuant to Article I Section 2 of this Constitution.

Section 3. If the requirements set forth in Sections 1 and 2 are met, the several States shall have exclusive power and jurisdiction as to the establishment of their electoral districts for the House of Representatives and the interpretation and enforcement of this article within each respective State.

[Section 4. The populations of all other electoral districts in any State shall not differ by more than ten percent from each other based upon the Enumeration made pursuant to Article I Section 2 of this Constitution. If this requirement is met, the several States shall have exclusive power and jurisdiction as to the establishment of electoral districts and the interpretation and enforcement of this Section within each respective State.]

With this amendment incumbent Representatives will again become accountable to their local communities, and the citizens who live together in them. As an ancillary benefit, this provision will also remove the federal courts from yet another arena where they have intruded on the States' management of their own affairs.

While reducing gerrymandering will certainly increase members of the House of Representatives' attention to their constituents, it does not address the fact that even popular congressmen and women become enmeshed over time in the Washington system of lobbyists and special interests, detached from the American people's thinking and concerns. It also does nothing to address the fact that Senators, who are elected at large by their entire State, are also susceptible to the same "Washingtonitis" as members of the House. The solution to this problem is term limits for members of Congress.

The idea here is to limit both Representatives and Senators to a certain number of terms, just like the twenty-second amendment (ratified in 1951) limits the President to two terms.[27] There was considerable enthusiasm in the 1990s for an amendment to the Constitution creating term limits for Congress. However, much of the momentum was sapped when Congress declined to pass the proposed amendment in 1995 and the Supreme Court ruled that the States could not impose term limits on members of the federal Congress.[28] However, the idea continues to enjoy wide support.

The primary issue in drafting a term limits amendment is how long members of Congress should be allowed to stay in office. Such limits are usually defined in terms of a certain number of terms or years.[29] This probably works well enough for presidential terms where we are only talking about two possible terms and, according to the twenty-second amendment, a "term" is anything that is two years or more. However, with members of Congress there are multiple terms involved. What about service for partial or non-consecutive terms, or terms that start late due to run-offs? And certainly someone will try somehow to "game' the system.

To deal with these issues, a workable term limits amendment needs to be expressed in days. The amendment below proposes a 6,000 day limit with both Senators and Representatives allowed to serve until the next congressional election after that period. Six thousand days is about sixteen and a half years. This allows for three full terms in the Senate or nine in the House, while minimizing the possibilities of gamesmanship or confusion with partial terms. The amendment would be new Section 11 if inserted in Article I of the Constitution.

> Section 11. No member of the Congress shall serve cumulatively for more than six thousand calendar days, except that at the end of said period they may continue to serve until the next election for the House of Representatives. The remainder of any senatorial term shall be filled in the manner prescribed by State law.

The Judiciary...has not corresponded with what was anticipated

As we saw in the quote from James Madison at the beginning of this chapter, the Supreme Court started usurping authority very early on. "The Court," Madison observed, "has manifested a propensity to enlarge the general authority in derogation of the local, and to amplify its own jurisdiction." Many of the amendments proposed in this book are designed to curb the Supreme Court's assumption of powers not granted by the Constitution, and its collaboration in the national government's seizure of powers intended to remain with the people and their local governments. However, let us ask ourselves why the Court has done this. Is there some systemic or psychological factor that has moved so many Supreme Court justices over such a long period of time to constantly write their own views and prejudices into the Constitution? Is there something about the Court itself that may require "a resort to the Nation for an amendment of the Tribunal"? Unfortunately, there may well be a feature of the original Constitution which inadvertently has contributed to this tendency. That is the life tenure of federal judges. If both of the elected branches of government are to be subject to term limits, shouldn't there be term limits for federal judges also?

Article III Section 1 of the Constitution provides that the "Judges, both of the supreme and inferior Courts, shall hold their Offices during good Behaviour." Judges can only be removed from office by impeachment and conviction for "Treason, Bribery, or other high Crimes and Misdemeanors."[30] The framers intended this to preserve the independence of the judiciary, a worthy aim. Of course, the constitutional system of checks and balances required that the judiciary be counter-balanced by checks. This was supposed to be supplied by the power of impeachment. However, as Jefferson discovered, impeachment was nothing but a "scare-crow." He concluded that a stronger check was needed on a judiciary which had assumed the right to declare acts of Congress unconstitutional. (This was not then, and is not now, in the Constitution, but rather was assumed by the Court in the 1803 case of Marbury vs. Madison.) Jefferson proposed that judges be limited to six year terms, like Senators, and subject to reappointment at the discretion of the President and Congress.[31]

However, Jefferson's proposal received little notice. This was mainly because at the time there was a reasonably rapid rotation on and off the Court in any case. Being a Supreme Court justice was hard work. A justice had to travel around on circuits hearing cases as well as attending the Court in Washington. The first Chief Justice, John Jay, only served a few years before jumping at the chance to resign to become the governor of New York. In addition, people did not live as long in those times. John Marshall's long tenure was the exception rather than the rule. The average tenure of the first Supreme Court was only eight years, and through 1970 the average tenure was still only fifteen years. However, since then the length of tenure for Supreme Court justices has extended tremendously. The justices retiring between 1971 and 2005 had served an average of 26.1 years and the average age of retirement has gone from a historical range of between 67 to 72 years old to 79.[32]

Certainly part of the reason for this is, in the words of one scholar, that "justices enjoy a job that has good pay, high prestige, manageable hours, great vacation opportunities, and no heavy lifting (or circuit riding)."[33] The Court can decide what cases it wants to hear, usually less than a hundred a year, and has summers off. However, beyond that, in the words of another scholar of the Court, the "exercise of great power without consequence leads...to a state of arrogance and permanent judicial activism.... [Judges] are free to 'evolve,' changing philosophies...and discarding the clothes they wore to gain appointment. Without any effective checks, they can 'discover' interpretations not found in the Constitution's text in order to validate their own personal political and moral choices...in sweeping judgments that sometimes lack convincing legal foundations," thereby writing "themselves into the history books and currying favor with the media and academic elites – all while ignoring original intent and casting off the wise restraints of prudence and caution"[34] And that is the judgment of an academic of progressive political leanings.

Beyond the issue of unchecked power, and the arrogance that can engender, there is the practical issue of the ability of older judges to carry on. With modern medicine, it is certainly true that many more older people today can be active longer into their advanced years. However, modern medicine also means that debilitated elderly people can hang on longer than they might have in earlier times. Unfortunately this had been the case with a number of modern Supreme Court justices. This issue cuts across ideology. It is widely agreed that both liberal icon William O. Douglas and conservative stalwart William Rehnquist stayed on the Court well past the point where their health allowed them to function adequately.[35] Other modern justices who have stayed on even when unable to function include Hugo Black, Thurgood Marshall, and Lewis Powell.[36]

Douglas was a particularly sad case. Debilitated by a stroke, he refused to resign while Gerald Ford was president because Ford had once proposed his impeachment. Even after he was finally forced to resign under pressure from the other members of the Court, he would still try to come to the Court conferences to vote on the cases.[37] Nor is this situation limited to Supreme Court justices. Even lower court judges who can take "senior" status linger on. How long they hang on to their positions can be seen from the fact that 90% of them die within a year of finally taking full retirement.[38]

Although Jefferson's proposal for limiting judicial terms did not go anywhere, the idea of a mandatory judicial retirement age has been around for a long time. In 1913, former President (and future Supreme Court Chief Justice) William Howard Taft wrote that "in a majority of cases when men come to be seventy, they have lost vigor, their minds are not as active,...and their willingness to undertake great labor is not so great as in younger men, and as we ought to have in Judges who are to perform the enormous task...of Supreme Court Justices."[39] In the 1930s there was widespread support for a

202

constitutional amendment providing for a mandatory retirement age of 75, but that was brushed aside by Franklin Roosevelt who instead impatiently pressed his doomed "court-packing" plan.[40] Mandatory retirement for federal judges was also part of a constitutional amendment proposal on judicial independence which was promoted by conservatives from 1946 through 1955.[41] In addition to Taft, Presidents Kennedy, Lyndon Johnson, and George H. W. Bush have favored mandatory retirement for federal judges, as have many modern Supreme Court justices.[42] Further, all of the other democratic nations as well as 49 of the American States apply some combination of mandatory retirement and fixed terms to the members of their high courts.[43]

More recently, it has also been proposed that Supreme Court justices serve for a fixed term. Although a number of different terms have been suggested, one that seems to nicely pull together several advantages is eighteen year terms staggered to begin one every two years.[44] If there continue to be nine justices on the Supreme Court, this will mean that every President will be able to nominate at least two Supreme Court justices in each presidential term. This will eliminate the phenomenon of Supreme Court appointments being bunched up in certain presidential terms while other Presidents are unable to appoint any. This will also eliminate the practice on the part of some Supreme Court justices of timing their retirement to give an advantage to a President of a particular political party to name their successor. It will also reduce the likelihood of Supreme Court justices staying on past their ability to fulfill their responsibilities. Most importantly, it will combat the image, and self-image, of the Supreme Court justice as someone who is superior to the constraints imposed by the Constitution on the other fixed term constitutional officers of the United States, and the people who elect them.

Another advantage of this schedule is that it minimizes the possibility of a President naming a majority of the Supreme Court, since only four of the nine Supreme Court terms will expire during an eight year, two term presidency. While we want to increase the Court's respect for the elected branches, enabling one President to name a majority of the Court could imbalance the constitutional checks and balances the other way. This consideration also argues against shorter Supreme Court terms. For example, if Supreme Court terms were made 12 or 15 years, there would need to be three appointments every four years to keep the Court staffed and the terms evenly staggered. This would mean that a President who served two terms could appoint six of nine justices. The only way to avoid giving a President that level of power would be to increase the size of the Court to 13 seats. While there are arguments to be made for a larger Supreme Court, the system can probably absorb only so much innovation at a time.

By combining the two proposals, mandatory retirement for all federal judges at age seventy-five and fixed terms for Supreme Court judges, we can preserve judicial independence but also assure a more frequent rotation in judicial personnel. Federal judges will then not be so removed and aloof from the rest of the American people and their views. Justices would be limited to filling a single term so that they would not be tempted to curry political favor with their decisions in order to secure reappointment. If a justice left before the end of her or his term, their replacement would only serve the remainder of the term, thus preserving the staggered relation of the terms. This would provide an opportunity for older judges to serve who might not be considered for a full eighteen year term. The fixed terms would be coordinated with the mandatory retirement age by shortening the justice's term by one year for every two years served past the age of seventy-five. The balance of this shortened term would be filled like any other vacancy. Supreme Court justices who are younger than seventy-five when their terms end could continue to serve as federal judges until the retirement age. As with our anti-gerrymandering amendment, even though this proposal directly affects the provisions of Article III of the Constitution, it is probably best treated as a free-standing amendment. It would read as follows:

Section 1. Except as provided in Section 3 of this article, Judges appointed under Article III of this Constitution shall hold their offices during good behavior until the thirty-first day of August of the year in which their seventy-fifth birthday occurs.

Section 2. Justices of the Supreme Court shall serve terms of eighteen years each. One of each of these terms shall expire on the thirty-first day of August of each year following an election pursuant to Article I Section 2 Clause 1 of this Constitution. No person may serve in more than one such term. In the event of a vacancy for any reason, a replacement shall be named in accordance with Article II Section 2 Clause 2 of this Constitution, but such replacement shall only serve for the remainder of the vacated term.

Section 3. The term of service for any justice of the Supreme Court whose term expires after such justice's seventy-fifth birthday shall be reduced by one year for every two years that such term would extend past the thirty-first day of August in the year in which such justice's seventy-fifth birthday occurs. A replacement for the balance of such justice's term shall be named as provided in Section 2 of this article.

Section 4. In the event that the Congress provides for a number of justices of the Supreme Court other than nine, it shall provide in such action for the expiration of terms over the maximum possible time.

The full text of the amendment in the Appendix also includes some transitional provisions for judges serving at the time the amendment is ratified. With this amendment the Supreme Court should come back down from Olympus and rejoin the Republic. Of course, as we have seen, restricted jurisdiction and tightened language can be of little avail if judicial lawyers still adhere to the "living Constitution" philosophy. To secure the restoration of the Constitution gained by the amendments proposed so far, one more is needed. An amendment is needed to put an end to the elitist attitude which has led so many judges to feel that they are entitled to rewrite the Constitution.

Chapter 12

A Right to Choose for Itself:
Restoring the Constitution

Laws and institutions must go hand in hand with the progress
of the human mind. As that becomes more developed, more
enlightened, as new discoveries are made, new truths disclosed,
and manners and opinions change with the change of
circumstances, institutions must advance also, and keep pace
with the times. We might as well require a man to wear still the
coat which fitted him when a boy, as civilized society to remain
ever under the regimen of their barbarous ancestors.... Each
generation has...a right to choose for itself the form of
government it believes most promotive of its own happiness....
This corporeal globe, and everything upon it, belong to its
present corporeal inhabitants, during their generation. They
alone have a right to direct what is the concern of themselves
alone, and to declare the law of that direction; .... But how to
collect their voice? This is the real difficulty.

Thomas Jefferson[1]

These words, from a private letter Jefferson wrote in July 1816, are
much quoted by the advocates of the "living Constitution"
philosophy. And there is more. "Some men," wrote Jefferson, "look
at constitutions with sanctimonious reverence, and deem them like
the arc of the covenant, too sacred to be touched. They ascribe to
the men of the preceding age a wisdom more than human, and
suppose what they did to be beyond amendment."[2] He suggests that
constitutions be rewritten every generation, "so that it may be handed
on, with periodical repairs, from generation to generation, to the end
of time, if anything human can so long endure."[3]

Of course, these advocates never mention that Jefferson is discussing the Virginia state constitution, not the United States Constitution. Otherwise he would not have had to ask "how to collect [the] voice" of the people. He recognized that the United States Constitution might also be "defective. This is the ordinary case of all human works." However, the United States Constitution provided a means for us "to go on perfecting it, by adding by way of amendment to the Constitution those powers which time and trial show are still wanting."[4]

Man of the Enlightenment that he was, Jefferson seems to assume in this letter that the "progress of the human mind" will lead "civilized society" beyond "the regimen of their barbarous ancestors." As we stand on the eve of the bicentennial of that writing, we "present corporeal inhabitants" of our generation are in a position to evaluate that assumption. What we see is the realization of developments which the "sage of Monticello" also foresaw.

In the same 1816 letter, Jefferson warns that to preserve our "independence, we must not let our rulers load us with perpetual debt. We must make our election between *economy and liberty, profusion and servitude.*" He cites the example of England, where the level of taxation forces the common people to devote so much of their income to taxes that they "have no time to think, no means of calling the mismanagers to account; but be glad to obtain subsistence by hiring ourselves to rivet their chains on the necks of our fellow-sufferers." Even those with some assets may technically retain "the title and stewardship of" their property, but they are "held really in trust for the treasury." He then continues that "private fortunes are destroyed by public as well as by private extravagance. And this is the tendency of all human governments. A departure from principle in one instance becomes a precedent for a second; that second for a third; and so on, till the bulk of the society is reduced to be mere automatons of misery, and to have no sensibilities left but for sinning and suffering.... And the fore horse of this frightful team is public debt. Taxation follows that, and in its train wretchedness and oppression."[5]

Even the US government's own official figures show the $15 trillion national debt in 2011 exceeding the entire national gross domestic product. In other words, our collective liabilities will be larger than our entire national income, of the poor as well as of the wealthy.[6] Those official government estimates see annual interest alone on the debt rising from $200 billion to over $700 billion before the end of the decade. At that level interest payments every year will exceed the combined federal 2010 budgets for education, energy, homeland security, and the wars in Iraq and Afghanistan.[7] And private researchers estimate that the real national debt, including unfunded liabilities for entitlement programs like Social Security and Medicare and the unresolved bailouts of Fannie Mae and Freddie Mac, is actually over $61 trillion.[8]

In letters written a few years later Jefferson warned that "when all government, domestic and foreign, in little as in great things, shall be drawn to Washington as the centre of power, it will render powerless the checks of one government upon another, and will become as venal and oppressive as the government from which we separated [Great Britain]."[9] Instead, he wrote, "I wish to see maintained that wholesome distribution of powers established by the Constitution for the limitation of both; and never to see all offices transferred to Washington, where, further withdrawn from the eyes of the people, they may more secretly be bought and sold as at market."[10]

As we saw at the end of the chapter 1, since 1913 the share of the national income consumed by the federal government has increased about fifteen times, there are over thirty times as many laws and regulations as measured by simple page count, and the number of workers either in the federal government or operating under federal direction has increased at ten times the rate of population growth. On top of this an alphabet soup of federal regulatory bureaucracies reach into every aspect of American life. In chapter 2 was saw how this Big Government regulatory state, which began to expand rapidly after 1913, was from the beginning in collusion with the interests of Big Business, which has used federal regulation to enhance its control of the national economy and impose complicated, burdensome, one-size-fits-all regulations on their small business competitors. In chapter 3 we saw how this Big Business/Big Government Washington-based complex has pulled power away from state and local governments, which are close to the people, and consolidated it in the Congress and federal bureaucracy in Washington, a centralized power which is "bought and sold" by Big Business and their lobbyists. And those bureaucrats who are supposedly "anti-business," such as in the Obama administration, use the existence of Big Business to justify increasing and centralizing their own power and reach. This has all confirmed Jefferson's observation that "the natural progress of things is for liberty to yield and government gain ground."[11]

It has been almost a century since the inauguration of Woodrow Wilson in 1913. The United States has had a century-long experiment with the Wilsonian program of highly centralized, ever-expanding, increasingly powerful federal government. Tightly bound to the interests of business, social and academic elites, this Wilsonian program has betrayed the principles of sincere progressives as much as it has stifled the nation's natural center-right majority. For a century liberty has yielded, and government has gained ground. Jefferson argued that it falls to each generation to "to choose for itself the form of government it believes most promotive of its own happiness." Academics of the "living Constitution" philosophy love to decry the influence of the dead hand of history, and advocate that "institutions must advance also, and keep pace with the times." What have our times taught us? Have they taught us that a highly centralized, ever-expanding, increasingly powerful national government is efficient, productive, or promotive of liberty and happiness?

These advocates would have us cast off the dead hand of James Madison and his Constitution of limited government because it is two centuries old. But why then are we not free to divest ourselves of something one hundred years old? If we can cast off the dead hand of Jefferson and Madison, why can we not also cast off the dead hand of Woodrow Wilson and Franklin Roosevelt? What claim do they have on us? Lawyers have a maxim which says that "hard cases make bad law." Even now the economic statistics are no where near as dire as in the Great Depression, which was used as the excuse to carry out the rapid and vast expansion of the national government called the New Deal. Why are we bound by a governmental philosophy which became ascendant over seven decades ago, in the worst of times? And why are we still bound by that outdated governmental philosophy which failed even in its own time, and is failing again in our time?

Age is supposed to bring wisdom. We have a hundred years of experience with the consolidation and centralization of power in Washington. As children of Hamilton as well as Jefferson, we want our country to be strong and prosperous, and our government to do well what it does do. However, Hamilton knew that government debt had to be manageable. He wrote that we should "cherish public credit as a means of strength and security. As one method of preserving it, use it as little as possible.... Avoid the accumulation of debt by avoiding occasions of expence and by vigorous exertions in time of peace to discharge the debts...not transferring to posterity the burden which we ought to bear ourselves."[12] What would he have thought of the debt-ridden monstrosity that our national government has become, foisting on generations to come the burden of paying for our special interest driven profligacy?

Hamilton also treasured the freedoms that made America the golden land of opportunity for striving immigrants such as himself. He declared that "as to whatever may depend on enterprise we need not fear to be out done by any people on Earth. It may almost be said that enterprise is our element."[13] He thought government could help expand private enterprise. If he could see our rapidly expanding government sector, voraciously taxing and borrowing capital away

211

from the private sector, I believe his reaction would not be so different than that of his old adversary.

The decision, Jefferson said, is ours. If our generation is free to choose its system of government, are we not free to decide that the decentralized government of the founders and framers is superior to the power-hungry Franklin Roosevelt's power-mad Leviathan State? Are we not free to conclude that James Madison was wiser about the affairs of men and governments than Woodrow Wilson?

To choose between reformation and revolution

Jefferson was clear as to the prime culprit in this process of centralization, which had begun even in his time. In the letter where he warned that a government centralized in Washington would "become as venal and oppressive as the government from which we separated" he wrote that it was "the Federal Judiciary...working like gravity by night and by day, gaining a little today and a little tomorrow," which would advance "its noiseless step like a thief over the field of jurisdiction until all shall be usurped from the States, and the government of all be consolidated into one."[14] Justice Owen Roberts admitted that his switch to support the New Deal would "reduce the states to administrative districts" where "not only local business activities but local social and community services may be taken from the states and...assumed by the federal government."[15] In the letter quoted at the beginning of the chapter, the one with language so often used to justify the Supreme Court's changes to the meaning of the Constitution, Jefferson also wrote that life tenure for federal judges was a mistake for "we have made them independent of the nation itself. They are irremovable...for any depravities of conduct, and even...for the imbecilities of dotage."[16]

Jefferson would have been appalled at Justice William Brennan's notorious definition of what decides the meaning of the Constitution (Brennan would hold up the fingers of one hand, indicating five votes on the Supreme Court).[17] Jefferson saw the Court removing "every

212

check, every counterpoise to the ingulfing power of which themselves are to make a sovereign part. If ever this vast country is brought under a single government, it will be one of the most extensive corruption, indifferent and incapable of wholesome care.... This will not be borne, and you will have to choose between reformation and revolution."[18]

This book has proposed reformation by restoration. These amendments are no cure-all. They simply aim to repair the damage that has been done to the Constitution by a century of judicial arrogance, the arrogance practiced by Hugo Black, William Brennan and their ilk in assuming to themselves the right to amend the Constitution by the vote of five judges unaccountable in any way to the people. The amendments proposed here simply attempt to restore the older, more decentralized government which placed power closer to the people, the government which prevailed before the depredations of Woodrow Wilson and his successors of the "living Constitution" cabal.

However, as we saw in chapter 4 and subsequent chapters, as long as the Supreme Court presumes the right to loosely construe the language of the written Constitution, no constitutional provision is safe from being turned inside out, upside down, and backwards. Therefore, one more amendment is needed, an amendment which will end the arrogance of the "living Constitution" advocates in the judiciary and legal academe, and enforce instead the rule of law. The rule of law is based on the understanding that the written language controls, not the personal views of a judge. To lock in that understanding, a new section should be added to Article III of the Constitution. (That is the article dealing with the judicial branch).

> Section 4. In construing any provision of this Constitution or any statue or regulation enacted hereunder, the Supreme Court and all inferior courts shall be bound first by the common meaning of the words of the provision at the time of its enactment, in case of more than one possible meaning

of those words shall construe the provision in the manner most restrictive to the power of government, and shall not use as authority any international or foreign law other than the received common law nor enforce any treaty which conflicts with this Constitution or purports to expand the authority of Congress beyond that granted by this Constitution. [Breach of this Section by any judicial Officer of the United States shall constitute a Misdemeanor under Article II Section 4.]

The second phrase will end Congress' habit of wording statues vaguely in order to hide their real objectives, and then relying on bureaucrats and judges to generously expand the scope of the statute to accomplish the real objective which the politicians were too scared to write forthrightly. The next phrase will end the recent tendency of Supreme Court justices to refer to foreign laws when they can not find any American law to support their position.[19] The exception for the "received common law" refers to the pre-1776 English law upon which our laws are based. Although rare, occasions do arise when courts must refer to that original body of law. The last phrase will prevent Congress from expanding its power or curtailing our constitutional liberties through treaties, which are normally given the effect of federal law by the courts.[20] Lastly, the additional bracketed language proposes that a violation by a federal judge of the interpretive rules set out in the amendment be made an impeachable offence. This is a harsh step, which it why it is not part of the core proposals. However, our imperial federal judiciary must be brought back under the control of the Republic and its people.

Of Peripheries and the People

In the 1816 letter, Jefferson advised his correspondent that the "mother principle" in forming constitutions was that "governments are republican only in proportion as they embody the will of their people, and execute it."[21] How has it come about that we have wandered so far from this "mother principle" of republican

214

government? How have we come to be subject in every way to Washington-based bureaucrats and their lobbyist friends from the revolving door of the elites? How has our very foundation, the Constitution itself, become subject to amendment by an unelected committee of five Harvard and Yale law school alumni?

We can again gain some insight from the most leftist of scholars. In studying the causes of Third World underdevelopment, some of these scholars came up with the concept of the "center-periphery" relationship.[22] They argued that all countries of the world were locked in a capitalist system where advanced economies (the center) drew resources of raw materials and cheap labor manufactures from Third World countries (the periphery) in an imbalanced relationship in which wealth was continually sapped from the economically peripheral countries. The peripheral countries then became dependent on the center countries, resulting in a persistent condition of underdevelopment. They also argued that this same process occurred inside countries where mammoth metropolises, like Mexico City, Lima, Nairobi or Bangkok, pulled resources out of, and dominated, the rest of the country. This center-periphery system was seen as a direct successor to the imperialist systems that persisted into the 1950s. One of the main solutions proposed by these scholars was for the peripheral countries to trade with each other to break their dependency on the imperialist centers.

One can argue about the validity of this idea as economics. One of the amazing aspects of capitalism is how countries can use education and enterprise to build themselves up through engagement in the international economy. (Obviously often at considerable social and environmental costs – but we must set that important aspect aside as, well, peripheral to the central point which follows.) However, this concept does suggest an interesting way of looking at politics. Unlike with capitalist economics, where new wealth has been generated in the periphery, being in a centralized imperialistic political system does not generate new power in the periphery. The periphery can only gain political power by seizing it from the imperial center.

All imperial centers act against this by the old strategy of "divide-and-conquer." The thirteen British North American colonies could never have individually challenged the imperial center in London. In order to succeed, the peoples of the periphery must unite against the imperial center. It was only when the thirteen colonies became the United States that they could challenge the imperial center of the 1700s. Today, there is a "divide-and-conquer"strategy at work in our modern politics. We are told that politics lies on a straight line continuum running from left to right. Now, that is a very good way of understanding political theory, and in fact many people live ideologically on that line. However, one consequence of forcing everyone on to that ideological line is that, if you want to talk to someone else in that political spectrum, you have to come to the center of the line and become "moderate." And, of course, that reasonable, moderate political center is located in Washington, D.C.

However, the center-periphery concept suggests another form of political geometry. Instead of a line, think of a big circle. At the middle of the circle is a small center, an imperial center. Everyone else is outside that center, in the periphery. Now ask yourself this question. If you want to reach someone in another part of the periphery, do you have to go through the center? No, you can go around the center. Indeed the shortest distance to most other parts of the periphery is by a straight line skipping the center. In our time, the center has been drawing power into itself from throughout the periphery, from all sides. Individually each part of the periphery is unable to stop this power drain. However, united the periphery can stop it and reverse it. The question we must ask ourselves is this. Can we reach past the center to directly make common cause with the vast majority of other Americans who are also under the domination of that imperial center?

New Hampshiremen and South Carolinians, New Yorkers and Virginians were able to make common cause against an imperial center over two centuries ago, despite vast differences in economies, religions, and even ethnic origins. The question today is whether we

216

can do that again, in our generation. It is not just a question of Alaskans and Floridians getting together. The elites who rule us from Washington, D.C. (and Manhattan) have also tried to divide us ideologically and culturally. A rapper is not supposed to talk to a country-western fan. A progressive and a conservative cannot talk to each other without getting "moderate," and doing it the Washington way. However, what if both realize that the problem *is* the Washington way? What if they realize that we are all subjects of the Big Business/Big Government complex which controls the imperial center in Washington, D.C.? Can we find enough common ground to make common cause against the imperial center which rules us all? This book has argued that the answer to that question is *yes*.

Whether your ideal is a Ron Paul libertarian minimalist state, a William Appleman Williams socialist community, or maybe just a nice town which gets to run its own affairs without multitudinous layers of federal bureaucracy on top of it, the first step is to create a method for the States to again take the initiative in determining what our fundamental law is. The amended amendment proposal in chapter 5 will break the Congressional monopoly on the amendment process and the Supreme Court's monopoly on changing the Constitution's meaning. If it is adopted, we can open a path to breaking Washington's power monopoly. With the ability to initiate constitutional amendments restored to the States, control of our nation's fundamental issues will again be in the hands of the people. This is a proposal that all Americans of the periphery (which is to say most Americans) can agree on. Both progressives and conservatives have many ideas for constitutional amendments which they would like to put before the American people.[23] Some have so many ideas that they want to call a full-fledged constitutional convention.[24] (The proposed "amendment amendment" in chapter 5 should make that uncertain step unnecessary.) Ralph Nader wants an amendment saying that corporations do not have the same rights as people and Robert Bork would like the Congress to be able to override a Supreme Court decision as it can with a presidential veto.[25]

While I believe that the other amendment proposals in this book will do much to restore a democratic equilibrium in our polity, and to restore our original constitutional liberties, these are hardly all of the proposals even I would put forth. Eventually, I would like to curb the unchecked power of the administrative agencies, the unaccountable bureaucratic "fourth branch," and promote a balanced budget by requiring super-majority approvals of spending and tax increases when the budget is in deficit. And we should clarify or modify the undefined requirement that the President be a "natural born Citizen."

Who knows what other worthy proposals might arise from a people again in possession of their Constitution? What is crucial is that they be decided in the public square, not in the courtroom. Whatever your view of particular proposals, we can all agree that it is the American people, "We, the People" as it says at the beginning of the Constitution, who should decide what the Constitution means. Let us begin by making the amendment process accessible to the American people. Let us begin taking back our Republic and its Constitution.

Appendix

The United States Constitution
(incorporating proposed amendments)[1]

Preamble

We the People of the United States, in Order to form a more perfect Union, establish Justice, insure domestic Tranquility, provide for the common defence, promote the general Welfare, and secure the Blessings of Liberty to ourselves and our Posterity, do ordain and establish this Constitution for the United States of America.

Article I: The Legislative Branch

Section 1

All legislative Powers herein granted shall be vested in a Congress of the United States, which shall consist of a Senate and House of Representatives.

Section 2

Clause 1:   The House of Representatives shall be composed of Members chosen every second Year by the People of the several States, and the Electors in each State shall have the Qualifications requisite for Electors of the most numerous Branch of the State Legislature.

Clause 2:   No Person shall be a Representative who shall not have attained to the Age of twenty five Years, and been seven Years a Citizen of the United States, and who shall not, when elected, be an Inhabitant of that State in which he shall be chosen.

Clause 3:   Representatives and direct Taxes shall be apportioned among the several States which may be included within this Union, according to their respective Numbers, which shall be determined by adding to the whole Number of free Persons, including those bound to Service for a Term of Years, and excluding Indians not taxed, three fifths of all other Persons. The actual Enumeration shall be made within three Years after the first Meeting of the Congress of the

---

[1]   Headings and proposed amended language are in **bold**.

United States, and within every subsequent Term of ten Years, in such Manner as they shall by Law direct. The Number of Representatives shall not exceed one for every thirty Thousand, but each State shall have at Least one Representative; and until such enumeration shall be made, the State of New Hampshire shall be entitled to chuse three, Massachusetts eight, Rhode-Island and Providence Plantations one, Connecticut five, New-York six, New Jersey four, Pennsylvania eight, Delaware one, Maryland six, Virginia ten, North Carolina five, South Carolina five, and Georgia three.

Clause 4: When vacancies happen in the Representation from any State, the Executive Authority thereof shall issue Writs of Election to fill such Vacancies.

Clause 5: The House of Representatives shall chuse their Speaker and other Officers; and shall have the sole Power of Impeachment.

Section 3

Clause 1: The Senate of the United States shall be composed of two Senators from each State, chosen by the Legislature thereof, for six Years; and each Senator shall have one Vote.

Clause 2: Immediately after they shall be assembled in Consequence of the first Election, they shall be divided as equally as may be into three Classes. The Seats of the Senators of the first Class shall be vacated at the Expiration of the second Year, of the second Class at the Expiration of the fourth Year, and of the third Class at the Expiration of the sixth Year, so that one third may be chosen every second Year; and if Vacancies happen by Resignation, or otherwise, during the Recess of the Legislature of any State, the Executive thereof may make temporary Appointments until the next Meeting of the Legislature, which shall then fill such Vacancies.

Clause 3: No Person shall be a Senator who shall not have attained to the Age of thirty Years, and been nine Years a Citizen of the United States, and who shall not, when elected, be an Inhabitant of that State for which he shall be chosen.

Clause 4: The Vice President of the United States shall be President of the Senate, but shall have no Vote, unless they be equally divided.

Clause 5:	The Senate shall chuse their other Officers, and also a President pro tempore, in the Absence of the Vice President, or when he shall exercise the Office of President of the United States.
Clause 6:	The Senate shall have the sole Power to try all Impeachments. When sitting for that Purpose, they shall be on Oath or Affirmation. When the President of the United States is tried, the Chief Justice shall preside: And no Person shall be convicted without the Concurrence of two thirds of the Members present.
Clause 7:	Judgment in Cases of Impeachment shall not extend further than to removal from Office, and disqualification to hold and enjoy any Office of honor, Trust or Profit under the United States: but the Party convicted shall nevertheless be liable and subject to Indictment, Trial, Judgment and Punishment, according to Law.

Section 4

Clause 1:	The Times, Places and Manner of holding Elections for Senators and Representatives, shall be prescribed in each State by the Legislature thereof; but the Congress may at any time by Law make or alter such Regulations, except as to the Places of chusing Senators.
Clause 2:	The Congress shall assemble at least once in every Year, and such Meeting shall be on the first Monday in December, unless they shall by Law appoint a different Day.

Section 5

Clause 1:	Each House shall be the Judge of the Elections, Returns and Qualifications of its own Members, and a Majority of each shall constitute a Quorum to do Business; but a smaller Number may adjourn from day to day, and may be authorized to compel the Attendance of absent Members, in such Manner, and under such Penalties as each House may provide.
Clause 2:	Each House may determine the Rules of its Proceedings, punish its Members for disorderly Behaviour, and, with the Concurrence of two thirds, expel a Member.
Clause 3:	Each House shall keep a Journal of its Proceedings, and from time to time publish the same, excepting such Parts as

may in their Judgment require Secrecy; and the Yeas and Nays of the Members of either House on any question shall, at the Desire of one fifth of those Present, be entered on the Journal.

Clause 4: Neither House, during the Session of Congress, shall, without the Consent of the other, adjourn for more than three days, nor to any other Place than that in which the two Houses shall be sitting.

Section 6

Clause 1: The Senators and Representatives shall receive a Compensation for their Services, to be ascertained by Law, and paid out of the Treasury of the United States. They shall in all Cases, except Treason, Felony and Breach of the Peace, be privileged from Arrest during their Attendance at the Session of their respective Houses, and in going to and returning from the same; and for any Speech or Debate in either House, they shall not be questioned in any other Place.

Clause 2: No Senator or Representative shall, during the Time for which he was elected, be appointed to any civil Office under the Authority of the United States, which shall have been created, or the Emoluments whereof shall have been increased during such time; and no Person holding any Office under the United States, shall be a Member of either House during his Continuance in Office.

Section 7

Clause 1: All Bills for raising Revenue shall originate in the House of Representatives; but the Senate may propose or concur with Amendments as on other Bills.

Clause 2: Every Bill which shall have passed the House of Representatives and the Senate, shall, before it become a Law, be presented to the President of the United States; If he approve he shall sign it, but if not he shall return it, with his Objections to that House in which it shall have originated, who shall enter the Objections at large on their Journal, and proceed to reconsider it. If after such Reconsideration two thirds of that House shall agree to pass the Bill, it shall be sent, together with the Objections, to the other House, by which it shall likewise be reconsidered, and if approved by two thirds of that House, it shall become a Law. But in all such Cases the Votes of both Houses shall be determined by yeas and Nays, and the Names of the Persons voting for and against the Bill shall be entered on the Journal of each House respectively. If any Bill shall not be returned by the President within ten Days (Sundays excepted) after it shall have been presented to him, the Same shall be a Law, in like Manner as if he had signed it, unless the Congress by their Adjournment prevent its Return, in which Case it shall not be a Law.

Clause 3: Every Order, Resolution, or Vote to which the Concurrence of the Senate and House of Representatives may be necessary (except on a question of Adjournment) shall be presented to the President of the United States; and before the Same shall take Effect, shall be approved by him, or being disapproved by him, shall be repassed by two thirds of the Senate and House of Representatives, according to the Rules and Limitations prescribed in the Case of a Bill.

Section 8

Clause 1: The Congress shall have Power To lay and collect Taxes, Duties, Imposts and Excises, and to pay the Debts of the United States;[2] **for, and only for, the following purposes;** but all Duties, Imposts and Excises shall be uniform throughout the United States;

Clause 2: To borrow Money on the credit of the United States;

Clause 3: To regulate Commerce with foreign Nations[3] **or** with the Indian Tribes; **or which substantively crosses the borders of the several States, but the latter only so as to directly either (a) promote the passage of persons, goods, services, information, funds, or other economic activity across state borders, or collective bargaining, or (b) prohibit the passage of criminals, criminal**

---

[2]   "and provide for the common Defence and general Welfare" deleted, see chapter 6.

[3]   "and among the several States" deleted, see chapter 6.

223

activities, and dangerous substances across state borders; and the costs of any such regulation [on the several States] are fully funded by the United States;

Clause 4: To establish an uniform Rule of Naturalization, and uniform Laws on the subject of Bankruptcies throughout the United States;

Clause 5: To coin Money, regulate the Value thereof, and of foreign Coin, and fix the Standard of Weights and Measures;

Clause 6: To provide for the Punishment of counterfeiting the Securities and current Coin of the United States;

Clause 7: To establish Post Offices and post Roads;

Clause 8: To promote the Progress of Science and useful Arts, by securing for limited Times to Authors and Inventors the exclusive Right to their respective Writings and Discoveries;

Clause 9: To constitute Tribunals inferior to the supreme Court;

Clause 10: To define and punish Piracies and Felonies committed on the high Seas, and Offences against the Law of Nations;

Clause 11: To declare War, grant Letters of Marque and Reprisal, and make Rules concerning Captures on Land and Water, **and approve any placement of the United States' armed forces outside the United States or its territories, but no such approval shall be for a term longer than two years [unless provided by a treaty approved in accordance with the second clause of Section 2 of Article II of this Constitution];**[4]

Clause 12: To raise and support Armies, but no Appropriation of Money to that Use shall be for a longer Term than two Years;

Clause 13: To provide and maintain a Navy;

Clause 14: To make Rules for the Government and Regulation of the land and naval Forces;

Clause 15: To provide for calling forth the Militia to execute the Laws of the Union, suppress Insurrections and repel Invasions;

Clause 16: To provide for organizing, arming, and disciplining, the Militia, and for governing such Part of them as may be employed in the Service of the United States, reserving to the States respectively, the Appointment of the Officers,

---

[4] See chapter 7.

and the Authority of training the Militia according to the discipline prescribed by Congress;

Clause 17: To exercise exclusive Legislation in all Cases whatsoever, over such District (not exceeding ten Miles square) as may, by Cession of particular States, and the Acceptance of Congress, become the Seat of the Government of the United States, and to exercise like Authority over all Places purchased by the Consent of the Legislature of the State in which the Same shall be, for the Erection of Forts, Magazines, Arsenals, dock-Yards, and other needful Buildings;

Clause 18: **To make expenditures to promote the general welfare, provided that the criteria for distributing such expenditures make them generally available in fact, any regulation thereunder only applies directly to the specific expenditure, is not applicable to any other expenditure from any source, and shall not be imposed unless its costs are fully funded by the expenditure;[5] and**

Clause 19: To make all Laws which shall be necessary and proper for carrying into Execution the foregoing Powers, and all other Powers vested by this Constitution in the Government of the United States, or in any Department or Officer thereof.

Section 9

Clause 1: The Migration or Importation of such Persons as any of the States now existing shall think proper to admit, shall not be prohibited by the Congress prior to the Year one thousand eight hundred and eight, but a Tax or duty may be imposed on such Importation, not exceeding ten dollars for each Person.

Clause 2: The Privilege of the Writ of Habeas Corpus shall not be suspended, unless when in Cases of Rebellion or Invasion the public Safety may require it.

Clause 3: No Bill of Attainder or ex post facto Law shall be passed.

Clause 4: No Capitation, or other direct, Tax shall be laid, unless in Proportion to the Census or Enumeration herein before

---

5   See chapter 6.

	directed to be taken.
Clause 5:	No Tax or Duty shall be laid on Articles exported from any State.
Clause 6:	No Preference shall be given by any Regulation of Commerce or Revenue to the Ports of one State over those of another: nor shall Vessels bound to, or from, one State, be obliged to enter, clear, or pay Duties in another.
Clause 7:	No Money shall be drawn from the Treasury, but in Consequence of Appropriations made by Law; and a regular Statement and Account of the Receipts and Expenditures of all public Money shall be published from time to time.
Clause 8:	No Title of Nobility shall be granted by the United States: And no Person holding any Office of Profit or Trust under them, shall, without the Consent of the Congress, accept of any present, Emolument, Office, or Title, of any kind whatever, from any King, Prince, or foreign State.

Section 10

Clause 1:	No State shall enter into any Treaty, Alliance, or Confederation; grant Letters of Marque and Reprisal; coin Money; emit Bills of Credit; make any Thing but gold and silver Coin a Tender in Payment of Debts; pass any Bill of Attainder, ex post facto Law, or Law impairing the Obligation of Contracts, or grant any Title of Nobility.
Clause 2:	No State shall, without the Consent of the Congress, lay any Imposts or Duties on Imports or Exports, except what may be absolutely necessary for executing it's inspection Laws: and the net Produce of all Duties and Imposts, laid by any State on Imports or Exports, shall be for the Use of the Treasury of the United States; and all such Laws shall be subject to the Revision and Controul of the Congress.
Clause 3:	No State shall, without the Consent of Congress, lay any Duty of Tonnage, keep Troops, or Ships of War in time of Peace, enter into any Agreement or Compact with another State, or with a foreign Power, or engage in War, unless actually invaded, or in such imminent Danger as will not admit of delay.

Section 11

Clause 1:	**No member of the Congress shall serve cumulatively**

for more than six thousand calendar days, except that at the end of said period they may continue to serve until the next election for the House of Representatives. The remainder of any senatorial term shall be filled in the manner prescribed by State law.[6]

Article II: The Executive Branch

Section 1

Clause 1: The executive Power shall be vested in a President of the United States of America. He shall hold his Office during the Term of four Years, and, together with the Vice President, chosen for the same Term, be elected, as follows:

Clause 2: Each State shall appoint, in such Manner as the Legislature thereof may direct, a Number of Electors, equal to the whole Number of Senators and Representatives to which the State may be entitled in the Congress: but no Senator or Representative, or Person holding an Office of Trust or Profit under the United States, shall be appointed an Elector.

Clause 3: The Electors shall meet in their respective States, and vote by Ballot for two Persons, of whom one at least shall not be an Inhabitant of the same State with themselves. And they shall make a List of all the Persons voted for, and of the Number of Votes for each; which List they shall sign and certify, and transmit sealed to the Seat of the Government of the United States, directed to the President of the Senate. The President of the Senate shall, in the Presence of the Senate and House of Representatives, open all the Certificates, and the Votes shall then be counted. The Person having the greatest Number of Votes shall be the President, if such Number be a Majority of the whole Number of Electors appointed; and if there be more than one who have such Majority, and have an equal Number of Votes, then the House of Representatives shall immediately chuse by Ballot one of them for President; and if no Person have a Majority, then from the five highest on the List the said House shall in like Manner chuse the President. But in

---

[6]   See chapter 11.

chusing the President, the Votes shall be taken by States, the Representation from each State having one Vote; A quorum for this Purpose shall consist of a Member or Members from two thirds of the States, and a Majority of all the States shall be necessary to a Choice. In every Case, after the Choice of the President, the Person having the greatest Number of Votes of the Electors shall be the Vice President. But if there should remain two or more who have equal Votes, the Senate shall chuse from them by Ballot the Vice President.

Clause 4:   The Congress may determine the Time of chusing the Electors, and the Day on which they shall give their Votes; which Day shall be the same throughout the United States.

Clause 5:   No Person except a natural born Citizen, or a Citizen of the United States, at the time of the Adoption of this Constitution, shall be eligible to the Office of President; neither shall any Person be eligible to that Office who shall not have attained to the Age of thirty five Years, and been fourteen Years a Resident within the United States.

Clause 6:   In Case of the Removal of the President from Office, or of his Death, Resignation, or Inability to discharge the Powers and Duties of the said Office, the Same shall devolve on the Vice President, and the Congress may by Law provide for the Case of Removal, Death, Resignation or Inability, both of the President and Vice President, declaring what Officer shall then act as President, and such Officer shall act accordingly, until the Disability be removed, or a President shall be elected.

Clause 7:   The President shall, at stated Times, receive for his Services, a Compensation, which shall neither be encreased nor diminished during the Period for which he shall have been elected, and he shall not receive within that Period any other Emolument from the United States, or any of them.

Clause 8:   Before he enter on the Execution of his Office, he shall take the following Oath or Affirmation:--"I do solemnly swear (or affirm) that I will faithfully execute the Office of President of the United States, and will to the best of my Ability, preserve, protect and defend the Constitution of the United States."

Section 2

Clause 1: The President shall be Commander in Chief of the Army and Navy of the United States, and of the Militia of the several States, when called into the actual Service of the United States, **all subject to authorization by the Congress under Section 8 of Article I;**[7] he may require the Opinion, in writing, of the principal Officer in each of the executive Departments, upon any Subject relating to the Duties of their respective Offices, and he shall have Power to grant Reprieves and Pardons for Offences against the United States, except in Cases of Impeachment.

Clause 2: He shall have Power, by and with the Advice and Consent of the Senate, to make Treaties, provided two thirds of the Senators present concur; and he shall nominate, and by and with the Advice and Consent of the Senate, shall appoint Ambassadors, other public Ministers and Consuls, Judges of the supreme Court, and all other Officers of the United States, whose Appointments are not herein otherwise provided for, and which shall be established by Law: but the Congress may by Law vest the Appointment of such inferior Officers, as they think proper, in the President alone, in the Courts of Law, or in the Heads of Departments.

Clause 3: The President shall have Power to fill up all Vacancies that may happen during the Recess of the Senate, by granting Commissions which shall expire at the End of their next Session.

Section 3

He shall from time to time give to the Congress Information of the State of the Union, and recommend to their consideration such Measures as he shall judge necessary and expedient; he may, on extraordinary Occasions, convene both Houses, or either of them, and in Case of Disagreement between them, with Respect to the Time of Adjournment, he may adjourn them to such Time as he shall think proper; he shall receive Ambassadors and other public Ministers; he shall take Care that the Laws be faithfully executed, and shall Commission all the Officers of the United States.

---

[7]   See chapter 7.

Section 4

The President, Vice President and all civil Officers of the United States, shall be removed from Office on Impeachment for, and Conviction of, Treason, Bribery, or other high Crimes and Misdemeanors.

Article III: The Judicial Branch

Section 1

The judicial Power of the United States, shall be vested in one supreme Court, and in such inferior Courts as the Congress may from time to time ordain and establish. The Judges, both of the supreme and inferior Courts, shall hold their Offices during good Behaviour,[8] and shall, at stated Times, receive for their Services, a Compensation, which shall not be diminished during their Continuance in Office.

Section 2

Clause 1:	The judicial Power shall extend to all Cases, in Law and Equity, arising under this Constitution, the Laws of the United States, and Treaties made, or which shall be made, under their Authority;--to all Cases affecting Ambassadors, other public Ministers and Consuls;--to all Cases of admiralty and maritime Jurisdiction;--to Controversies to which the United States shall be a Party;--to Controversies between two or more States;--between a State and Citizens of another state;--between Citizens of different States,--between Citizens of the same State claiming Lands under Grants of different States, and between a State, or the Citizens thereof, and foreign States, Citizens or Subjects.
Clause 2:	In all Cases affecting Ambassadors, other public Ministers and Consuls, and those in which a State shall be Party, the supreme Court shall have original Jurisdiction. In all the other Cases before mentioned, the supreme Court shall have appellate Jurisdiction, both as to Law and Fact, with such Exceptions, and under such Regulations as the Congress shall make.
Clause 3:	The Trial of all Crimes, except in Cases of Impeachment,

---

8   See the proposed 28th Amendment below and chapter 11.

230

shall be by Jury; and such Trial shall be held in the State where the said Crimes shall have been committed; but when not committed within any State, the Trial shall be at such Place or Places as the Congress may by Law have directed.

Section 3

Clause 1: Treason against the United States, shall consist only in levying War against them, or in adhering to their Enemies, giving them Aid and Comfort. No Person shall be convicted of Treason unless on the Testimony of two Witnesses to the same overt Act, or on Confession in open Court.

Clause 2: The Congress shall have Power to declare the Punishment of Treason, but no Attainder of Treason shall work Corruption of Blood, or Forfeiture except during the Life of the Person attainted.

Section 4. [9]

In construing any provision of this Constitution or any statue or regulation enacted hereunder, the Supreme Court and all inferior courts shall be bound first by the common meaning of the words of the provision at the time of its enactment, in case of more than one possible meaning of those words shall construe the provision in the manner most restrictive to the power of government, and shall not use as authority any international or foreign law other than the received common law nor enforce any treaty which conflicts with this Constitution or purports to expand the authority of Congress beyond that granted by this Constitution. [Breach of this Section by any judicial Officer of the United States shall constitute a Misdemeanor under Article II Section 4.]

[Section 5.

Upon any amendment of this Constitution, all judicial Officers of the United States shall renew their Oath or Affirmation to support this Constitution as amended under Article VI Clause 3. The judicial appointment of any judicial Officer of the United States who fails to submit this renewal within ninety days of the date of adoption of the amendment shall automatically terminate without further action by any

---

[9]   See chapter 12.

officer of the United States.]

Article IV: The States

Section 1: Full Faith and Credit shall be given in each State to the public Acts, Records, and judicial Proceedings of every other State. And the Congress may by general Laws prescribe the Manner in which such Acts, Records and Proceedings shall be proved, and the Effect thereof.

Section 2

Clause 1: The Citizens of each State shall be entitled to all Privileges and Immunities of Citizens in the several States.

Clause 2: A Person charged in any State with Treason, Felony, or other Crime, who shall flee from Justice, and be found in another State, shall on Demand of the executive Authority of the State from which he fled, be delivered up, to be removed to the State having Jurisdiction of the Crime.

Clause 3: No Person held to Service or Labour in one State, under the Laws thereof, escaping into another, shall, in Consequence of any Law or Regulation therein, be discharged from such Service or Labour, but shall be delivered up on Claim of the Party to whom such Service or Labour may be due.

Section 3

Clause 1: New States may be admitted by the Congress into this Union; but no new State shall be formed or erected within the Jurisdiction of any other State; nor any State be formed by the Junction of two or more States, or Parts of States, without the Consent of the Legislatures of the States concerned as well as of the Congress.

Clause 2: The Congress shall have Power to dispose of and make all needful Rules and Regulations respecting the Territory or other Property belonging to the United States; and nothing in this Constitution shall be so construed as to Prejudice any Claims of the United States, or of any particular State.

Section 4: The United States shall guarantee to every State in this Union a Republican Form of Government, and shall protect each of them against Invasion; and on Application of the Legislature, or of the Executive (when the Legislature cannot be convened) against domestic Violence.

232

Article V: Amendment Process[10]

Section 1:   This Constitution may be amended by either: (a) five eighths of both Houses of Congress and five eighths of the States, which approvals by the Congress and the States may occur concurrently, or (b) two thirds of the States with a majority of the nation's population as determined by the most recent Enumeration made pursuant to Article I Section 2 of this Constitution prior to the completion of the procedures set forth in this Section. If the first approval of a proposed amendment is by States, at least five States must approve the proposed amendment within a period of not more than one hundred twenty calendar days. Each State may determine whether actions under this article are to be by its legislature or by referendum.

Section 2: All approvals of any proposed amendment shall expire if the proposed amendment has not been fully approved (a) for proposed amendments initiated by the Congress seven years after the vote of whichever House of Congress was the first to approve it, or (b) for proposed amendments initiated by States nine years after the first State approval.

Section 3:   The operative text of any amendment must be approved with identical wording.

---

[10]   The prior Article is deleted in its entirety: "The Congress, whenever two thirds of both Houses shall deem it necessary, shall propose Amendments to this Constitution, or, on the Application of the Legislatures of two thirds of the several States, shall call a Convention for proposing Amendments, which, in either Case, shall be valid to all Intents and Purposes, as Part of this Constitution, when ratified by the Legislatures of three fourths of the several States, or by Conventions in three fourths thereof, as the one or the other Mode of Ratification may be proposed by the Congress; Provided that no Amendment which may be made prior to the Year One thousand eight hundred and eight shall in any Manner affect the first and fourth Clauses in the Ninth Section of the first Article; and that no State, without its Consent, shall be deprived of its equal Suffrage in the Senate." See chapter 5.

Section 4: Congress and any State may rescind approval of a proposed amendment except during the thirty calendar days prior to the date upon which the proposed amendment is fully approved under Section 1 of this article.

Section 5: An amendment shall be valid to all intents and purposes as part of this Constitution upon completion of the procedures set out in Section 1 of this article unless the amendment itself sets a future effective date. An approval or rescission of an approval of a proposed amendment shall be effective upon the completion of Congress' or a State's procedures for ordinary legislative or ballot actions, or as the legislature or a State's constitution may otherwise provide, except that no executive assent or veto shall apply to any action under this article.

Section 6: Congress' and each State's approvals and rescissions of approvals of proposed amendments must be promptly transmitted to the Speaker of the House of Representatives, who must promptly: (a) publicly post all such actions, (b) transmit them to the Senate and the legislatures of the States, and (c) declare the enactment of an amendment upon fulfillment of the requirements of this article. In the event of any failure to perform an executory action under this article, upon the application of any member of Congress, or with respect to any State any member of that State's legislature, the courts constituted under Article III of this Constitution must decree such action to be effected.

Section 7: No amendment shall deprive any State of its equal suffrage in the Senate without its consent.

Article VI: Legal Status of the Constitution

Clause 1:   All Debts contracted and Engagements entered into, before the Adoption of this Constitution, shall be as valid against the United States under this Constitution, as under the Confederation.

Clause 2:   This Constitution, and the Laws of the United States which shall be made in Pursuance thereof; and all Treaties made, or which shall be made, under the Authority of the United States, shall be the supreme Law of the Land; and the

Clause 3:

Judges in every State shall be bound thereby, any Thing in the Constitution or Laws of any State to the Contrary notwithstanding.

The Senators and Representatives before mentioned, and the Members of the several State Legislatures, and all executive and judicial Officers, both of the United States and of the several States, shall be bound by Oath or Affirmation, to support this Constitution; but no religious Test shall ever be required as a Qualification to any Office or public Trust under the United States.

Article VII: Signatures

The Ratification of the Conventions of nine States, shall be sufficient for the Establishment of this Constitution between the States so ratifying the Same. Done in Convention by the Unanimous Consent of the States present the Seventeenth Day of September in the Year of our Lord one thousand seven hundred and Eighty seven and of the Independence of the United States of America the Twelfth In witness whereof We have hereunto subscribed our Names,

GEO. WASHINGTON--Presidt. and deputy from Virginia

[Signed also by the deputies of twelve States.]

New Hampshire:John Langdon, Nicholas Gilman

Delaware:	Geo. Read, Gunning Bedford jun, John Dickinson, Richard Bassett, Jacob Broom
Massachusetts:	Nathaniel Gorham, Rufus King,
Maryland:	James MCHenry, Dan. of St. Thos. Jenifer, Danl. Carroll,
Connecticut:	Wm. Saml. Johnson, Roger Sherman
New York:	Alexander Hamilton
Virginia:	John Blair, James Madison Jr.,
New Jersey:	Wil. Livingston, David Brearley, Wm. Paterson, Jona. Dayton
North Carolina:	Wm. Blount, Richd. Dobbs Spaight, Hu Williamson,
Pennsylvania:	B. Franklin, Thomas Mifflin, Robt. Morris, Geo. Clymer, Thos. FitzSimons, Jared Ingersoll, James

	Wilson, Gouv Morris
South Carolina:	J. Rutledge, Charles Cotesworth Pinckney, Charles Pinckney, Pierce Butler
Georgia:	William Few, Abr Baldwin
Attest:	William Jackson, Secretary

The Bill of Rights Amendments I - 10 (Adopted 1791)

Amendment 1
Congress shall make no law[11] **preferring a religion or irreligion**, or prohibiting the free exercise thereof; or abridging the freedom of speech, or of the press; or the right of the people peaceably to assemble, and to petition the government for a redress of grievances.

Amendment 2[12]
The right of the people to keep and bear arms, shall not be infringed, **except for regulations restricting possession by persons convicted of a felony, or individually found by due process to be a threat to public or personal safety, or to assure public safety in the use of arms.**

Amendment 3
No soldier shall, in time of peace be quartered in any house, without the consent of the owner, nor in time of war, but in a manner to be prescribed by law.

Amendment 4
The right of the people to be secure in their persons, houses, papers, and effects, against unreasonable searches and seizures, shall not be violated, and no warrants shall issue, but upon probable cause, supported by oath or affirmation, and particularly describing the place to be searched, and the persons or things to be seized.

Amendment 5
No person shall be held to answer for a capital, or otherwise infamous crime, unless on a presentment or indictment of a grand jury, except in cases arising in the land or naval forces, or in the militia, when in actual service in time of war or public danger; nor shall any person be subject for the same offense to be twice put in jeopardy of life or limb; nor shall be compelled in any criminal case to be a witness against himself, nor be deprived of life, liberty, or

---

[11] "respecting an establishment of religion" deleted, see chapter 8.

[12] "A well regulated militia, being necessary to the security of a free state," deleted, see chapter 10.

property, without due process of law; nor shall private property be taken for public use, without just compensation.

Amendment 6
In all criminal prosecutions, the accused shall enjoy the right to a speedy and public trial, by an impartial jury of the state and district wherein the crime shall have been committed, which district shall have been previously ascertained by law, and to be informed of the nature and cause of the accusation; to be confronted with the witnesses against him; to have compulsory process for obtaining witnesses in his favor, and to have the assistance of counsel for his defense.

Amendment 7
In suits at common law, where the value in controversy shall exceed twenty dollars, the right of trial by jury shall be preserved, and no fact tried by a jury, shall be otherwise reexamined in any court of the United States, than according to the rules of the common law.

Amendment 8
Excessive bail shall not be required, nor excessive fines imposed, nor cruel and unusual punishments inflicted.

Amendment 9
The enumeration in the Constitution, of certain rights, shall not be construed to deny or disparage others retained by the people.

Amendment 10[13]
Section 1. The powers not **expressly** delegated to the United States by the Constitution, nor prohibited by it to the states, are reserved to the states respectively, or to the people.

Section 2. Without limitation to Section 1 of this Amendment, any state may require a declaratory judgment from the Supreme Court as to the violation of this Constitution by any act of Congress or any regulation or action of the executive as soon as such act takes effect under Section 7 of Article 1 of this Constitution or such executive regulation or action becomes effective.   The Supreme Court shall exercise original

---

[13]   See chapter 6.

jurisdiction over such causes, except that it may designate a Master or inferior Court to discover factual matters relating to the cause, but it shall not be bound by any such findings.

Section 3. Upon any successful action under Section 2 of this article, the state or states prosecuting the action shall be reimbursed by the United States treasury in an amount equal to three times the reasonable costs of prosecuting the action.

Section 4. Without limitation to Section 1 of this Amendment, five eighths of the states may rescind any act of Congress or any regulation or action of the executive within one year of the time such act takes effect under Section 7 of Article 1 of this Constitution or such executive regulation or action becomes effective.

Amendments 11 - 27 (Adopted 1798 - 1992)

Amendment 11 (1798)
The judicial power of the United States shall not be construed to extend to any suit in law or equity, commenced or prosecuted against one of the United States by citizens of another state, or by citizens or subjects of any foreign state.

Amendment 12 (1804)
The electors shall meet in their respective states and vote by ballot for President and Vice-President, one of whom, at least, shall not be an inhabitant of the same state with themselves; they shall name in their ballots the person voted for as President, and in distinct ballots the person voted for as Vice-President, and they shall make distinct lists of all persons voted for as President, and of all persons voted for as Vice-President, and of the number of votes for each, which lists they shall sign and certify, and transmit sealed to the seat of the government of the United States, directed to the President of the Senate;--The President of the Senate shall, in the presence of the Senate and House of Representatives, open all the certificates and the votes shall then be counted;--the person having the greatest number of votes for President, shall be the President, if such number be a majority of the whole number of electors appointed; and if no person have such majority, then from the persons having the highest numbers not exceeding three on the list of those voted for as President, the House of Representatives shall choose immediately, by ballot, the President. But in choosing the President, the votes

shall be taken by states, the representation from each state having one vote; a quorum for this purpose shall consist of a member or members from two-thirds of the states, and a majority of all the states shall be necessary to a choice. And if the House of Representatives shall not choose a President whenever the right of choice shall devolve upon them, before the fourth day of March next following, then the Vice-President shall act as President, as in the case of the death or other constitutional disability of the President. The person having the greatest number of votes as Vice-President, shall be the Vice-President, if such number be a majority of the whole number of electors appointed, and if no person have a majority, then from the two highest numbers on the list, the Senate shall choose the Vice-President; a quorum for the purpose shall consist of two-thirds of the whole number of Senators, and a majority of the whole number shall be necessary to a choice. But no person constitutionally ineligible to the office of President shall be eligible to that of Vice-President of the United States.

Amendment 13 (1865)
Section 1. Neither slavery nor involuntary servitude, except as a punishment forcrime whereof the party shall have been duly convicted, shall exist within the United States, or any place subject to their jurisdiction.

Section 2. Congress shall have power to enforce this article by appropriate legislation.

Amendment 14 (1868) [14]

Section 1.[15] **Equality of rights under the law shall not be denied or**

---

[14]   See chapter 9.

[15]   Prior Sections 1 through 4 are deleted in their entirety:
"Section 1. All persons born or naturalized in the United States, and subject to the jurisdiction thereof, are citizens of the United States and of the state wherein they reside. No state shall make or enforce any law which shall abridge the privileges or immunities of citizens of the United States; nor shall any state deprive any person of life, liberty, or property, without due process of law; nor deny to any person within its jurisdiction the equal protection of the laws.
Section 2. Representatives shall be apportioned among the several states according to their respective numbers, counting the whole number of

abridged by the United States or by any state on account of race, ethnic origin or sex. This article shall not prohibit laws or regulations taking account of sex which relate to physical differences, privacy, athletic competition or the military. This article shall not apply to homosexual orientation, transgenderness or the internal government of any religion.

Section 2. The Congress shall have power to enforce, by appropriate legislation, the provisions of this article, **except with regard to laws taking account of sex regarding family, domestic relations, property rights or criminal laws.**

Section 3. Without limitation to any other powers prohibited to the states by the Constitution, no state shall deny or abridge the rights set forth in the first, second, third, fourth, fifth, sixth, and eighth

---

persons in each state, excluding Indians not taxed. But when the right to vote at any election for the choice of electors for President and Vice President of the United States, Representatives in Congress, the executive and judicial officers of a state, or the members of the legislature thereof, is denied to any of the male inhabitants of such state, being twenty-one years of age, and citizens of the United States, or in any way abridged, except for participation in rebellion, or other crime, the basis of representation therein shall be reduced in the proportion which the number of such male citizens shall bear to the whole number of male citizens twenty-one years of age in such state. Section 3. No person shall be a Senator or Representative in Congress, or elector of President and Vice President, or hold any office, civil or military, under the United States, or under any state, who, having previously taken an oath, as a member of Congress, or as an officer of the United States, or as a member of any state legislature, or as an executive or judicial officer of any state, to support the Constitution of the United States, shall have engaged in insurrection or rebellion against the same, or given aid or comfort to the enemies thereof. But Congress may by a vote of two-thirds of each house, remove such disability.
Section 4. The validity of the public debt of the United States, authorized by law, including debts incurred for payment of pensions and bounties for services in suppressing insurrection or rebellion, shall not be questioned. But neither the United States nor any state shall assume or pay any debt or obligation incurred in aid of insurrection or rebellion against the United States, or any claim for the loss or emancipation of any slave; but all such debts, obligations and claims shall be held illegal and void." See chapter 9.

amendments to the Constitution, as amended from time to time. The several states shall have exclusive jurisdiction as to the interpretation and enforcement of this Section within each respective state. No state shall be bound in such interpretation or enforcement by any prior decisions of the courts of the United States.

Amendment 15 (1870)
Section 1. The right of citizens of the United States to vote shall not be denied or abridged by the United States or by any state on account of race, color, or previous condition of servitude.

Section 2. The Congress shall have power to enforce this article by appropriate legislation.

Amendment 16 (1913)
The Congress shall have power to lay and collect taxes on incomes, from whatever source derived, without apportionment among the several states, and without regard to any census of emuneration.

Amendment 17 (1913)
The Senate of the United States shall be composed of two Senators from each state, elected by the people thereof, for six years; and each Senator shall have one vote. The electors in each state shall have the qualifications requisite for electors of the most numerous branch of the state legislatures.

When vacancies happen in the representation of any state in the Senate, the executive authority of such state shall issue writs of election to fill such vacancies: Provided, that the legislature of any state may empower the executive thereof to make temporary appointments until the people fill the vacancies by election as the legislature may direct.

This amendment shall not be so construed as to affect the election or term of any Senator chosen before it becomes valid as part of the Constitution.

Amendment 18 (1919)
Section 1. After one year from the ratification of this article the manufacture, sale, or transportation of intoxicating liquors within, the importation thereof into, or the exportation thereof from the United States and all territory subject to the jurisdiction thereof for beverage purposes is hereby prohibited.

Section 2. The Congress and the several states shall have concurrent power to enforce this article by appropriate legislation.

Section 3. This article shall be inoperative unless it shall have been ratified as an amendment to the Constitution by the legislatures of the several states, as provided in the Constitution, within seven years from the date of the submission hereof to the states by the Congress.

Amendment 19 (1920)
The right of citizens of the United States to vote shall not be denied or abridged by the United States or by any state on account of sex.
Congress shall have power to enforce this article by appropriate legislation.

Amendment 20 (1933)
Section 1. The terms of the President and Vice President shall end at noon on the 20th day of January, and the terms of Senators and Representatives at noon on the 3d day of January, of the years in which such terms would have ended if this article had not been ratified; and the terms of their successors shall then begin.

Section 2. The Congress shall assemble at least once in every year, and such meeting shall begin at noon on the 3d day of January, unless they shall by law appoint a different day.

Section 3. If, at the time fixed for the beginning of the term of the President, the President elect shall have died, the Vice President elect shall become President. If a President shall not have been chosen before the time fixed for the beginning of his term, or if the President elect shall have failed to qualify, then the Vice President elect shall act as President until a President shall have qualified; and the Congress may by law provide for the case wherein neither a President elect nor a Vice President elect shall have qualified, declaring who shall then act as President, or the manner in which one who is to act shall be selected, and such person shall act accordingly until a President or Vice President shall have qualified.

Section 4. The Congress may by law provide for the case of the death of any of the persons from whom the House of Representatives may choose a President whenever the right of choice shall have devolved upon them, and for the case of the death of any of the persons from whom the Senate may choose a Vice President whenever the right of choice shall have devolved upon them.

Section 5. Sections 1 and 2 shall take effect on the 15th day of October following the ratification of this article.

Section 6. This article shall be inoperative unless it shall have been ratified as an amendment to the Constitution by the legislatures of three-fourths of the several states within seven years from the date of its submission.

Amendment 21 (1933)
Section 1. The eighteenth article of amendment to the Constitution of the United States is hereby repealed.

Section 2. The transportation or importation into any state, territory, or possession of the United States for delivery or use therein of intoxicating liquors, in violation of the laws thereof, is hereby prohibited.

Section 3. This article shall be inoperative unless it shall have been ratified as an amendment to the Constitution by conventions in the several states, as provided in the Constitution, within seven years from the date of the submission hereof to the states by the Congress.

Amendment 22 (1951)
Section 1. No person shall be elected to the office of the President more than twice, and no person who has held the office of President, or acted as President, for more than two years of a term to which some other person was elected President shall be elected to the office of the President more than once. But this article shall not apply to any person holding the office of President when this article was proposed by the Congress, and shall not prevent any person who may be holding the office of President, or acting as President, during the term within which this article becomes operative from holding the office of President or acting as President during the remainder of such term.

Section 2. This article shall be inoperative unless it shall have been ratified as an amendment to the Constitution by the legislatures of three-fourths of the several states within seven years from the date of its submission to the states by the Congress.

Amendment 23 (1961)
Section 1. The District constituting the seat of government of the United States shall appoint in such manner as the Congress may direct:
A number of electors of President and Vice President equal to the whole

number of Senators and Representatives in Congress to which the District would be entitled if it were a state, but in no event more than the least populous state; they shall be in addition to those appointed by the states, but they shall be considered, for the purposes of the election of President and Vice President, to be electors appointed by a state; and they shall meet in the District and perform such duties as provided by the twelfth article of amendment.

Section 2. The Congress shall have power to enforce this article by appropriate legislation.

Amendment 24 (1964)
Section 1. The right of citizens of the United States to vote in any primary or other election for President or Vice President, for electors for President or Vice President, or for Senator or Representative in Congress, shall not be denied or abridged by the United States or any state by reason of failure to pay any poll tax or other tax.

Section 2. The Congress shall have power to enforce this article by appropriate legislation.

Amendment 25 (1967)
Section 1. In case of the removal of the President from office or of his death or resignation, the Vice President shall become President.

Section 2. Whenever there is a vacancy in the office of the Vice President, the President shall nominate a Vice President who shall take office upon confirmation by a majority vote of both Houses of Congress.

Section 3. Whenever the President transmits to the President pro tempore of the Senate and the Speaker of the House of Representatives his written declaration that he is unable to discharge the powers and duties of his office, and until he transmits to them a written declaration to the contrary, such powers and duties shall be discharged by the Vice President as Acting President.

Section 4. Whenever the Vice President and a majority of either the principal officers of the executive departments or of such other body as Congress may by law provide, transmit to the President pro tempore of the Senate and the Speaker of the House of Representatives their written declaration that the

President is unable to discharge the powers and duties of his office, the Vice President shall immediately assume the powers and duties of the office as Acting President. Thereafter, when the President transmits to the President pro tempore of the Senate and the Speaker of the House of Representatives his written declaration that no inability exists, he shall resume the powers and duties of his office unless the Vice President and a majority of either the principal officers of the executive department or of such other body as Congress may by law provide, transmit within four days to the President pro tempore of the Senate and the Speaker of the House of Representatives their written declaration that the President is unable to discharge the powers and duties of his office. Thereupon Congress shall decide the issue, assembling within forty-eight hours for that purpose if not in session. If the Congress, within twenty-one days after receipt of the latter written declaration, or, if Congress is not in session, within twenty-one days after Congress is required to assemble, determines by two-thirds vote of both Houses that the President is unable to discharge the powers and duties of his office, the Vice President shall continue to discharge the same as Acting President; otherwise, the President shall resume the powers and duties of his office.

Amendment 26 (1971)
Section 1. The right of citizens of the United States, who are 18 years of age or older, to vote, shall not be denied or abridged by the United States or any state on account of age.

Section 2. The Congress shall have the power to enforce this article by appropriate legislation.

Amendment 27 (1992)
No law varying the compensation for the services of the Senators and Representatives shall take effect until an election of Representatives shall have intervened.

Amendment 28 (proposed)[16]
Section 1. Except as provided in Section 3 of this article, Judges appointed under Article III of this Constitution shall hold their offices during good behavior until the thirty-first day of August of the year in which their seventy-fifth birthday occurs.

---

[16]   See chapter 11.

Section 2. Justices of the Supreme Court shall serve terms of eighteen years each. One of each of these terms shall expire on the thirty-first day of August of each year following an election pursuant to Article I Section 2 Clause 1 of this Constitution. No person may serve in more than one such term. In the event of a vacancy for any reason, a replacement shall be named in accordance with Article II Section 2 Clause 2 of this Constitution, but such replacement shall only serve for the remainder of the vacated term.

Section 3. The term of service for any justice of the Supreme Court whose term expires after such justice's seventy-fifth birthday shall be reduced by one year for every two years that such term extends past the thirty-first day of August in the year in which such justice's seventy-fifth birthday occurs. A replacement for the balance of such justice's term shall be named as provided in Section 2 of this article.

Section 4. In the event that the Congress provides for a number of justices of the Supreme Court other than nine, it shall provide in such action for the expiration of terms over the maximum possible time.

Section 5. Upon ratification of this article, all judicial officers of the United States then serving who would be disqualified by this article upon ratification shall be ranked by length of service as a judicial officer of the United States and divided in accordance with such ranking into two classes of equal numbers. This article shall be effective as of the thirty-first day of August of the year following its ratification as to the more senior class and as of the thirty-first day of August of the second year following its ratification as to the more junior class.

Section 6. Justices of the Supreme Court serving upon ratification of this article may continue to serve until the thirty-first day of August of the year in which their seventy-fifth birthday occurs. Justices already past such age upon ratification of this article shall be included in the process provided by Section 5 of this article, and shall retire in accordance therewith. The replacements of justices serving upon ratification of this article shall be assigned to the next available term established under Section 2 of this article. However, such replacements' terms of service shall expire on the thirty-first day of August of the year in which occurs the eighteenth anniversary of their confirmation by the Senate or any shorter term in accordance with Section 3 of this article, the balance of such term shall be considered vacant, and it shall be filled as provided in Section 2 of this article.

Amendment 29 (proposed)[17]

Section 1. In any State entitled to more than one seat in the House of Representatives, the sum of the lengths of all of the boundaries of the districts for such seats shall not be more than five percent longer than the shortest possible distances for such boundaries consistent with Section 2 of this article. For purposes of this article, boundaries which follow any body of water or a state line shall be measured as a straight line between the two points where the other boundaries intersect the boundary which follows a body of water or state line.

Section 2. The populations of all districts referred to in Section 1 shall not differ by more than one percent from each other based upon the Enumeration made pursuant to Article I Section 2 of this Constitution.

Section 3. If the requirements set forth in Sections 1 and 2 are met, the several States shall have exclusive power and jurisdiction as to the establishment of their electoral districts for the House of Representatives and the interpretation and enforcement of this article within each respective State.

[Section 4. The populations of all other electoral districts in any State shall not differ by more than ten percent from each other based upon the Enumeration made pursuant to Article I Section 2 of this Constitution. If this requirement is met, the several States shall have exclusive power and jurisdiction as to the establishment of electoral districts and the interpretation and enforcement of this Section within each respective State.]

Section 4 [5]. The exclusive power and jurisdiction provided by this article shall be effective for any State in compliance herewith following ratification of this article. This article shall become mandatory upon the completion of the Enumeration made pursuant to Article I Section 2 of this Constitution next following the ratification of this article.

---

[17]   See chapter 11.

Appendix - Texts of Proposed Amendments

A Proposed Amendment to Restore the Allocation of Authority Among the State and Federal Governments

Section 1. The first clause of Article I Section 8 shall be amended to strike the words "and provide for the common Defence and general Welfare" and to insert after "the United States": "; for, and only for, the following purposes;".

Section 2. The third clause of Article I Section 8 shall be amended to strike ", and among the several States," and to insert at the end of the clause: ", or which substantively crosses the borders of the several States, but the latter only so as to directly either (a) promote the passage of persons, goods, services, information, funds, or other economic activity across state borders, or collective bargaining, or (b) prohibit the passage of criminals, criminal activities, and dangerous substances across state borders; and the costs of any such regulation [on the several States] are fully funded by the United States".

Section 3. A new penultimate clause shall be added to Article I section 8 reading in full: "To make expenditures to promote the general welfare, provided that the criteria for distributing such expenditures make them generally available in fact, any regulation thereunder only applies directly to the specific expenditure, is not applicable to any other expenditure from any source, and shall not be imposed unless its costs are fully funded by the expenditure;".

Section 4. This amendment shall be immediately effective upon its ratification as to all laws thereafter enacted, and on the second anniversary of its ratification as to all laws already in effect upon its ratification.

Section 5. The textual amendments provided by this article shall be incorporated in all official publications of this Constitution. Congress is authorized determine whether this article shall also be included in such official publications.

A Proposed Amendment to Provide a Mechanism to
Enforce the Restoration of the Allocation of Governmental
Authority Among the State and Federal Governments

Section 1. The tenth amendment shall be amended to insert the word "expressly" between the words "not" and "delegated."

Section 2. The original text of the tenth amendment as amended by Section 1 of this article shall be designated as "Section 1."

Section 3. The following shall thereafter be inserted and designated as "Section 2": "Section 2. Without limitation to Section 1 of this Amendment, any state may require a declaratory judgment from the Supreme Court as to the violation of this Constitution by any act of Congress or any regulation or action of the executive as soon as such act takes effect under Section 7 of Article 1 of this Constitution or such executive regulation or action becomes effective. The Supreme Court shall exercise original jurisdiction over such causes, except that it may designate a Master or inferior Court to discover factual matters relating to the cause, but it shall not be bound by any such findings."

Section 4. The following shall be added to the tenth amendment and designated as "Section 3": "Section 3. Upon any successful action under Section 2 of this article, the state or states prosecuting the action shall be reimbursed by the United States treasury in an amount equal to three times the reasonable costs of prosecuting the action."

Section 5. The following shall be added to the tenth amendment and designated as "Section 4": "Section 4. Without limitation to Section 1 of this Amendment, five eighths of the states may rescind any act of Congress or any regulation or action of the executive within one year of the time such act takes effect under Section 7 of Article 1 of this Constitution or such executive regulation or action becomes effective."

Section 6. Sections 2, 3 and 4 newly added to the tenth amendment shall be immediately effective upon ratification of this article as to all laws thereafter enacted, and on the second anniversary of its ratification as to all laws already in effect upon its ratification.

Section 7. The textual amendments provided by this article shall be incorporated in all official publications of this Constitution. Congress is authorized determine whether this article shall also be included in such official publications.

A Proposed Amendment to Improve the Process
for Amending the Constitution and Facilitate the
Initiation of Amendment Proposals by the States

Section 1. Article V shall be amended to read in its entirety as follows:

"Section 1:   This Constitution may be amended by either:
(a) five eighths of both Houses of Congress and five eighths
of the States, which approvals by the Congress and the
States may occur concurrently, or (b) two thirds of the
States with a majority of the nation's population as
determined by the most recent Enumeration made pursuant
to Article I Section 2 of this Constitution prior to the
completion of the procedures set forth in this Section. If
the first approval of a proposed amendment is by States, at
least five States must approve the proposed amendment
within a period of not more than one hundred twenty
calendar days. Each State may determine whether actions
under this article are to be by its legislature or by
referendum.

Section 2:   All approvals of any proposed amendment shall
expire if the proposed amendment has not been fully
approved (a) for proposed amendments initiated by the
Congress seven years after the vote of whichever House of
Congress was the first to approve it, or (b) for proposed
amendments initiated by States nine years after the first
State approval.

Section 3:   The operative text of any amendment must be
approved with identical wording.

Section 4:   Congress and any State may rescind approval of
a proposed amendment except during the thirty calendar
days prior to the date upon which the proposed amendment
is fully approved under Section 1 of this article.

Section 5:   An amendment shall be valid to all intents and
purposes as part of this Constitution upon completion of

the procedures set out in Section 1 of this article unless the amendment itself sets a future effective date. An approval or rescission of an approval of a proposed amendment shall be effective upon the completion of Congress' or a State's procedures for ordinary legislative or ballot actions, or as the legislature or a State's constitution may otherwise provide, except that no executive assent or veto shall apply to any action under this article.

Section 6: Congress' and each State's approvals and rescissions of approvals of proposed amendments must be promptly transmitted to the Speaker of the House of Representatives, who must promptly: (a) publicly post all such actions, (b) transmit them to the Senate and the legislatures of the States, and (c) declare the enactment of an amendment upon fulfillment of the requirements of this article. In the event of any failure to perform an executory action under this article, upon the application of any member of Congress, or with respect to any State any member of that State's legislature, the courts constituted under Article III of this Constitution must decree such action to be effected.

Section 7: No amendment shall deprive any State of its equal suffrage in the Senate without its consent."

Section 2. The textual amendments provided by this article shall be incorporated in all official publications of this Constitution. Congress is authorized determine whether this article shall also be included in such official publications.

A Proposed Amendment to Restore to the Congress
the Exclusive Responsibility for Sending the Armed
Forces Beyond the Territory of the United States and
to Clarify the Limits of Presidential War Powers

Section 1.   The eleventh clause of Article I Section 8 shall be amended to insert at the end: ", and approve any placement of the United States' armed forces outside the United States or its territories, but no such approval shall be for a term longer than two years [unless provided by a treaty approved in accordance with the second clause of Section 2 of Article II of this Constitution]".

Section 2. The first clause of Article 2 Section 2 shall be amended to insert the following between the words "United States" and "he may require": ", all subject to authorization by the Congress under Section 8 of Article I,".

Section 3. Section 1 of this amendment shall be immediately effective upon its ratification as to all placements of the United States' armed forces made thereafter.   All placements in existence upon its ratification shall require re-approval on the second anniversary of its ratification.

Section 4. The textual amendments provided by this article shall be incorporated in all official publications of this Constitution. Congress is authorized determine whether this article shall also be included in such official publications.

A Proposed Amendment to Establish Rules of Judicial Interpretation [and Enforce Judicial Compliance Therewith]

Section 1. Article III shall be amended to add the following new Section 4:

> "Section 4. In construing any provision of this Constitution or any statue or regulation enacted hereunder, the Supreme Court and all inferior courts shall be bound first by the common meaning of the words of the provision at the time of its enactment, in case of more than one possible meaning of those words shall construe the provision in the manner most restrictive to the power of government, and shall not use as authority any international or foreign law other than the received common law nor enforce any treaty which conflicts with this Constitution or purports to expand the authority of Congress beyond that granted by this Constitution. [Breach of this Section by any judicial Officer of the United States shall constitute a Misdemeanor under Article II Section 4.]

[Section 2. Article III shall be amended to add the following new Section 5:

> "Upon any amendment of this Constitution, all judicial Officers of the United States shall renew their Oath or Affirmation to support this Constitution as amended under Article VI Clause 3. The judicial appointment of any judicial Officer of the United States who fails to submit this renewal within ninety days of the date of adoption of the amendment shall automatically terminate without further action by any officer of the United States."]

Section 3. The textual amendments provided by this article shall be incorporated in all official publications of this Constitution. Congress is authorized determine whether this article shall also be included in such official publications.

A Proposed Amendment to Restore the Original Understanding of the Relationship Between Religion and Government

Section 1. The first amendment shall be amended to delete the words "respecting an establishment of religion" and to insert between the words "Congress shall make no law" and "or prohibiting the free exercise thereof" the following: "preferring a religion or irreligion,".

Section 2. The textual amendment provided by this article shall be incorporated in all official publications of this Constitution. Congress is authorized determine whether this article shall also be included in such official publications.

A Proposed Amendment to Restore the Original Understanding of the Right to Bear Arms

Section 1. The second amendment shall be amended to delete the words "A well regulated militia, being necessary to the security of a free state," and to insert at the end ", except for regulations restricting possession by persons convicted of a felony, or individually found by due process to be a threat to public or personal safety, or to assure public safety in the use of arms."

Section 2. The textual amendments provided by this article shall be incorporated in all official publications of this Constitution. Congress is authorized determine whether this article shall also be included in such official publications.

A Proposed Amendment to Clarify the
Fourteenth Amendment and the Allocation of Authority
Thereunder Among the State and Federal Governments

Section 1. Section 1 of the fourteenth amendment shall be amended to read in its entirety as follows:

> "Section 1. Equality of rights under the law shall not be denied or abridged by the United States or by any state on account of race, ethnic origin or sex. This article shall not prohibit laws or regulations taking account of sex which relate to physical differences, privacy, athletic competition or the military. This article shall not apply to homosexual orientation, transgenderness or the internal government of any religion."

Section 2. Sections 2, 3 and 4 are deleted.

Section 3. Section 5 of the fourteenth amendment shall be renumbered as Section 2 and amended to add at the end: ", except with regard to laws taking account of sex regarding family, domestic relations, property rights or criminal laws."

Section 3. The textual amendments provided by this article shall be incorporated in all official publications of this Constitution. Congress is authorized determine whether this article shall also be included in such official publications.

A Proposed Amendment to Make Portions of
the Bill of Rights Applicable to the States and to
Provide for the Allocation of Authority Thereunder
Among the State and Federal Governments

Section 1. The fourteenth amendment shall be amended to add a
new final Section as follows:

> "Section [3][6]. Without limitation to any other
> powers prohibited to the states by the Constitution,
> no state shall deny or abridge the rights set forth in
> the first, second, third, fourth, fifth, sixth, and eighth
> amendments to the Constitution, as amended from
> time to time. The several states shall have exclusive
> jurisdiction as to the interpretation and enforcement
> of this Section within each respective state. No state
> shall be bound in such interpretation or enforcement
> by any prior decisions of the courts of the United
> States."

The numeration of this Section shall be adjusted based upon other
amendments of the fourteenth amendment.

Section 2. The textual amendment provided by this article shall be
incorporated in all official publications of this Constitution. Congress
is authorized determine whether this article shall also be included in
such official publications.

A Proposed Amendment to provide for
Mandatory Judicial Retirement and
Fixed Terms for Justices of the Supreme Court

Section 1. Except as provided in Section 3 of this article, Judges appointed under Article III of this Constitution shall hold their offices during good behavior until the thirty-first day of August of the year in which their seventy-fifth birthday occurs.

Section 2. Justices of the Supreme Court shall serve terms of eighteen years each. One of each of these terms shall expire on the thirty-first day of August of each year following an election pursuant to Article I Section 2 Clause 1 of this Constitution. No person may serve in more than one such term. In the event of a vacancy for any reason, a replacement shall be named in accordance with Article II Section 2 Clause 2 of this Constitution, but such replacement shall only serve for the remainder of the vacated term.

Section 3. The term of service for any justice of the Supreme Court whose term expires after such justice's seventy-fifth birthday shall be reduced by one year for every two years that such term extends past the thirty-first day of August in the year in which such justice's seventy-fifth birthday occurs. A replacement for the balance of such justice's term shall be named as provided in Section 2 of this article.

Section 4. In the event that the Congress provides for a number of justices of the Supreme Court other than nine, it shall provide in such action for the expiration of terms over the maximum possible time.

Section 5. Upon ratification of this article, all judicial officers of the United States then serving who would be disqualified by this article upon ratification shall be ranked by length of service as a judicial officer of the United States and divided in accordance with such ranking into two classes of equal numbers. This article shall be effective as of the thirty-first day of August of the year following its ratification as to the more senior class and as of the thirty-first day of August of the second year following its ratification as to the more junior class.

Section 6. Justices of the Supreme Court serving upon ratification of this article may continue until the thirty-first day of August of the year in which their seventy-fifth birthday occurs. Justices already past such age upon ratification of this article shall be included in the process provided by Section 5 of this article, and shall retire in accordance therewith. The replacements of justices serving upon ratification of this article shall be assigned to the next available term established under Section 2 of this article. However, such replacements' terms of service shall expire on the thirty-first day of August of the year in which occurs the eighteenth anniversary of their confirmation by the Senate or any shorter term in accordance with Section 3 of this article, the balance of such term shall be considered vacant, and it shall be filled as provided in Section 2 of this article.

A Proposed Amendment to Improve the Cohesiveness of the
Districts of Members of the House of Representatives
[and Assure Equal Representation in Electoral Districts]

Section 1. In any State entitled to more than one seat in the House of Representatives, the sum of the lengths of all of the boundaries of the districts for such seats shall not be more than five percent longer than the shortest possible distances for such boundaries consistent with Section 2 of this article. For purposes of this article, boundaries which follow any body of water or a state line shall be measured as a straight line between the two points where the other boundaries intersect the boundary which follows a body of water or state line.

Section 2. The populations of all districts referred to in Section 1 shall not differ by more than one percent from each other based upon the Enumeration made pursuant to Article I Section 2 of this Constitution.

Section 3. If the requirements set forth in Sections 1 and 2 are met, the several States shall have exclusive power and jurisdiction as to the establishment of their electoral districts for the House of Representatives and the interpretation and enforcement of this article within each respective State.

[Section 4. The populations of all other electoral districts in any State shall not differ by more than ten percent from each other based upon the Enumeration made pursuant to Article I Section 2 of this Constitution. If this requirement is met, the several States shall have exclusive power and jurisdiction as to the establishment of electoral districts and the interpretation and enforcement of this Section within each respective State.]

Section 4 [5]. The exclusive power and jurisdiction provided by this article shall be effective for any State in compliance herewith following ratification of this article. This article shall become mandatory upon the completion of the Enumeration made pursuant to Article I Section 2 of this Constitution next following the ratification of this article.

A Proposed Amendment to Limit the
Time of Service of Member of Congress

Section 1: Article I of the Constitution shall be amended to add the following Section:

> "Section 11. No member of the Congress shall serve cumulatively for more than six thousand calendar days, except that at the end of said period they may continue to serve until the next election for the House of Representatives. The remainder of any senatorial term shall be filled in the manner prescribed by State law."

Section 2: This article shall take effect upon the next election for the House of Representatives following this article's enactment, except that any Senator serving at the time of enactment may complete their then current full term.

Section 3: The textual amendment provided by this article shall be incorporated in all official publications of this Constitution. Congress is authorized determine whether Section 2 and this Section 3 shall also be included in such official publications.

NOTES

NOTES to Chapter 1

1. Richard Beeman. Plain, Honest Men: The Making of the American Constitution. New York: Random House, 2009, p. 412, from The Records of the Federal Convention of 1787, edited by Max Farrand, New Haven, CT: Yale University Press, 1937, 1966, volume 3, p. 85.

2. Beeman, Plain Honest Men, pp. 360-361.

3. The Federalist, edited by Robert Scigliano. New York: The Modern Library, 2000, quotation from Federalist No. 62, p. 400.

4. Catherine Drinker Bowen. Miracle at Philadelphia: The Story of the Constitutional Convention May to September 1787. Boston: Little, Brown & Company, 1966, pp. 8-10.

5. Randy E. Barnett, "The Original Meaning of the Commerce Clause," *The University of Chicago Law Review*, volume 68, No. 1 (Winter 2001), pp. 101-147.

6. This scenario tracks the facts of Wickard v. Filburn, 317 U.S. 111 (1942), the Supreme Court case which established the right of the national government to regulate local farming activities such as these. Although current US Department of Agriculture regulations are not quite so intrusive, they nonetheless have immensely burdened many organic farmers. See, for example, the experience of Josh Slotnick and his wife, Kim Murchison, who were faced with thousand dollars in fees and numerous forms and inspections to be certified organic by the USDA, even though those regulations ignore many of the tenets of organic farming. Ari Levaux, "Homegrown Standards: An attractive alternative to national organic certification," *Orion*, January/February 2007, at http://www.orionmagazine.org/index.php/articles/ article/100/ (retrieved March 26, 2010).

7.   The government agents are supposed to have some reasonable suspicion that the person being tapped is a foreign agent or terrorist, but that is solely up to them to determine. They are required to notify a special court within a week of the surveillance.

8.   This scenario is based on the actual case of New York City school teacher Mildred Rosario. Macarena Hernandez. "Furor Over School Prayer Stuns a Fired Teacher," *New York Times*, June 30, 1998, p. B3.

9.   Michael W. McConnell, "Establishment and Disestablishment at the Founding, Part I: Establishment of Religion," *William and Mary Law Review*, volume 44 (April 2003), pp. 2105-2208.

10.   Saul Cornell. A Well-Regulated Militia: The Founding Fathers and the Origins of Gun Control in America. New York: Oxford University Press, 2006, pp 9-65.

11.   554 U.S. 290 (2008).

12.   http://www.supremecourt.gov/opinions/09pdf/08-1521.pdf (retrieved September 3, 2010).

13.   Richard Brust, "The 'Super Median': On an ideological court, it's all about keeping Justice Kennedy," *ABA Journal*, July 2010, pp. 20-21, 43.

14.   Federalist No. 43, Modern Library edition, p. 282.

15.   5 U.S.137 (1803).

16.   5 U.S. 137, 177.

17.   The Writings of Thomas Jefferson: being his Autobiography, Correspondence, Reports, Messages, Addresses, and Other Writings, Official and Private, edited by H. A. Washington. Washington, DC: Taylor & Maury, 1854, volume 5, p. 85 (letter to George Hay, June 2, 1807).

18.   The Writings of Thomas Jefferson, edited by Paul Leicester Ford. New York: G. P. Putnam's Sons, 1899, volume 10, pp. 140, 141 (letter to Judge Spencer Roane, September 6, 1819).

19.   The Writings of Thomas Jefferson, 1854 edition, volume 7, p. 404 (letter to Edward Livingston, March 25, 1825).

20.   See http://en.wikipedia.org/wiki/Revenue_Act_of_1913 (retrieved March 26, 2010).

21.   The Writings of Thomas Jefferson, 1854 edition, volume 4, p. 506 (letter to Wilson C. Nicholas, September 7, 1803).

22.   Office of Management and Budget. Budget of the U. S. Government, Fiscal Year 2010, Historical Tables, Table 1.2, at http://www.whitehouse.gov/omb/budget/fy2010/ assets/hist.pdf (retrieved March 26, 2010).

23.   Louis D. Johnston and Samuel H. Williamson, "What Was the U.S. GDP Then?" MeasuringWorth, 2008, at http://www. measuringworth.org/ usgdp/ (retrieved March 27, 2010).

24.   Office of Management and Budget, Budget Fiscal 2010, Historical Tables, Table 1.2.

25.   Bureau of the Census. Historical Statistics of the United States: Colonial Times to 1970, Part 2. Washington, DC: Government Printing Office, 1975, p. 1102 (1913 figure); Office of Management and Budget, Budget Fiscal 2010, Historical Tables, Table 17.1 (2009 figure).

26.   Paul C. Light. The True Size of Government. Washington, D.C.: Brookings Institution Press, 1999.

27.   US Government Bookstore at http://bookstore.gpo.gov/ index.jsp (retrieved March 27, 2010).

28.   Office of the Federal Register at http://www.llsdc.org/ attachments/wysiwyg/544/fed-reg- pages.pdf (retrieved March

27, 2010).

NOTES to Chapter 2

1.   Thomas Jefferson. First Inaugural Address, in The Papers of Thomas Jefferson, edited by Barbara B. Oberg, et. al., Princeton NJ: Princeton University Press, 2006, volume 33, pp. 148-152, quotations at pp. 149-150.

2.   There are numerous biographies of both men. A dual biography comparing the two is John S. Pancake's "Thomas Jefferson and Alexander Hamilton," Woodbury, NY: Barron's Educational Series, Inc., 1974. Noble E. Cunningham's "Jefferson vs. Hamilton: Confrontations That Shaped a Nation, Boston: Bedford/St. Martin's, 2000, summarizes their conflict with original documents.

3.   Richard Beeman. Plain, Honest Men: The Making of the American Constitution. New York: Random House, 2009, pp. 164-170, 202-203.

4.   The Federalist, edited by Robert Scigliano, New York: The Modern Library, 2000. Quotations from Federalist No. 9, pp. 48, 49, 52 (capitalization in original).

5.   Federalist No. 11, Modern Library edition, pp. 62, 65.

6.   Federalist No. 12, Modern Library edition, pp. 69, 70.

7.   Alexander Hamilton, "Report on the Subject of Manufactures," reprinted in The Papers of Alexander Hamilton, edited by Harold C. Syrett, et al. New York and London: Columbia University Press, 1961-79, volume 10, pp. 230-340, quotations at pp. 255-256.

8.   Hamilton, Report on the Subject of Manufactures, in Papers, volume 10, pp. 277-283.

9.   Thomas Jefferson, "Memoranda of Conversations with the

President,"in The Papers of Thomas Jefferson, edited by Charles T. Cullen, et. al., Princeton, NJ: Princeton University Press, 1990, volume 23, pp. 184-187 (March 1, 1790), quotation at p. 187.

10. The Writings of Thomas Jefferson: being his Autobiography, Correspondence, Reports, Messages, Addresses, and Other Writings, Official and Private, edited by H. A. Washington. Washington, DC: Taylor & Maury, 1854, volume 7, p 216 (letter to C. Hammond, August 18, 1821).

11. The Writings of Thomas Jefferson, being his Autobiography, Correspondence, Reports, Messages, Addresses, and Other Writings, Official and Private, edited by H. A. Washington. New York: John C. Riker, Washington, DC: Taylor & Maury, 1853, volume 1, p. 82 (from the Autobiography, 1821).

12. The Writings of Thomas Jefferson, 1854 edition, volume 7, p. 256 (letter to William. T. Barry, July 2, 1822).

13. Frederick A. Cleveland and Fred W. Powell, "Railroad Finance," reprinted in Alfred D. Chandler, Jr. (editor and compiler), The Railroads: The Nation's First Big Business. New York: Harcourt, Brace & World, Inc., 1965, pp. 48-50, 52-53, and Chandler, The Railroads, pp. 185-187.

14. Richard B. Du Boff. Accumulation & Power: An Economic History of the United States. Armonk, NY: M. E. Sharpe, Inc., 1989, pp. 45-46, 55-56.

15. Grover Cleveland, "Veto Message – Distribution of Seeds," *Congressional Record, Forty-ninth Congress Second Session,* February 17, 1887, Washington, DC: Government Printing Office, 1887, volume XVIII, p. 1875.

16. Michael Kazin. A Godly Hero: the Life of William Jennings Bryan. New York: Alfred A. Knopf, 2006 is an excellent biography.

17. See Kazin, A Godly Hero, pp. 153, 182-183, 217, 235, 238, 248-

249, 259 on Wilson's personal opinion of Bryan. Even Wilson hagiographer John Milton Cooper could not cover up Wilson's privately expressed disdain for Bryan. See John Milton Cooper, Jr., Woodrow Wilson: A Biography, New York: Alfred A. Knopf, 2009, pp. 73, 87, 279, 293.

18. Gabriel Kolko. The Triumph of Conservatism: A Reinterpretation of American History, 1900-1916. New York: The Free Press, 1963, pp. 247-253; Martin J. Sklar, "Woodrow Wilson and the Political Economy of Modern United States Liberalism" in A New Leviathan: Essays on the Rise of the American Corporate State, edited by Ronald Radosh and Murray N. Rothbard, New York: E. P. Dutton & Co. Inc., 1972, pp. 51-57; Kazin, A Godly Hero, p. 226.

19. James Weinstein. The Corporate Ideal in the Liberal State, 1900-1918. Boston, MA: Beacon Press, 1968, pp. 86-91; Kolko, The Triumph of Conservatism, pp. 267-278.

20. Sklar, Wilson and Modern Liberalism, pp. 17-24.

21. Sklar, Wilson and Modern Liberalism, pp. 25-51, 59-64; William Appleman Williams. Americans in a Changing World: A History of the United States in the Twentieth Century. New York: Harper& Row, 1978, pp. 126-133.

22. This phenomenon is so common that Nobel Prize winning economist George Stigler has formulated it as an economic theory called "regulatory capture." George J. Stigler. "The Theory of Economic Regulation," originally published in the *Bell Journal of Economics and Management Science*, (Spring 1971) and reprinted in George J. Stigler, The Citizen and the State: Essays on Regulation, Chicago: The University of Chicago Press, 1975, pp. 114-141 with a supplementary note, "The Process of Economic Regulation," in the same volume (pp.145-166) where he shows how even well-meaning professional regulators will find it easier to cooperate with the regulated businesses to assure non-controversial acceptance of their regulations and support for their budgetary requests to the legislature. See also Kenneth Prewitt

and Alan Stone, The Ruling Elites: Elite Theory, Power, and American Democracy, New York: Harper & Row, 1973, pp. 35-44 for a summary of this phenomenon up to the New Deal era.

23.   Quoted in Thomas Frank, "Obama and 'Regulatory Capture?': It's time to take the quality of our watchdogs," *Wall Street Journal,* June 24, 2009; p. A13. See Chandler, The Railroads, pp. 185-187 and quotes from the Interstate Commerce Commission at pp. 204-208 to show how, in Chandler's words, "the commissioners came to their problems with the same assumptions as railroad managers and analysts" and thus "soon analyzed the problems of costing, pricing, and competition in much the same way as" the railroads, including favoring "legalized pooling to unrestricted competition"(p. 187).

24.   Wilson praised Hamilton's view of government as wiser than that of the other founders and more like his own view of government as an evolving Darwinian organism. Woodrow Wilson. Constitutional Government in the United States (1908), reprinted in The Papers of Woodrow Wilson, edited by Arthur S. Link, Princeton, NJ: Princeton University Press, 1974, volume 18, pp. 200-201. Also see Cooper, Woodrow Wilson, pp. 143-144, 335.

25.   Woodrow Wilson. The Study of Administration, *Political Science Quarterly II* (July 1887) pp. 197-222, reprinted in The Papers of Woodrow Wilson, volume 5, pp. 359-380, quotation at p. 369.

26.   Wilson, Administration, p. 370.

27.   Wilson, Administration, p. 373.

28.   Wilson, Administration, p. 374.

29.   Wilson, Administration, p. 376.

30.   Frank Fischer. Technology and the Politics of Expertise. New York: Sage, 1990, p. 16.

31.   Ronald J. Pestritto. Woodrow Wilson and the Roots of Modern

Liberalism. Lanham, MD: Rowman & Littlefield Publishers, Inc., 2005, pp. 221-262.

32.   Gary Gerstle, "Race and Nation in the Thought and Politics of Woodrow Wilson," in Reconsidering Woodrow Wilson: Progressivism, Internationalism, War and Peace, edited by John Milton Cooper, Jr., Baltimore: The Johns Hopkins University Press, 2008, pp. 93-123; Williams, Americans in a Changing World, pp. 108-113; Kazin, A Godly Hero, p. 227.

33.   Kazin, A Godly Hero, pp. 232-238.

34.   Williams, Americans in a Changing World, pp. 134-145, quotation at pp. 142-143.

35.   Geoffrey R. Stone, "Mr. Wilson's First Amendment," in Cooper (ed.), Reconsidering Woodrow Wilson, pp. 189-224; Williams, Americans in a Changing World, pp. 145-148.

36.   Kazin, A Godly Hero, p. 254.

37.   A good recent survey is Mike Hawkins. Social Darwinism in European and American Thought 1860 - 1945. Cambridge, UK: Cambridge University Press, 1997.

38.   Robert C. Bannister. Social Darwinism: Science and Myth in Anglo-American Social Thought. Philadelphia: Temple University Press, 1979, pp. 201, 243-245; Kazin, A Godly Hero, pp. 273-275.

39.   Edwin Black. War Against the Weak: Eugenics and America's Campaign to Create a Master Race. New York: Four Walls, Eight Windows, 2003, pp. 68-69, 322. Years later the doctor Wilson asked to draft the bill, Edwin Katzen-Ellenbogen, was on the staff of the Nazi concentration camp at Buchenwald performing horrific medical experiments on its inmates. Black, War Against the Weak, pp. 329-335.

40.   Kazin, A Godly Hero, pp. 244-245, 249; Cooper, Woodrow Wilson, p. 201.

41.   Edward J. Larson. Summer for the Gods: The Scopes Trial and America's Continuing Debate Over Science and Religion. New York: Basic Books, 1997, pp. 72-72, 103-104, 165.

42.   Kazin, A Godly Hero, pp. 298-299. An example of this attitude can be found in the popular writer Irving Stone's 1941 biography of Darrow, where he describes Bryan as acting with "abysmal ignorance" as Secretary of State making "of his office an object of ridicule throughout the world"and who in debating "entangled himself and his listeners in a mass of illogical and irrelevant material." Irving Stone. Clarence Darrow for the Defense. Garden City, NY: Doubleday, Doran & Company, 1941, pp. 450-451.

43.   See Jeff Taylor, Where Did the Party Go? William Jennings Bryan, Hubert Humphrey and the Jeffersonian Legacy, Columbia, MO: University of Missouri Press, 2006.

44.   These include Federal Reserve chairman and Great Depression scholar Ben Bernanke. Ben S. Bernanke and Ilian Mihov, "Deflation and Monetary Contraction in the Great Depression: An Analysis of Simple Ratios," in Essays on the Great Depression, edited by Ben S. Bernanke. Princeton, NJ: Princeton University Press, 2000, pp. 108-160.

45.   Burt Solomon. FDR v. The Constitution: The Court-Packing Fight and the Triumph of Democracy. New York: Walker & Company, 2009, p. 222.

46.   One historian concludes that "Hamilton, with his deficit spending and his daring spirit of experiment, would doubtless have found a warm reception among the 'Brain Trusters' of the New Deal. The result of Hamilton's program was a concentration of power in the central government and the attraction of the 'rich and well-born' to his standard." John S. Pancake. Thomas Jefferson & Alexander Hamilton. Woodbury, NY: Barron's Educational Series, Inc., 1974, pp. 404-405.

47.   Paul K. Conkin. The New Deal. New York: Thomas Y. Crowell

Company, 1969, p. 36.

48.   Ellis W. Hawley. The New Deal and the Problem of Monopoly.
        Princeton, NJ: Princeton University Press, 1966, p. 479. On the
        NRA and its integration with the big companies see Hawley, New
        Deal and Monopoly, pp. 19-146 and Gene Smiley. Rethinking the
        Great Depression. Chicago: Ivan R. Dee, 2002, pp. 93-103.

49.   G. William Domhoff. State Autonomy or Class Dominance?:
        Case Studies on Policy Making in America. New York: Aline de
        Gruyter, 1996, pp. 51-100.

50.   Conkin, New Deal, pp. 100-101; Barton J. Bernstein, "The New
        Deal: The Conservative Achievements of Liberal Reform," in
        Towards a New Past: Dissenting Essays in American History,
        edited by Barton J. Bernstein, New York: Random House, 1968,
        pp. 269-270, 280.

51.   Bernstein, Conservative Achievements of Liberal Reform, p. 268.

52.   295 U.S. 495 (1935).

53.   Williams, Americans in a Changing World, p. 259.

54.   David M. Kennedy. Freedom From Fear: The American People
        in Depression and War, 1929-1945. New York: Oxford
        University Press, 1999, pp. 275-286.

55.   Kennedy, Freedom From Fear, pp. 278, 284; Conkin, New Deal,
        pp. 70-75.

56.   Thomas Ferguson, "Industrial Conflict and the Coming of the
        New Deal: The Triumph of Multinational Liberalism in
        America,"in Rise and Fall of the New Deal Order, 1930-1980,
        edited by Steve Fraser and Gary Gerstle. Princeton, NJ:
        Princeton University Press, 1989, pp. 20-21.

57.   Butler Shaffer. In Restraint of Trade: The Business Campaign
        Against Competition 1918-1938. Lewisburg, PA: Bucknell

273

University Press and Cranbury, NJ: Associated University Presses, 1997, pp. 118-122, 166-170, 179-181; Hawley, New Deal and Monopoly, pp. 273-274.

58. Hawley, New Deal and Monopoly, pp. 132, 190-246, 483-484.

59. Hawley, New Deal and Monopoly, p. 270.

60. Domhoff, State Autonomy or Class Dominance, pp. 117-176.

61. Ronald Radosh. "The Myth of the New Deal" in A New Leviathan: Essays on the Rise of the American Corporate State, edited by Ronald Radosh and Murray N. Rothbard, New York: E. P. Dutton & Co. Inc., 1972, pp. 154-159.

62. Radosh, The Myth of the New Deal, pp. 173-185.

63. Bernstein, Conservative Achievements of Liberal Reform, pp. 273-274.

64. Conkin, The New Deal, pp. 74-79; Prewitt and Stone, The Ruling Elites, pp. 44-50.

65. Kennedy, Freedom From Fear, p. 376; Conkin, The New Deal, pp. 70-72.

66. Ferguson, Industrial Conflict, pp. 19-23; Thomas Ferguson and Joel Rogers. Right Turn: The Decline of the Democrats and the Future of American Politics. New York: Hill and Wang, 1986, pp. 46-49.

67. Philip La Follette. Adventure in Politics, edited by Donald Young. New York: Holt, Rinehart and Winston, 1970, p. 247.

68. 163 U.S. 537 (1896). The *Plessy* decision allowed racially segregated facilities if they were "equal," a condition almost always honored in the breach.

69. Howard Jay Graham, "An Innocent Abroad: The Constitutional

Corporate 'Person'," UCLA Law Review, volume 2, no. 1, pp. 155-211.

70.   Citizens United vs. Federal Election Commission, 558 U.S. 50 (2010), overturning limits on corporate political spending independent of specific candidates.

71.   Smiley, Rethinking the Great Depression, pp.111-132.

72.   Hawley, New Deal and Monopoly, pp. 439-455, 464-465; Bernstein, Conservative Achievements of Liberal Reform, pp. 275-276; Alan Brinkley, "The New Deal and the Idea of the State," in Rise and Fall of the New Deal Order, 1930-1980, edited by Steve Fraser and Gary Gerstle. Princeton, NJ: Princeton University Press, 1989, pp. 90-92.

73.   John P. Diggins, "Flirtation with Fascism," *American Historical Review*, volume 71, no. 2 (January 1966), pp. 487-506, describes the attraction of many American liberals to the Mussolini regime.

74.   Rexford G. Tugwell and Howard C. Hill. Our Economic Society and Its Problems: A Study of American Levels of Living and How to Improve Them. New York: Harcourt, Brace and Company, 1934, pp. 542, 541. See Arthur A. Ekrich, Jr., The Decline of American Liberalism, New York: Atheneum, 1967, pp. 268-282, on the triumph of the New Deal's collectivist planning impulses over concern for individual liberties.

75.   Quoted in Solomon, FDR v. The Constitution, p. 140.

76.   Peter Temin. Lessons from the Great Depression. Cambridge, MA: The MIT Press, 1989, pp. 89-137.

77.   Norman and Jeanne Mackenzie. The Fabians. New York: Simon & Schuster, 1977.

78.   Donald R. Brand, "Competition and the New Deal Regulatory State," in The New Deal and the Triumph of Liberalism, edited by Sidney M. Milkis and Jerome M. Mileus, Amherst and Boston,

MA: University of Massachusetts Press, 2002, pp. 166-192, particularly pp. 187-188; Hawley, New Deal and Monopoly, pp. 466, 480-481; Brinkley, The New Deal and the Idea of the State, p. 90.

79.   Robert M. Collins, "Positive Business Responses to the New Deal: The Roots of the Committee for Economic Development," *The Business History Review*, volume 52, no. 3 (Autumn 1978), pp. 371-380.

80.   Conkin, The New Deal, p. 79.

81.   Bernstein, Conservative Achievements of Liberal Reform, p. 270. See also pp. 264, 278, 281.

82.   Williams, Americans in a Changing World, p. 249. See also pp.280-281, 291-292.

83.   Harold L. Cole and Lee E. Ohanian, "New Deal Policies and the Persistence of the Great Depression: A General Equilibrium Analysis," *Journal of Political Economy*, volume 112, no. 4 (August 2004), pp. 779-816.

84.   Quoted from Morgenthau's diary in John Morton Blum, Roosevelt and Morgenthau: A Revision and Condensation of *From the Morgenthau Diaries*, Boston: Houghton Mifflin, 1970, p. 256.

85.   Smiley, Rethinking the Great Depression, pp.132-147.

86.   Kim McQuaid, "Corporate Liberalism in the American Business Community 1920-1940, *The Business History Review*, volume 52, no. 3 (Autumn 1978), pp. 364-368.

87.   Collins, Positive Business Responses, pp. 386-391. The failure of the Roosevelt and Truman administrations to achieve any real progressive change and the growing power of big business in government are discussed in Barton J. Bernstein, "America in War and Peace: The Test of Liberalism," in Bernstein (editor),

Towards a New Past, pp. 289-321.

88.   See Williams, Americans in a Changing World, pp. 415-431 for a discussion of how John F. Kennedy neatly fit into the centralized, corporate-dominated, elitist system inherited from Franklin Roosevelt, and Ferguson and Rogers, Right Turn, pp. 51-52, 55-57, 63, 67-68, 85, 108-111, 138-139, 145-151, 155-157, 160, 181-186 for further detail regarding corporate support and control of the Democratic Party through the 1984 election.

89.   G. William Domhoff. Fat Cats and Democrats: The role of the big rich in the party of the common man. Englewood Cliffs, NJ: Prentice-Hall, 1972.

90.   Domhoff, Fat Cats and Democrats, quotes at pp. 145, 157, 175, 176. This continues to accurately describe the Democratic Party according to David Korten in his "When Corporations Rule the World," San Francisco: Berrett-Koehler Publishers, Inc., 2001, pp. 148-149 and Ralph Nader in "Crashing the Party: Taking on the Corporate Government in an Age of Surrender," New York: St. Martin's Press, 2002, pp. 22-24, 27-37.

91.   Bruce Bartlett. Imposter: How George W. Bush Bankrupted America and Betrayed the Reagan Legacy. New York: Doubleday, 2006.

92.   For an academic description of the process see G. William Domhoff's "The Powers That Be: Processes of Ruling-Class Domination in America," New York: Random House, 1978. Timothy P. Carney's "The Big Ripoff: How Big Business and Big Government Steal Your Money, Hoboken, NJ: John Wiley & Sons, Inc., 2006, gives a more recent book-length description, with specific examples, of how the system works.

93.   Dan Eggen. "Investments Can Yield More on K Street, Study Indicates: One Tax Break Brought Companies 22,000% Rate of Return on Lobbying Costs," *Washington Post*, April 12, 2009, p. A8.

94.   Ralph Nader. The Good Fight: Declare Your Independence & Close the Democracy Gap. New York: HarperCollins, 2004, pp. 192-193, quotation at p. 193.

95.   Jane Hamsher. Fact Sheet: The Truth About the Health Care Bill, March 19, 2010, at http://static1.firedoglake.com/ 1/files/2010/03/ mythfactshcr-2.pdf (retrieved April 2, 2010).

96.   Katharine Q. Seelye. "Senators Add the Ornaments and Trimmings," *New York Times*, December 20, 2009, p. A36.

97.   Dave Lindorff. Worse Than Nothing: Krugman's Health Care Sell-Out, December 29, 2009; http://www.counterpunch.org/ lindorff12292009. html (retrieved April 2, 2010).

98.   Dave Lindorff. Obama's Fog Machine: SOTU Whoppers, January 29 - 31, 2010; http://www.counterpunch.org/lindorff 01292010. html (retrieved April 2, 2010).

99.   Hamsher, Fact Sheet: The Truth About the Health Care Bill.

100.   Timothy P. Carney. "Obama gives sugar plums to the special interests," *Washington Examiner*, March 24, 2010; Editors, "ObamaCare's Secret History," *Wall Street Journal*, June 12, 2012, p. A12.

101.   Seelye, Senators Add the Ornaments and Trimmings.

102.   Howard Fineman. "'Socialism,' Chicago Style: Why the health industry quietly loves Obamacare." *Newsweek*, April 5, 2010, p. 23.

103.   Dave Lindorff. Obamacare and health industry: Death to Obamacare! March 10, 2010; http://www.counterpunch.org/ lindorff 03102010.html (retrieved April 2, 2010).

104.   Fineman, Socialism Chicago Style. Also see David Sirota's withering analysis "What's the Matter with Democrats?," *In These Times*, March 19, 2010 at hhtp://inthesetimes.com /main/article/5710/ (retrieved April 2, 2010).

105. The Center for Public Integrity. "New Center Story Names Top 12 Health Reform Lobby Firms: Record Amount Spent Lobbying on a Single Issue, Experts Say," March 26, 2010; http://www. publicintegrity.org /news/entry/2015/ (retrieved April 2, 2010).

106. Calculated from public election filings collected by the Center for Responsive Politics; opensecrets.org - Politicians and Elections - Presidential - Industries for each candidate (retrieved April 13, 2010).

107. From public election filings collected by the Center for Responsive Politics; opensecrets.org - Politicians and Elections - Presidential - Selected Industry Totals (retrieved April 17, 2010).

108. From public election filings collected by the Center for Responsive Politics; opensecrets.org - Politicians and Elections - Presidential - Donors for each candidate (retrieved April 17, 2010).

109. From public election filings collected by the Center for Responsive Politics; opensecrets.org - Influence and Lobbying - Money to Congress - Industries - (retrieved April 17, 2010).

110. From public election filings collected by the Center for Responsive Politics; opensecrets.org - Elections - Contributions by Sector (retrieved April 26, 2010).

111. Pam Martens. "The Guys Who Got It Wrong: Obama's Economic Brain Trust," April 2 - 4, 2010; http://www. counterpunch.org/ martens04022010.html (retrieved April 17, 2010).

112. Joshua Green. "Inside Man." *Atlantic*, April 2010, pp. 36-51. The FDIC reports that 318 banks failed during 2008, 2009, and 2010, http://www.fdic.gov/bank/individual/failed/ banklist.html (retrieved January 3, 2011).

113. Randall Smith and Robin Sidel. "Banks Keep Failing, No End in

279

Sight: Since WaMu Fell, 279 Lenders Have Collapsed; Lost Jobs, Curtailed Lending and the Big Get Bigger," *Wall Street Journal*, September 27, 2010, p. C6.

114.   Charles Gasparino. Bought and Paid For: The Unholy Alliance Between Barack Obama and Wall Street. New York: Sentinel/Penguin Group, 2010, gives a detailed book length account of the deep connections between Wall Street and Barack Obama and his administration.

115.   Calculated from public election filings collected by the Center for Responsive Politics; opensecrets.org - Politicians and Elections - Presidential - Top Industries and Top Donors for each candidate (retrieved April 13, 2010).

116.   Kenneth P. Vogel and Mike Allen. "Obama finds room for lobbyists," January 30, 2009; http://www.politico.com/news/stories/0109/18128.html (retrieved April 13, 2010); and Timothy P. Carney. "Obama, who excluded lobbyists, has appointed 50," *Washington Examiner*, March 31, 2010. See generally http://www.opensecrets.org/revolving/.

117.   Calculated from public election filings collected by the Center for Responsive Politics; opensecrets.org - Politicians and Elections - Presidential - Donor Demographics for each candidate (retrieved April 13, 2010).

118.   Chris Hedges. "Ralph Nader Was Right About Barack Obama," March 1, 2010; http://truthdig.com/report.item/ralph_nader_was_right_about_barack_obama_20100301/ (retrieved March 29, 2010).

119.   Andrew J. Bacevich. Washington Rules: America's Path to Permanent War. New York: Henry Holt and Company LLC, 2010, pp. 248, 210, 228.

120.   Roger D. Hodge. The Mendacity of Hope: Barack Obama and the Betrayal of American Liberalism. New York: HarperCollins, 2010, quotations at pp. 20, 233-235. See also pp. 23-28, 39-53

(Obama's long-standing obeisance to his money sources), 90-98 (despite his token anti-bank rhetoric Obama's financial regulation reform is nugatory due his, his advisors', Dodd's and Frank's long-time dependence on Wall Street money), 132-144 (Obama's health care reform simply locks in the power of the existing "health-industrial complex"), 167-169 (as a reactionary, business dominated politician with a messianic ego, Obama is most comparable to Woodrow Wilson), and 182-199 (with token exceptions, Obama has continued all of the Bush military policies, civil liberties abuses, and claims to expansive executive power). Another book-length progressive criticism is Tariq Ali. The Obama Syndrome: Surrender at Home, War Abroad. Brooklyn, NY: Verso Books, 2010.

121.   John W. Whitehead. "America Under Barack Obama: An Interview with Nat Hentoff," December 11, 2009; at http://www.rutherford.org/oldspeak/articles/interviews /oldspeak-Hentoff_ 2009.html (retrieved March 24, 2010).

122.   Ferguson, Industrial Conflict and the Coming of the New Deal, p. 24.

NOTES to Chapter 3

1.   E. F. Schumacher. Small Is Beautiful: Economics as if People Mattered. New York: Harper & Row, 1973, p. 230.

2.   The Writings of Thomas Jefferson: being his Autobiography, correspondence, Reports, Messages, Addresses, and Other Writings, Official and Private, edited by H. A. Washington. New York: Derby & Jackson, 1859, volume 6, p. 543 (letter to Joseph C. Cabell, Esq., February 2, 1816).

3.   Schumacher, Small Is Beautiful, p. 59.

4.   Schumacher, Small Is Beautiful, pp. 59-60, quotation on p. 59.

5.   Schumacher, Small Is Beautiful, p. 61.

6.   Schumacher, Small Is Beautiful, p. 62.

7.   Schumacher. Small Is Beautiful, p. 70.

8.   Schumacher, Small Is Beautiful, pp. 149-151, quotations at p. 149.

9.   Schumacher, Small Is Beautiful, p. 229.

10.   E. F. Schumacher. This I Believe and Other Essays. Totnes, UK: Green Books, Ltd., 1997, p. 31.

11.   Leopold Kohr. The Overdeveloped Nations: the Diseconomies of Scale. Swansea, UK: Christopher Davies (Publisher) Ltd., 1976.

12.   Kohr, The Overdeveloped Nations, pp. 1-46, quotations at p. 24.

13.   Kohr, The Overdeveloped Nations, pp. 34-35 (italics in original).

14.   Kohr, The Overdeveloped Nations, p. 93.

15.   Kohr, The Overdeveloped Nations, p. 22, note 1.

16.   Louis D. Johnston and Samuel H. Williamson, "What Was the U.S. GDP Then?" MeasuringWorth, 2008, at http://www.measuringworth.org /usgdp/ (retrieved March 27, 2010) (1913 figure); Office of Management and Budget, Budget Fiscal 2010, Historical Tables, Table 1.2 (2009 figure) at http://www.whitehouse.gov/omb/budget/fy2010/assets/hist.pdf (retrieved March 26, 2010).

17.   US Government Bookstore at http://bookstore.gpo.gov /index.jsp (retrieved March 27, 2010); Office of the Federal Register (retrieved March 27, 2010) at http://www.llscdc.org/ attachments/wysiwyg/ 544 /fed-reg-pages.pdf .

18.   Kohr, The Overdeveloped Nations, p.93.

19.   Woodrow Wilson. Address in Scranton, reprinted in The Papers of Woodrow Wilson, edited by Arthur S. Link, Princeton, NJ: Princeton University Press, 1974, volume 25, p. 222.

20.   Wilson, Address in Scranton, pp. 223-224.

21.   Richard B. Du Boff. Accumulation & Power: An Economic History of the United States. Armonk, NY: M. E. Sharpe, Inc., 1989, p. 43.

22.   Du Boff, Accumulation & Power, pp. 57-61.

23.   United States Small Business Administration Office of Advocacy. The 2009 Small Business Economy: A Report to the President. Washington, DC: U. S. Government Printing Office, 2009, p. 2.

24.   Small Business Administration, 2009 Report, p. 111.

25.   Small Business Administration, 2009 Report, pp. 9-10, 44, 104.

26.   Small Business Administration, 2009 Report, p. 11.

27.   Small Business Administration, 2009 Report, p. 45.

28.   Small Business Administration, 2009 Report, pp. 46-47.

29.   Fortune 500 statistics from Jim Collins, "The Secret of Enduring Greatness," Fortune, May 5, 2008, p. 72; DJIA statistics derived from tables at http://en.wikipeida.org/wiki /Historical_components_of _the_ Dow_Jones _Industrial_ Average (retrieved February 19, 2010).

30.   W. Mark Crain. The Impact of Regulatory Costs on Small Firms. United States Small Business Administration Office of Advocacy, September 2005, at http://www.sba.gov/advo/ research /rs264tot.pdf (retrieved April 23, 2010).

31.   Crain, The Impact of Regulatory Costs, p. v.

32.   Timothy P. Carney. Obamanomics: How Barack Obama Is Bankrupting You and Enriching His Wall Street Friends, Corporate Lobbyists, and Union Bosses. Washington, DC: Regnery Publishing, Inc., 2009, pp. 112-113.

33.   Carney, Obamanomics, pp. 180-185.

34.   Carney, Obamanomics, pp. 185-192; Timothy P. Carney, "The Big Ripoff: How Big Business and Big Government Steal Your Money, Hoboken, NJ: John Wiley & Sons, Inc., 2006, pp. 120-125.

35.   For a general overview see http://www.sustainabletable.org /issues/ organic/. For corporate influence on the process see "Organic Watchdog's Lawsuit Forces Release of Suppressed USDA Documents, Secrecy of National Organic Program Successfully Challenged," Natural Newswire, March 2, 2007, at http://www.naturalnewswire.com/2007/03/organic_watchdo.\ html, Kimberly Kindy and Lyndsey Layton, "Purity of Federal 'Organic' Label Is Questioned," *Washington Post*, July 3, 2009, pp. A1, A6, and Stephanie Strom, "Has 'Organic' Been Oversized?," *New York Times*, July 8, 2012, p. BU1. The sourcing of "organic" food from China and the dodging inspection process there are discussed in Alexandra Gross and Eliza Murphy, "Seal of Disapproval Concerns Arise Over China-Sourced Food Labeled USDA Organic," *E / The Environmental Magazine*, January/February 2010, at http://www.emagazine.com/ view/?4987. The USDA's National List of Allowed and Prohibited Substances showing the artificial chemicals allowed in connection with food labeled "organic" are at http://www.ams.usda.gov/AMSv1.0/getfile?dDocName= STELPRDC5068682&acct;=nopgeninfo (all websites retrieved April 26, 2010).

36.   Linda Baker, "The not-so-sweet success of organic farming: Pesticide-free, non-genetically modified food is a big, global business now but, ironically, small farmers are getting the shaft," *Salon*, July 29, 2002, at http://www.salon.com /technology/feature/2002/ 07/29/organic (retrieved April 26,

2010).

37.   Charles Gasparino. Bought and Paid For: The Unholy Alliance Between Barack Obama and Wall Street. New York: Sentinel/Penguin Group, 2010, pp. 157-243.

38.   Gretchen Morgenson, "Do You Have Any Reforms in Size XL?," *New York Times*, April 23, 2010, p. BU1.

39.   Binyamin Appelbaum, "On Finance Bill, Lobbying Shifts to Regulations," *New York Times*, June 27, 2010, p. A1.

40.   Sarah Wallace, "The End of Community Banking: creditworthy borrowers will be denied loans as small banks devote more and more energy to regulatory compliance," *Wall Street Journal*, June 29, 2010, p. A19; David Weidner, "Too Small to Fail: Banks Can Drive an Economic Recovery. No, Not Those Banks," *Wall Street Journal*, October 7, 2010, at http://online.wsj.com/article/ SB10001424052748703735804575536094104047302.html (retrieved October 18, 2010).

41.   Christine Hauser, "Banks Likely to Offset Impact of New Law, Analysts Say," *New York Times*, June 25, 2010 at http:// www.nytimes.com/2010/06/26/business/ 26reax.html?pagewanted =1&ref;=politics (retrieved July 7, 2010).

42.   Gasparino, Bought and Paid For, pp. 237-239.

43.   Eric Lichtblau, "Lawmakers Regulate Banks, Then Flock to Them," *New York Times*, April 14, 2010, p. B1; Eric Lichtblau, "Ex-Regulators Get Set to Lobby on New Financial Rules," *New York Times*, July 28, 2010, p. B1.

44.   Steven Gorelick. Small Is Beautiful, Big Is Subsidized: how our taxes contribute to social and environmental breakdown. Berkeley, CA: ISEC, 1998.

45.   Gorelick, Small Is Beautiful, Big Is Subsidized, pp. 47-48.

285

46.   Joel Salatin. Everything I Want To Do Is Illegal. White River Junction, VT: Chelsea Green, 2007, quotation at p. 23.

47.   Ralph Nader. The Good Fight: Declare Your Independence & Close the Democracy Gap. New York: HarperCollins, 2004, pp. 30-31, 72-73. Other examples are at pp. 83-89.

48.   http://www.ncsl.org/documents/standcomm/scbudg/Catalog/une2009.pdf (retrieved April 26, 2010).

49.   http://www.ncsl.org/default.aspx?tabid=15850 (retrieved April 26, 2010).

50.   http://www.ncsl.org/Default.aspx?TabID=773&tabs;=854,14,825#854 (retrieved April 26, 2010).

51.   Kohr, The Overdeveloped Nations, p. 35, note1.

52.   US Census Bureau Historical Income Tables - Income Equality, hhtp://www.census.gov/hhes/www/income/_histinc/ie1.html (retrieved April 26, 2010).

53.   In fact, big businesses often oppose tax reductions. See Carney, The Big Ripoff, pp. 155-172.

54.   Kohr, The Overdeveloped Nations, p. 73.

55.   Kohr, The Overdeveloped Nations, pp. 75-77.

56.   Kohr, The Overdeveloped Nations, p. 73.

57.   Joseph Pearce. Small Is Still Beautiful. London: HarperCollins, 2001, p. 114.

58.   Pearce, Small Is Still Beautiful, pp. 103-109, quotation at pp. 103-104.

59.   David C. Korten. When Corporations Rule the World (second edition). San Francisco: Berret-Koehler Publishers, Inc. and

Kumarian Press, 2001, pp. 240-241.

60.   Korten, When Corporations Rule the World, pp. 245, 251.

61.   William Appleman Williams, "Let Us Make Our Own Future With the Help of the Past," in A William Appleman Williams Reader: Selections from His Major Historical Writings, edited by Henry W. Berger. Chicago: Ivan R. Dee, 1992, pp. 345-359, quotation at p. 355.

62.   Williams, Let Us Make Our Own Future, pp. 355-356.

63.   Roderick M. Hills, Jr., "Is Federalism Good for Localism? The Localist Case for Federal Regimes," *The Journal of Law & Politics*, volume 21 (Spring/Summer, 2005), pp. 187-221.

64.   The Pew Research Center for the People & the Press, "Distrust, Discontent, Anger and Partisan Rancor," April 18, 2010, at http://pewresearch.org/pubs/1569/trust-in-government-distrust - discontent-anger-partisan-rancor (retrieved April 22, 2010).

65.   The Papers of Thomas Jefferson, Retirement Series, edited by J. Jefferson Looney, et. al., Princeton, NJ: Princeton University Press, 2007, volume 4, p. 570 (letter to Francis Adrian Van der Kemp, March 22, 1812).

66.   The Papers of Thomas Jefferson, edited by Julian P. Boyd, Princeton, NJ: Princeton University Press, 1956, volume 13, p. 208-209 (letter to Edward Carrington, May 27, 1788).

NOTES to Chapter 4

1.   The Writings of Thomas Jefferson: being his Autobiography, Correspondence, Reports, Messages, Addresses, and Other Writings, Official and Private, edited by H. A. Washington. Washington, DC: Taylor & Maury, 1854, volume 4, p. 506 (letter to Wilson C. Nicholas, September 7, 1803).

2.   Thomas Jefferson, "Opinion on the Constitutionality of

Establishing a National Bank," February 15, 1791, reprinted in "Jefferson vs. Hamilton: Confrontations That Shaped a Nation," edited by Noble E. Cunningham, Jr., Boston: Bedford/St. Martin's, 2000, p. 51.

3.   Jefferson, Opinion, pp. 52-54, quotation at p. 52.

4.   Alexander Hamilton, "Opinion on the Constitutionality of Establishing a National Bank," February 23, 1791, reprinted in "Jefferson vs. Hamilton: Confrontations That Shaped a Nation," edited by Noble E. Cunningham, Jr., Boston: Bedford/St. Martin's, 2000, pp. 55-62, quotation at p. 57.

5.   Hamilton, Opinion, p. 61.

6.   17 U.S. 316 (1819).

7.   17 U.S. 316, at 406, 414-415.

8.   James M. McPherson. Battle Cry of Freedom: The Civil War Era. New York: Oxford University Press, 1988, pp. 78-81, 120.

9.   The Slaughter-House Cases, 83 U.S. 36 (1873).

10.   The earliest cases are Santa Clara County vs. Southern Pacific Railroad Co., 118 U.S. 394 (1886), and Minneapolis & St. Louis Railroad vs. Beckwith, 129 U.S. 26 (1889).

11.   Jeff Shesol. Supreme Power: Franklin Roosevelt vs. The Supreme Court. New York: W. W. Norton & Company, Inc., 2010, p. 24, 29-30 indicates that more laws were overturned in the 1920s alone than in the country's first century, and more in the period 1920-1926 than in the prior five decades.

12.   Howard Gillman, "The Collapse of Constitutional Originalism and the Rise of the Notion of the 'Living Constitution' in the Course of American Sate-Building," *Studies in American Political Development*, volume 11, No. 2 (Fall 1997), pp. 191-247, see particularly pp. 197-213.

13.   Woodrow Wilson. Constitutional Government in the United States, March 24, 1908, reprinted in The Papers of Woodrow Wilson, edited by Arthur S. Link, Princeton, NJ: Princeton University Press, 1974, volume 18, pp. 69-216.

14.   Wilson, Constitutional Government, p. 83.

15.   Wilson, Constitutional Government, p. 98.

16.   Wilson, Constitutional Government, pp. 106, 105.

17.   Wilson, Constitutional Government, p. 106.

18.   Wilson, Constitutional Government, pp. 200, 195.

19.   Wilson, Constitutional Government, pp. 172, 173, 179.

20.   Wilson, Constitutional Government, pp. 196, 197.

21.   Wilson, Constitutional Government, p. 215.

22.   The Federalist, edited by Robert Scigliano. New York: The Modern Library, 2000, quotations from Federalist No. 10, pp. 55, 57.

23.   Federalist No. 51, Modern Library edition, pp. 331, 332.

24.   For example, in writing about the federal power to regulate interstate commerce Wilson asked if that gave the federal government power to "regulate the conditions of labor in field and factory? Clearly not,...that would be to destroy all lines of division between the field of state legislation and federal legislation." Constitutional Government, p. 181. Yet the New Deal was to do that and much more.

25.   Paul K. Conkin. The New Deal. New York: Thomas Y. Crowell Company, 1969, p. 19.

26.   295 U.S. 495 (1935).

27.   298 U.S. 238 (1936).

28.   297 U.S. 1 (1936).

29.   295 U.S. 602 (1935).

30.   Joseph Alsop and Turner Catledge, quoted in William E. Leuchtenburg. The Supreme Court Reborn: The Constitutional Revolution in the Age of Roosevelt. New York: Oxford University Press, 1995, p. 80.

31.   Shesol, Supreme Power, pp. 120, 145, 203.

32.   Rexford G. Tugwell. The Democratic Roosevelt: A Biography of Franklin D. Roosevelt. Garden City, NY: Doubleday & Company, Inc., 1957, pp. 390-391.

33.   Gillman, The Collapse of Constitutional Originalism, p. 241.

34.   David E. Kyvig, "The Road Not Taken: FDR, the Supreme Court and Constitutional Amendment, *Political Science Quarterly*, volume 104, no. 3 (1989), pp. 463-481, see p. 475. These ranged from former Republican turned progressive Democrat Senator Edward Costigan to labor unions to rabble-rousing radio preacher Father Coughlin. See "Roosevelt Firm for Law to Retain NRA Principles," *New York Times*, May 30, 1935, pp. A1, A11 (including text of Senator Costigan's proposed amendment); Louis Stark, "Union Labor Maps Out a Militant Program, Demands Speedy Revival of NRA, New Laws, Constitutional Amendment," *New York Times*, June 9, 1935, p. E3; "Coughlin For Amendment, Priest, Closing Radio Services, Assails 'Obsolete' Interstate Law," *New York Times*, June 10, 1935, p. A12.

35.   There are many book-length accounts of the "court-packing" drama. These include William E. Leuchtenburg's "The Supreme Court Reborn," Jeff Shesol's "Supreme Power," Marian C. McKenna's "Franklin Roosevelt and the Great Constitutional War: The court-packing crisis of 1937," New York: Fordham

University Press, 2002, and Burt Solomon's "FDR v. The Constitution: The Court-Packing Fight and the Triumph of Democracy," New York: Walker & Company, 2009.

36. Kyvig, The Road Not Taken, pp. 468, 479-481.

37. Leuchtenburg, The Supreme Court Reborn, p. 111.

38. Kyvig, The Road Not Taken, p. 480.

39. Tugwell, The Democratic Roosevelt, p. 400.

40. Quoted in Doris Kearns Goodwin, "Franklin D. Roosevelt, 1933-1945," in Character Above All: Ten Presidents from FDR to George Bush, edited by Robert A. Wilson, New York: Simon & Schuster, 1995, p. 35. Also see the analysis in McKenna, Franklin Roosevelt and the Great Constitutional War, pp. 557-563. Professor McKenna concludes that the court-packing plan was "marked by [Roosevelt's] characteristic deviousness" and "was in large part a reflection of political arrogance" (pp. 558, 559).

41. West Coast Hotel Co. vs. Parrish, 300 U.S. 379 (1937), effectively overruling Morehead vs. New York ex. rel. Tiplado, 298 U.S 587 (1936).

42. McKenna, Franklin Roosevelt and the Great Constitutional War, p. 411; Shesol, Supreme Power, p. 415; David M. Kennedy, Freedom From Fear: The American People in Depression and War, 1929-1945, New York: Oxford University Press, 1999, p. 335.

43. Owen J. Roberts. The Court and the Constitution. Cambridge, MA: Harvard University Press, 1951, pp. 61-62.

44. Roberts, The Court and the Constitution, pp . 63, 61, 62.

45. Roberts, The Court and the Constitution, p. 56.

46. Arthur Krock, "In Washington: Flexibility of Constitution

Conceded by High Court," *New York Times*, March 30, 1937, p. 22.

47.   Quoted in Solomon, FDR v. the Constitution, p. 161 from correspondence in the papers of Harlan Fiske Stone in the Library of Congress, Frankfurter letter dated March 30, 1937 and Stone reply dated April 2, 1937.

48.   Leuchtenburg, The Supreme Court Reborn, p. 176, quoting Attorney General Homer Cummings and Texas Congressman Maury Maverick, who also described Justice Roberts' vote as "the Greatest Constitutional Somersault in History."

49.   Leuchtenburg, The Supreme Court Reborn, pp. 161, 236.

50.   Federalist No. 43, Modern Library edition, p. 282.

51.   The Writings of James Madison: Comprising His Public Papers and His Private Correspondence, including Numerous Letters and Documents Now for the First Time Printed, edited by Gaillard Hunt, New York: G. P. Putnam's Sons, volume 9, 1910, p. 375 (letter to M. L. Hurlburt, May 1830).

52.   Philip A. Hamburger, "The Constitution's Accommodation of Social Change," *Michigan Law Review*, volume 88, no. 2 (November 1989), pp. 239-327.

53.   5 U.S. 137, 176-178.

54.   Gillman, The Collapse of Constitutional Originalism, pp. 204-205; Hamburger, The Constitution's Accommodation of Social Change, pp. 263-265.

55.   The Writings of Thomas Jefferson, 1854 edition, volume 7, p. 404 (letter to Edward Livingston, March 25, 1825).

56.   Abraham Lincoln, First Inaugural Address (March 4, 1861), in The Life and Writings of Abraham Lincoln, edited by Philip Van Doren Stern, New York: The Modern Library, 1999, quotation at

p.654.

57. Hearings before the Committee on the Judiciary, United States Senate, Seventy-fifth Congress, First Session on S.1392, *Reorganization of the Federal Judiciary*, Washington, DC: United States Government Printing Office, 1937, Part I, p. 48.

58. Progressive sociologists have produced a vast literature on this subject. A recent book-length study is Robert Perrucci and Earl Wysong, "The New Class Society: Goodbye American Dream?," Lanham, MD: Rowman & Littlefield Publishers, Inc, 2008 (third edition).

59. Perrucci and Wysong, The New Class Society, p. 351.

60. Perrucci and Wysong, The New Class Society, p. 353.

61. Thomas R. Dye. Who's Running America?: the Bush Era (5th edition). Englewood Cliffs, NJ: Prentice Hall, 1990, p. 115.

62. Thomas R. Dye. Who's Running America?: The Bush Restoration (7th edition). Upper Saddle River, NJ: Prentice Hall, 2002, pp. 88-89.

63. Adam Liptak, "Rare Breed Now: a Justice Who Wasn't a Judge," *New York Times*, May 1, 2010, p. A1.

64. Although Justice Ruth Bader Ginsburg received her law degree from Columbia she spent her first two years of law school at Harvard, and then transferred to Columbia only because her husband had taken a job in New York City.

65. Descriptions of the Supreme Court clerkship can be found in Todd C. Peppers, "Courtiers of the Marble Palace: The Rise and Influence of the Supreme Court Law Clerk," Stanford, CA: Stanford University Press, 2006, and Edward Lazarus, "Closed Chambers: The First Eyewitness Account of the Epic Struggles Inside the Supreme Court," New York: Random House, 1998.

66.   Peppers, Courtiers of the Marble Palace, pp. 2-10; Lazarus, Closed Chambers, pp. 261-278; Todd C. Peppers and Christopher Zorn, "Law Clerk Influence on Supreme Court Decision-Making: An Empirical Assessment,"*DePaul Law Review*, volume 58, no. 1 (Fall 2008), pp. 51-77.

67.   For a critique of law reviews and the writing published in them see Robert J. Spitzer, "Saving the Constitution From Lawyers: How Legal Training and Law Reviews Distort Constitutional Meaning," New York: Cambridge University Press, 2008, pp. 36-59.

68.   An extended argument describing the use of the courts by the modern American elite to dominate the majority can be found in David Lebedoff, "The Uncivil War: How a New Elite Is Destroying Our Democracy," Lanham, MD: Rowman-Littlefield Publishing Group, Inc., 2004, pp. 19-84.

69.   He was speaking on the occasion of the observance of the 150th anniversary of the Constitution on September 17, 1937. The Public Papers and Addresses of Franklin D. Roosevelt: The constitution prevails, 1937 volume, edited by Samuel I. Rosenman, New York: Macmillan, 1941, p. 362.

70.   For a description of this situation on the current Supreme Court see Adam Liptak, "Justices Are Long on Words but Short on Guidance," *New York Times*, November 18, 2010, p. A1.

71.   James MacGregor Burns. Packing the Court: The Rise of Judicial Power and the Coming Crisis of the Supreme Court. New York: The Penguin Press, 2009, p. 251.

72.   Jamin B. Raskin. Overruling Democracy: The Supreme Court vs. The American People. New York: Routledge, 2003, quotation at p. 6. Another book-length progressive critique of the current Court's constitutional jurisprudence is Cass R. Sunstein, "Radicals in Robes: Why Extreme Right-Wing Courts Are Wrong for America," Cambridge, MA: Basic Books, 2005. Recently analysts have claimed that this rightward movement of the Supreme

294

Court can be shown by objective measures. Adam Liptak, "Court Under Roberts is Most Conservative in Decades," *New York Times*, July 25, 2010, p. A1.

73. Algernon Sidney. Discourses Concerning Government, edited by Thomas G. West. Indianapolis, IN: Liberty Fund, 1990, II:13:3, p. 150. On Sidney's influence on the American revolutionaries and founders, see Alan Craig Houston, "Algernon Sidney and the Republican Heritage in England and America," Princeton, NJ: Princeton University Press, 1991, pp. 223-267. A famous quote from Sidney is the Massachusetts state motto, "Ense petit placidam sub libertate quietem" (By the sword we seek peace, but peace only under liberty).

74. See Keith E. Whittington's "Constitutional Interpretation: Textual Meaning, Original Intent, and Judicial Review," Lawrence, KS: University Press of Kansas, 1999, for a book-length discussion of originalism in relation to modern academic theories.

75. A good one-volume summary of the debate is "Interpreting the Constitution: the Debate over Original Intent," edited by Jack N. Rakove, Boston: Northeastern University Press, 1990. The terms "original meaning" and "original intent" are sometimes used interchangeably. However, a critical distinction must be made. Most "originalists" do not pretend that we can or should divine the inner intentions of the framers and ratifiers in enacting a particular constitutional provision. The records are incomplete, the framers and ratifiers could well have had different intentions and, in any case, how can we know the minds of men who lived more than two centuries ago? However, we can come to reliable conclusions as to how the words they used were commonly understood at the time. This is done by looking at their use of the words in context, at how the words were generally used in common discourse, and at contemporary dictionaries of the time. It is this "original meaning" rather than "original intent" that most proponents of this view look to. See Randy E. Barnett, Restoring the Lost Constitution: The Presumption of Liberty, Princeton, NJ: Princeton University Press, 2004, pp. 89-117.

76.   Hamburger, The Constitution's Accommodation of Social Change.

77.   The Writings of James Madison, volume 9, p. 72 (letter to Thomas Ritchie, September 15, 1821).

78.   The Writings of James Madison, volume 9, pp. 191, 192 (letter to Henry Lee, June 25, 1824).

79.   The first such analysis is Donald S. Lutz. "Toward a Theory of Constitutional Amendment," in Responding to Imperfection: the Theory and Practice of Constitutional Amendment, edited by Sanford Levinson, Princeton, NJ: Princeton University Press, 1995, pp. 237-274. At the time he did his analysis, Professor Lutz thought the constitution of Yugoslavia was more difficult to amend than that of the United States, but with that nation's dissolution, the United States moves into the unenviable first position. We will not go into the question of whether the rigidity of its constitution had anything to do with Yugoslavia's dissolution. Subsequent studies which have confirmed Professor Lutz' conclusion about the rigidity of the U.S. Constitution include Arend Lijphart, "Patterns of Democracy: Government Forms and Performance in Thirty-six Countries," New Haven, CT: Yale University Press, 1999, pp. 206-221, 308-309; Astrid Lorenz, "How to Measure Constitutional Rigidity," *Journal of Theoretical Politics*, volume 17, number 3 (2005), pp. 339, 359; Steven L. Taylor, Matthew S. Shugart, Arend Lijphart and Bernard Grofman, "A Different Democracy: American Government in a Twenty-one Country Perspective," New Haven, CT: Yale University Press, 2014, pp. 78-81.

NOTES to Chapter 5

1.   The Writings of George Washington, edited by John C. Fitzpatrick. Washington, DC: United States Government Printing Office, 1939, volume 29, p. 278 (letter to Patrick Henry, September 24, 1787). Henry was to become one of the leading opponents of the Constitution's ratification. Washington repeatedly noted the availability of the procedure for amendment

in his correspondence during this period. See The Writings of George Washington, volume 29, pp. 287 (David Humphreys, October 10, 1787), 289 (Henry Knox, October 15, 1787), 311 (Bushrod Washington, November 10, 1787), 411 (Marquis De Lafayette, February 7, 1788) and 465 (John Armstrong, April 25, 1788).

2. George Washington, Farewell Address (September 19, 1796), in The Writings of George Washington, edited by John C. Fitzpatrick, Washington, DC: United States Government Printing Office, 1940, volume 35, quotation at p. 224.

3. Ezra Klein, "Elena Kagan Must Talk: With great supremacy comes great responsibility," *Newsweek*, May 24 & 31, 2010, p. 20.

4. Larry J. Sabato, "A More Perfect Constitution: 23 Proposals to Revitalize Our Constitution and Make American a Fairer Country," New York: Walker & Company, 2007, pp. 108-110 discusses the widespread dissatisfaction with the courts.

5. James MacGregor Burns. Packing the Court: The Rise of Judicial Power and the Coming Crisis of the Supreme Court. New York: The Penguin Press, 2009, pp. 252-259. See also Larry D. Kramer, The People Themselves: Popular Constitutionalism and Judicial Review, New York: Oxford University Press, 2004. Kramer argues for the validity of constitutional interpretation outside of the courts or formal Article V amendment, although it is unclear what practical steps he is advocating as a consequence of that view.

6. Akhil Reed Amar and Alan Hirsch. For the People: What the Constitution Really Says About Your Rights. New York: The Free Press, 1998, pp. 3-33 and Akhil Reed Amar, "Popular Sovereignty and Constitutional Amendment," in Responding to Imperfection: the Theory and Practice of Constitutional Amendment, edited by Sanford Levinson, Princeton, NJ: Princeton University Press, 1995, pp. 89-115.

7. Kirk Johnson, "States' Rights Is Rallying Cry for Lawmakers,"

New York Times, March 17, 2010, p. A1; Thomas E. Woods, Jr. Nullification: How to Resist Federal Tyranny in the 21st Century. Washington, DC: Regnery Publishing, Inc., 2010.

8.   Thomas R. Dye. Top Down Policymaking. New York: Seven Bridges Press, 2001, pp. 8-9, 118-119. The survey of presidential staff and senior officials was made during the Clinton administration. However, there is no indication that the Obama administration is any different, especially considering how many Clinton administration veterans it contains and the highly elite backgrounds of most of its personnel.

9.   The Federalist, edited by Robert Scigliano. New York: The Modern Library, 2000, quotation from Federalist No. 43, p. 282.

10.   Donald S. Lutz. "Toward a Theory of Constitutional Amendment," in Responding to Imperfection: the Theory and Practice of Constitutional Amendment, edited by Sanford Levinson, Princeton, NJ: Princeton University Press, 1995, pp. 237-274.

11.   Lutz, Theory of Constitutional Amendment, pp. 247-259.

12.   Lutz, Theory of Constitutional Amendment, pp. 260-264.

13.   The Writings of James Madison: Comprising His Public Papers and His Private Correspondence, including Numerous Letters and Documents Now for the First Time Printed, edited by Gaillard Hunt, New York: G. P. Putnam's Sons, volume 8, 1910, p. 451 (letter to Spencer Roane, September 2, 1819).

14.   David E. Kyvig. Explicit & Authentic Acts: Amending the Constitution 1776-1995. Lawrence, KS: University of Kansas Press, 1996, p. 192.

15.   Kyvig, Explicit & Authentic Acts, pp. 193, 249-253, 473; Charles James Antieau. A U. S. Constitution for the Year 2000. Chicago: Loyola University Press, 1995, pp. 99-107.

16.   Lutz, Theory of Constitutional Amendment, p. 265.

17.   Federalist No. 43, Modern Library edition, p. 282.

18.   For a summary of the myriad issues surrounding a prospective Article V convention (as well as a more technical discussion of the Amendment Amendment), see James W. Lucas, "To Originate the Amendment of Errors: Reforming Article V to Facilitate State and Popular Engagement in Constitutional Amendment" at (http://papers.ssrn.com/sol3/papers.cfm? Abstract_id=2275124) and Michael B. Rappaport, Reforming Article V: The Problems Created by the National Convention Method and How to Fix Them, *Virginia Law Review*, volume 96, No. 7 (November 2010), pp. 1511-1581. (Professor Rappaport provides an excellent analysis of the defects and detrimental consequences of the convention method, but then unfortunately proposes solutions which introduce new and unnecessary complications to the amendment process.)

19.   The Records of the Federal Convention of 1787, edited by Max Farrand, New Haven, CT: Yale University Press, 1937, volume 2, pp. 629-630.

20.   Kyvig, Explicit & Authentic Acts, pp. 210, 213, 372-373, 432-435, 440-443, 471-472.

21.   Kyvig, Explicit & Authentic Acts, pp. 223-224, 248, 414-415, 421, 468.

22.   Kyvig, Explicit & Authentic Acts, pp. 174-175, 408-409, 414-416.

23.   Kyvig, Explicit & Authentic Acts, pp. 283-287.

24.   Hawke v. Smith, 253 U.S. 221 (1920).

NOTES to Chapter 6

1.   The Writings of Thomas Jefferson, being his Autobiography, Correspondence, Reports, Messages, Addresses, and Other

Writings, Official and Private, edited by H. A. Washington. New York: John C. Riker, Washington, DC: Taylor & Maury, 1853, volume 1, p. 82 (from the Autobiography, 1821).

2. James Madison, "Report on the Alien and Sedition Acts to the General Assembly of Virginia," January 7, 1800, reprinted in James Madison Writings, edited by Jack N. Rakove, New York: Library of America, 1999, pp. 608-662, quotations at pp. 617-619 (italics in original).

3. 301 U.S. 619 (1937). The actual decision declaring that the general welfare clause was not limited by the enumerated powers was U.S. vs. Butler, 297 U.S. 1 (1936). However, *Butler* had overturned the statute in question on other grounds. *Helvering* was the first case where a tax and spending statute based only on "general welfare" was upheld.

4. 301 U.S. 548 (1937).

5. 483 U.S. 203 (1987).

6. The Social Security Fund trustees themselves calculate the unfunded obligation of the Trust Fund to be $15.1 trillion. Annual outflows for old age pensions will begin to exceed income from payroll taxes starting in 2016. After this, the Fund will have to start redeeming the US Treasury securities which it holds. These will have to be paid out of general tax revenues. Even this resource will be exhausted by 2037. However, the disability insurance fund is in far worse shape. It will completely exhaust its US Treasury securities holdings in 2020. See The 2009 Annual Report of the Board of Trustees of the Federal Old-Age and Survivors Insurance and Federal Disability Insurance Trust Funds, Washington, DC: US Government Printing Office, 2009, pp. 2, 9, 13. Also available at http://www.ssa.gov/OACT/TR/2009 /tr09.pdf.

7. Alexander Hamilton, "Report on the Subject of Manufactures," reprinted in The Papers of Alexander Hamilton, edited by Harold C. Syrett, et al. New York and London: Columbia University

Press, 1961-79, volume 10, p. 303 (italics in original).

8.   Leslie A. Gillum, Christopher Gouveia, E. Ray Dorsey, Mark Pletcher, Colin D. Mathers, Charles E. McCulloch and S. Claiborne Johnston, "NIH Disease Funding Levels and Burden of Disease," *PLoS ONE* 6(2) (2011):e16837.doi:10.1371/ journal.pone.0016837, at http://www.plosone.org/article/ info%3Adoi%2F10.1371%2Fjournal.pone.0016837 (retrieved July 7, 2012).

9.   http://febp.newamerica.net/background-analysis/no-child-left-behind-funding (retrieved May 17, 2010).

10.   James Madison Writings, p. 815 (letter to Joseph Cabell, September 18, 1828).

11.   Randy E. Barnett, "The Original Meaning of the Commerce Clause," *The University of Chicago Law Review*, volume 68, No. 1 (Winter 2001), pp. 101-147, see pp. 111-125.

12.   The Federalist, edited by Robert Scigliano. New York: The Modern Library, 2000, quotation from Federalist No. 11, p. 67. See also Barnett, The Original Meaning of the Commerce Clause, pp. 132-138.

13.   Barnett, The Original Meaning of the Commerce Clause, pp. 139-145. On the narrow original meaning of the words in the interstate commerce clause also see Richard A. Epstein, "The Proper Scope of the Commerce Clause," *Virginia Law Review*, volume 73, No. 8 (November 1987), pp. 1387-1455.

14.   22 U.S. 1 (1824).

15.   298 U.S. 238 (1936).

16.   301 U.S. 1 (1937).

17.   317 U.S. 111 (1942).

18.   317 U.S. 111, 128-129 (italics added).

19.   In Gonzales v. Raich, 545 U.S. 1, 45-46 (2005) (O'Connor, J dissenting).

20.   545 U.S. 1, 49-50. Justice Thomas was even more blunt in his dissent, arguing that "the Federal Government may now regulate quilting bees, clothes drives, and potluck suppers throughout the 50 States. This makes a mockery of Madison's assurance to the people of New York that the 'powers delegated' to the Federal Government are 'few and defined,' while those of the States are 'numerous and indefinite.'" 545 U.S. 1, 69.

21.   Lopez vs. United States, 514 U.S. 549 (1995) and United States vs. Morrison, 529 U.S. 598 (2000).

22.   See Gonzales v. Raich, 545 U.S. 1 (2005), holding that a seriously ill woman who grew a few marijuana plants at home for her own use in conformance with California's medical marijuana law was nonetheless acting in "interstate" commerce and subject to federal drug laws.

23.   Federalist No. 11, Modern Library edition, pp. 68, 65.

24.   Federalist No. 42, Modern Library edition, p.270.

25.   James Madison. Letters and Other Writings of James Madison. Philadelphia: J. B. Lippincott & Co., 1865, volume 4, p. 15 (letter to Joseph C. Cabell, February 13, 1829).

26.   Federalist No. 45, Modern Library edition, p. 298.

27.   Adam Smith. An Inquiry Into The Nature and Causes of The Wealth of Nations, edited by R. H. Campbell and A. S. Skinner. Indianapolis, IN: Liberty Fund, Inc., 1981 (originally published 1776), Chapter xiii.12, pp. 83-84.

28.   Smith, Wealth of Nations, Chapter x..61, pp. 157-158.

29. Smith, Wealth of Nations, Chapter xiii.44, p. 99.

30. Smith, Wealth of Nations, Book V, Chapter iii.90-92, pp. 944-947; The Correspondence of Adam Smith, edited by Ernest Campbell Mosner and Ian Simpson Ross, Oxford: Clarendon Press, 1977, pp. 380-385.

31. The Papers of Thomas Jefferson, edited by Julian P. Boyd, et. al. Princeton, NJ: Princeton University Press, 1961, volume 16, p. 449 (letter to Thomas Mann Randolph, Jr., May 30, 1790).

32. This suggestion comes from Andrew P. Napolitano, "The Constitution in Exile: How the Federal Government Has Seized Power by Rewriting the Supreme Law of the Land," Nashville, TN: Thomas Nelson, Inc., 2006, at p. 240.

33. See Alec Stone Sweet, "Governing with Judges: Constitutional Politics in Europe," Oxford, UK: Oxford University Press, 2000, pp. 31-60 for a concise summary of the history and operation of constitutional courts in western Europe and Louis Favoreu, "Constitutional Review in Europe," in Constitutionalism and Rights: The Influence of the United States Constitution Abroad, edited by Louis Henkin and Albert J. Rosenthal, New York: Columbia University Press, 1990, pp. 38-42, 50-62 for more background and a comparison of constitutional review in European constitutional courts with the American system of judicial review.

34. This section is based on what is sometimes referred to as the "Repeal Amendment," a version of which has been introduced in Congress without success. The five eighths threshold (32 of 50 states) tracks the proposed reform of Article V discussed in chapter 5 and is also a compromise between the original version proposed by Professor Randy Barnett which called for action by three fourths of the States (http://www.forbes.com/2009/05/bill-of-federalism-constitution-states-supreme-court-opinions-contributors-randy-barnett.html) and the more recent proposal by Mark Levin which would allow three fifths of the states to override (Mark R. Levin, "The Liberty Amendments: Restoring

the American Republic," New York, NY: Simon & Schuster, 2013, pp. 169-181).

NOTES to Chapter 7

1.   George Washington, Farewell Address (September 19, 1796), in The Writings of George Washington, edited by John C. Fitzpatrick, Washington, DC: United States Government Printing Office, 1940, volume 35, quotations at pp. 221-222, 228, 229.

2.   Office of Management and Budget. Budget of the U. S. Government, Fiscal Year 2010, Historical Tables, Table 3.1, at http://www.whitehouse.gov/omb/budget/fy2010/assets/hist.pdf (retrieved May 18, 2010).

3.   Department of Defense, "Active Duty Military Personnel Strengths by Regional Area and by Country (309A) March 31, 2008" at http://siadapp.dmdc.osd.mil/personnel/MILITARY/history/hst0803.pdf; Department of Defense, "Base Structure Report Fiscal Year 2007 Baseline," p. DoD-22, at http://www.defense.gov/pubs/BSR_2007_Baseline.pdf (retrieved May 18, 2010).

4.   Information from the Departments of Defense and Veterans Affairs collected at http://www.infoplease.com/ipa /A0778300.html and http://www.infoplease.com/ipa /A0004615.html (retrieved May 18, 2010).

5.   Federalist No. 69, Modern Library edition, pp. 441-442 (italics in original).

6.   Alexander Hamilton, Pacificus No. I (June 29, 1793), reprinted in The Papers of Alexander Hamilton, edited by Harold C. Syrett, et al. New York and London: Columbia University Press, 1961-79, volume 15, p. 43.

7.   Pacificus No. I, The Papers of Alexander Hamilton, volume 15, p. 42 (italics in original).

8.   Washington, Farewell Address, p. 236.

9.   The articles, related documents and an introductory background can be found in Alexander Hamilton and James Madison, "The Pacificus-Helvidius Debates of 1793 - 1794: The Completion of the American Founding," edited by Morton J. Frisch, Indianapolis, IN: Liberty Fund, Inc., 2007.

10.   In a fascinating essay, Professor Garrett Sheldon attributes this realistic approach in part to Madison's Calvinist religious education. Garrett Ward Sheldon, "Religion and Politics in the Thought of James Madison," in The Founders on God and Government, edited by Daniel L. Dreisbach, Mark D. Hall and Jeffry H. Morrison, Lanham, MD: Rowman & Littlefield Publishers, Inc., 2004, pp. 83-115.

11.   James Madison, Helvidius No. IV (September 14, 1793) , reprinted in The Writings of James Madison: Comprising His Public Papers and His Private Correspondence, Including Numerous Letters and Documents Now for the First Time Printed, edited by Gaillard Hunt, New York: G. P. Putnam's Sons, 1906, volume 6, p. 174.

12.   Madison, Helvidius No. I (August 24, 1793), The Writings Of James Madison, volume 6, p. 148 (italics in original).

13.   This process is described in detail in Gerald Astor, "Presidents at War: From Truman to Bush, the Gathering of Military Power to Our Commander-in-Chief," Hoboken, NJ: John Wiley & Sons, Inc., 2006 and Kenneth B. Moss, "Undeclared War and the Future of U.S. Foreign Policy," Baltimore, MD: The Johns Hopkins University Press, 2008, pp. 74-111.

14.   David M. Kennedy. Freedom From Fear: The American People in Depression and War, 1929-1945. New York: Oxford University Press, 1999, pp. 427-429, 460-463, 473-474, 490-493, 496-499; William Appleman Williams. Americans in a Changing World: A History of the United States in the Twentieth Century. New York: Harper& Row, 1978, pp. 312-315.

15.   See, for example, Peter Irons, "War Powers: How the Imperial Presidency Hijacked the Constitution," New York: Henry Holt and Company, 2005.

16.   Louis Fisher. Congressional Abdication on War and Spending. College Station, TX: Texas A&M University Press, 2000.

17.   The text of the War Powers Resolution and official documents issued for subsequent foreign military operations under the Resolution can be found in "The War Powers Resolution," edited by Richard F. Grimmett, New York: Novinka Books, 2002.

18.   Irons, War Powers, pp. 198-204; Moss, Undeclared War, pp. 97-107.

19.   Edward Keynes. Undeclared War: Twilight Zone of Constitutional Power. University Park, PA: The Pennsylvania State University Press, 1982.

20.   Robert F. Turner. Repealing the War Powers Resolution: Restoring the Rule of Law in US Foreign Policy. McLean, VA: Brassey's (US) Inc., 1991.

21.   Federalist No. 41, Modern Library edition, pp. 258-259.

22.   Moss, Undeclared War, pp. 132-148.

23.   Andrew J. Bacevich, "Washington Rules: America's Path to Permanent War," New York: Henry Holt and Company LLC, 2010, gives a history of the growth of US military presence overseas and argues that the national security establishment is now seeking a state of permanent engagement in global conflict.

24.   Donald L. Westerfield. War Powers: The President, Congress, and the Question of War. Westport, CT: Praeger, 1996.

25.   Moss, Undeclared War, pp. 107-111.

26.   The need to restrain our military commitments in light of our

straightened economic situation is becoming very topical. For example, see David M. Walker, "Comeback America: Turning the Country Around and Restoring Fiscal Responsibility," New York: Random House, 2009, pp. 140-158 and Michael Mandelbaum, "The Frugal Superpower: America's Global Leadership in a Cash-Strapped Era," New York: PublicAffairs, 2010.

27. Paul Kennedy. The Rise and Fall of Great Powers: Economic and Military Conflict from 1500 to 2000. New York: Random House, 1987. See particularly pp. 514-535 regarding the United States.

28. The War Powers Initiative Committee. Deciding to Use Force Abroad: War Powers in a System of Checks and Balances. Washington, DC: The Constitution Project, 2005.

29. Bacevich, Washington Rules, pp. 238-250.

NOTES to Chapter 8

1. George Washington, Farewell Address (September 19, 1796), in The Writings of George Washington, edited by John C. Fitzpatrick., Washington, DC: United States Government Printing Office, 1940, volume 35, quotation at pp. 229-230.

2. There was one moderate Republican, Harold Burton, a friend of Harry Truman's from his time in the Senate. It is hard to imagine today that there once was a time when a President would practice bipartisanship in Supreme Court nominations.

3. 330 U.S. 1 (1947).

4. 330 U.S. 1, 15-16.

5. 330 U.S. 1, 11-12.

6. Barry Adamson. Freedom of Religion, the First Amendment and the Supreme Court: How the Court Flunked History. Gretna, LA: Pelican Publishing Company, Inc., 2008, pp. 29-55.

7.   Michael W. McConnell, "Establishment and Disestablishment at the Founding, Part I: Establishment of Religion," *William and Mary Law Review*, volume 44 (April 2003), pp. 2105-2208.

8.   Thomas J. Curry. The First Freedoms: Church and State in America to the Passage of the First Amendment. New York: Oxford University Press, 1986, pp. 134-192.

9.   Curry, First Freedoms, pp. 191-192, 208-210, quotation at p. 209.

10.   Adamson, Freedom of Religion, pp. 19-24.

11.   Curry, First Freedoms, pp. 217-221.

12.   On Washington's views see Vincent Phillip Munoz, "Religion and the Common Good: George Washington on Church and State," in The Founders on God and Government, edited by Daniel L. Dreisbach, Mark D. Hall and Jeffry H. Morrison, Lanham, MD: Rowman & Littlefield Publishers, Inc., 2004, pp. 1-22. That they represented a common view in this period is pointed out by McConnell, Establishment and Disestablishment, p. 2196.

13.   McConnell, Establishment and Disestablishment, pp. 2193-2205.

14.   Quoted in Adamson, Freedom of Religion, p. 159.

15.   Quoted in Patrick M. Garry. Wrestling with God: the Courts' Treatment of Religion. Washington, DC: The Catholic University of America Press, 2006, at p. 101 (italics added).

16.   The congressional history is detailed in Adamson, Religious Freedom, pp. 72-106.

17.   Edwin S. Corwin, "The Supreme Court as National School Board," *Law and Contemporary Problems*, volume 14, no. 1 (Winter 1949), pp. 3-22 (see particularly pp. 9-16); Garry, Wrestling with God, pp. 94-102.

18.   Adamson, Freedom of Religion, pp. 136-148.

19.   Garry, Wrestling with God, p. 102.

20.   In fact, Madison tried to add the word "national" to the first amendment but had to take it out because of Congressman Elbridge Gerry's long-standing prejudice against the word. At the Constitutional Convention, he had also insisted that it be removed from the Constitution because he felt it had an anti-states rights connotation. See Adamson, Freedom of Religion, pp. 108-122.

21.   Dumas Malone. Jefferson the President: First Term, 1801-1805. Boston: Little, Brown and Company, 1970, pp. 190-192, 200-205.

22.   Thomas Jefferson, "Reply to Committee of the Danbury Baptist Association," reprinted in The Writings of Thomas Jefferson, edited by Andrew A. Lipscomb and Albert Ellery Bergh, Washington, DC: Thomas Jefferson Memorial Association, 1905, volume 16, pp. 281-282 (January 1, 1802).

23.   Daniel L. Dreisbach. Thomas Jefferson and the Wall of Separation between Church and State. New York: New York University Press, 2002, pp. 95-102. It was quoted in Reynolds vs. US (98 U.S. 145), an 1878 Mormon polygamy case, but did not receive any particular notice until Black repeated it in his *Everson* opinion. Eminent constitutional scholar Edwin Corwin famously wrote that the letter "was not improbably motivated by an impish desire to heave a brick at the Congregationalist-Federalist hierarchy of Connecticut, whose leading members had denounced him two years before as an 'infidel' and 'atheist.'" Corwin, The Supreme Court as National School Board, p. 14.

24.   Philip Hamburger. Separation of Church and State. Cambridge, MA: Harvard University Press, 2002, pp. 163-180; Dreisbach, Thomas Jefferson and the Wall of Separation, pp. 51-53.

25.   Dreisbach, Thomas Jefferson and the Wall of Separation, pp. 55-70, 125-128 argues that even Jefferson meant the "wall" to only refer to the Constitution as a jurisdictional barrier to involvement by the federal government in religion, and had no reference to

relations between religion and state governments.

26. Hamburger, Separation of Church and State, p. 162.

27. Thomas E. Buckley, "The Religious Rhetoric of Thomas Jefferson," in The Founders on God and Government, edited by Daniel L. Dreisbach, Mark D. Hall and Jeffry H. Morrison, Lanham, MD: Rowman & Littlefield Publishers, Inc., 2004, pp. 53-82. Buckley also describes Jefferson's resentment of the accusations of personal irreligion and his conflicts with the established New England clergy as background to the letter to the Connecticut Baptists.

28. Thomas Jefferson. First Inaugural Address, in The Papers of Thomas Jefferson, edited by Barbara B. Oberg, et. al., Princeton NJ: Princeton University Press, 2006, volume 33, pp. 148-152, quotation at p. 150.

29. Buckley, The Religious Rhetoric of Thomas Jefferson, p. 53.

30. This discussion follows Hamburger, Separation of Church and State, pp. 193-251.

31. Jay P. Dolan. In Search of an American Catholicism: A History of Religion and Culture in Tension. New York: Oxford University Press, 2002, pp. 47-70; David O'Brien. Public Catholicism. New York: Macmillan, 1989, pp. 41-56; Jay P. Dolan. The American Catholic Experience: A History from Colonial Times to the Present. Garden City, NY: Doubleday & Company, Inc., 1985, pp. 262-293.

32. On secularist support for separation see Hamburger, Separation of Church and State, pp. 288-321, for the role of the Ku Klux Klan and other nativists see pp. 399-422.

33. Ira Katznelson. Fear Itself: The New Deal and the Origins of Our Time. New York: Liveright Publishing Corp., 2013, pp. 156-168, 251-260.

34.   Hamburger, Separation of Church and State, pp. 422-434; Stephen Mansfield. Ten Tortured Words: How the Founding Fathers Tried to Protect Religion in America -- and What's Happened Since. Nashville, TN: Thomas Nelson, 2007, pp. 55-60.

35.   Hamburger, Separation of Church and State, p. 433.

36.   Hugo Black, Jr. My Father: A Remembrance. New York: Random House, 1975, p. 104.

37.   Hamburger, Separation of Church and State, pp. 448-463.

38.   Justice Black was not alone in this even on the Supreme Court. Hamburger, Separation of Church and State, p. 474 notes that Justice Felix Frankfurter also had a "distaste for Catholicism."

39.   333 U.S. 203 (1948). This case led Professor Edwin Corwin to write a widely noted article in 1949 pointing out the historical and legal errors of this interpretation of the Establishment clause (see note 17). Thus, since the very beginning the Supreme Court has had access to correct information and is without excuse in still persisting in its erroneous *Everson* line of cases, of which there have been almost 60 since 1947 according to Adamson, Freedom of Religion, p. 241.

40.   Roberts vs. Madigan, 921 F.2d 1047 (10th Circuit 1990).

41.   Bishop vs. Aronov, 926 F.2d 1066 (11th Circuit 1991).

42.   Hansen vs. Ann Arbor Public Schools, 293 F.Supp.2d 780 (Eastern Dist. Mich. 2003).

43.   Reed vs. van Hoven, 237 F.Supp. 48 (Western Dist. Mich. 1965).

44.   Warsaw vs. Tehachapi, CV-F-90-404 (Eastern Dist. Cal. 1990).

45.   Wallace vs. Jaffree, 472 U.S. 38 (1985).

46. Metzl vs. Leininger, 57 F.3d 618 (7th Circuit 1995).

47. Harris vs. City of Zion, 927 F.2d 1401 (7th Circuit 1991).

48. County of Allegheny vs. ACLU, 492 U.S. 573 (1989).

49. Alexander vs. Nacogdoches School District, CA 9:91CV144 (Eastern Dist. Texas 1991).

50. Collins vs. Chandler Unified School District, 644 F.2d 759 (9th Circuit 1981).

51. See Garry, Wrestling with God, notes to pp. 54 and 122 for sources.

52. Garry, Wrestling with God, pp. 18-35.

53. Compare Lee vs. Weisman, 505 U.S. 577 (1992) and Mozert vs. Hawkins County Board of Education, 827 F.2d 1058 (6th Circuit 1987).

54. 392 U.S. 83 (1968). The *Flast* decision was somewhat narrowed in Valley Forge Christian College vs. Americans United for Separation of Church and State, 454 U.S. 464 (1982), which held that standing under *Flast* only applied where actual tax money was being spent by legislative action, not where an administrative agency was simply transferring surplus government property.

55. 403 U.S. 602 (1971).

56. 403 U.S. 602, 612-613.

57. Leonard W. Levy. The Establishment Clause: Religion and the First Amendment. New York: Macmillan, 1986, pp. 128, 129.

58. 473 U.S. 402 (1985). Although this case was subsequently overruled in Agostini vs. Felton, 521 U.S. 203 (1997), that was by a narrow 5-4 majority, with the dissenters vigorously defending the *Aguilar* decision.

59. Levy, The Establishment Clause, p. 142.

60. Levy, The Establishment Clause, p. 162.

61. Marsh vs. Chambers, 463 U.S. 783 (1983) and County of Allegheny vs. ACLU, 492 U.S. 573 (1989).

62. Corporation of the Presiding Bishop vs. Amos, 483 U.S. 327 (1987) and Estate of Thornton vs. Caldor, 472 U.S. 703 (1985).

63. McCreary County vs. ACLU of Kentucky, 545 U.S. 844 (2005) and Van Orden vs. Perry, 545 U.S. 677 (2005).

64. Jeffrey Rosen, "Lemon Law," *New Republic*, March 29, 1993, pp. 17-18, quotation at p. 17.

65. Garry, Wrestling with God, pp. 55-86, 145-146.

66. Kent Greenawalt. Religion and the Constitution: Volume 2: Establishment and Fairness. Princeton, NJ: Princeton University Press, 2008, pp. 46, 160-161.

67. In 1985, 38 years after *Everson*, Justice William Rehnquist finally reviewed the actual history of the first amendment's anti-establishment clause and correctly concluded that it prohibited the creation of a national church and preferential aid to particular religions, but in no way barred non-preferential government benefits to religions. Wallace vs. Jaffree, 472 U.S. 38, 91-114. A few years later Justice David Souter tried to rebut Rehnquist's research in an opinion which repeated Hugo Black's error of focusing on James Madison's writings regarding the Virginia religious freedom act in 1786 rather than what he did in the First Congress in 1789 when framing the first amendment. Souter also cites some scholarly articles which ludicrously try to defend a twentieth century strict separationist interpretation by anachronistically reading twentieth century legal issues and methods of statutory interpretation back into the eighteenth century record. Rosenberger vs. University of Virginia, 515 U.S. 819, 863-899 (1995). Both Rehnquist and Souter's opinions were

313

dissents, so neither offered any controlling solution to the disarray of the Court's establishment clause rulings.

68. Akhil Reed Amar. The Bill of Rights: Creation and Reconstruction. New Haven, CT: Yale University Press, 1998, p. 34.

69. Vincent Phillip Munoz, "The Original Meaning of the Establishment Clause and the Impossibility of Its Incorporation," *University of Pennsylvania Journal of Constitutional Law*, volume 8, No. 4 (August 2006), pp. 585-639; Dreisbach, Thomas Jefferson and the Wall of Separation, pp. 55-70, 125-128; Amar, The Bill of Rights, pp. 32-42.

70. American Civil Liberties Union, Inc. and Consolidated Entities, Consolidated Financial Statements for the Year Ended March 31, 2009, Note 2 - Legal Awards at p. 11, at http://www.aclu.org/files/pdfs/about/fy2009_aclu_fs.pdf (retrieved June 2, 2010).

71. Mansfield, Ten Tortured Words, pp. 96-100.

72. Levy, The Establishment Clause, p. 177.

73. 374 U.S. 203, 306 (1963). This was the case which banned Bible reading in public schools.

74. 403 U.S. 602, 614.

75. Frederick Mark Gedicks, The Rhetoric of Church and State: A Critical Analysis of Religion Clause Jurisprudence, Durham, NC: Duke University Press, 1995, argues that the "Supreme Court's religion clause jurisprudence is limited and controlled by the rhetorical resources of secular individualist discourse. By confining religion to private life, secular individualism can subordinate religion to secularism in public life, or exclude it altogether. As ruled by secular individualist discourse, religion clause jurisprudence is neither plausible nor popular.... While secular individualist discourse is the discourse within which most

314

cultural elites make their intellectual home, its assumptions are rejected by a large number of Americans.... As a result religion clause doctrine [currently] stands in the same position as economic due process in the 1930s - a failed jurisprudence ripe for dismantling" (pp. 117, 122).

76.   The Pew Forum on Religion & Public Life, U.S. Religious Landscape Survey (2007) at http://religions.pewforum.org /reports (retrieved June 2, 2010).

77.   Steve Crabtree, "Religiosity Highest in World's Poorest Nations: United States is among the rich countries that buck the trend," August 31, 2010, at http://www.gallup.com/poll/142727/ religiosity-highest-world-poorest-nations.aspx   (retrieved September 4, 2010).

NOTES to Chapter 9

1.   The Federalist, edited by Robert Scigliano. New York: The Modern Library, 2000, quotation from Federalist No. 78, pp. 502-503.

2.   Michael Les Benedict. A Compromise of Principle: Congressional Republicans and Reconstruction 1863-1869. New York: W. W. Norton & Company, Inc., 1974, pp. 122-123. This is an excellent overview of the entire period and is the basis of the following historical summary.

3.   Eric Foner. Reconstruction: America's Unfinished Revolution 1863 - 1877. New York: Harper & Row, 1998, pp. 134-135, 198-208.

4.   United States Code, Title 42, Section 1981.

5.   This account of Stevens' life follows Hans L. Trefousse, Thaddeus Stevens: Nineteenth Century Egalitarian, Chapel Hill, NC: The University of North Carolina Press, 1997.

6.   Quoted in Alexander M. Bickel, "The Original Understanding

and the Segregation Decision," *Harvard Law Review*, volume 69, no. 1 (November 1955), at p. 30.

7.   Bickel, The Original Understanding, pp. 29-40.

8.   Bickel, The Original Understanding, pp. 40-41. Stevens told Owen that "we've had nothing before us that comes anywhere near being as good as this or complete." Quoted in Trefousse, Thaddeus Stevens, p. 184.

9.   Bickel, The Original Understanding, p. 25.

10.   Garrett Epps. Democracy Reborn: The Fourteenth Amendment and the Fight for Equal Rights in Post-Civil War America. New York: Henry Holt and Company, 2006, pp. 168-169.

11.   Quoted in Benedict, A Compromise of Principle, p. 170.

12.   Lambert Gingras, "Congressional Misunderstandings and the Ratifiers' Understanding: The Case of the Fourteenth Amendment," *The American Journal of Legal History*, volume 40, no. 1 (January 1996), pp. 41-71.

13.   Charles Fairman, "Does the Fourteenth Amendment Incorporate the Bill of Rights?: The Original Understanding, *Stanford Law Review*, volume 2, no. 1 (November 1949), pp. 44-48, 72-74; Raoul Berger, Government By Judiciary: The Transformation of the Fourteenth Amendment, Indianapolis, IN: Liberty Fund, Inc., 1997 (second edition), pp. 32-33, 48-52.

14.   Jacobus tenBroek. Equal Under Law. Toronto: Macmillan, 1951, 1965 (revised edition), p. 232.

15.   The Papers of Alexander Hamilton, edited by Harold C. Syrett, et al. New York and London: Columbia University Press, 1961-79, volume 4, p. 35.

16.   tenBroek, Equal Under Law, pp. 237-239.

17. Fairman, Does the Fourteenth Amendment Incorporate the Bill of Rights?, pp. 50-51, 135.

18. Bickel, The Original Understanding, p. 58.

19. Benedict, A Compromise of Principle, pp. 184-209.

20. Quoted in Benedict, A Compromise of Principle, p. 182 ("offspring of cowardice") and Bickel, The Original Understanding, p. 46 ("shilly-shally bungling thing").

21. The Selected Papers of Thaddeus Stevens, edited by Beverly Wilson Palmer and Holly Byers Ochoa. Pittsburgh, PA: University of Pittsburgh Press, 1998, volume 2, p. 156.

22. Trefousse, Thaddeus Stevens, p. xi. On his tombstone are these words: I repose in this quiet and secluded spot, not from any natural preference for solitude but, finding other Cemeteries limited by Charter rules, I have chosen this that I might illustrate in my death the Principles which I advocated through a long life: EQUALITY OF MAN BEFORE HIS CREATOR.

23. The Slaughter-House Cases, 83 U.S. 36 (1873).

24. Fairman, "Does the Fourteenth Amendment Incorporate the Bill of Rights?, pp. 44, 50, 61.

25. Edward Keynes, Life, Liberty and Privacy: Toward a Jurisprudence of Substantive Due Process, University Park, PA: Pennsylvania State University Press, 1996, pp. 95-111.

26. The earliest cases are Santa Clara County vs. Southern Pacific Railroad Co., 118 U.S. 394 (1886), and Minneapolis & St. Louis Railroad vs. Beckwith, 129 U.S. 26 (1889).

27. Chicago, Milwaukee & St. Paul Ry. Co. vs. Minnesota, 134 U.S. 418 (1890).

28. 165 U.S. 578 (1897).

29.   198 U.S. 45 (1905).

30.   198 U.S. 45, 53.

31.   236 U.S. 1 (1915).

32.   208 U.S. 161 (1908).

33.   163 U.S. 538 (1896).

34.   163 U.S. 538, 551.

35.   347 U.S. 483 (1954).

36.   Herbert Wechsler, "Toward Neutral Principles of Constitutional Law," *Harvard Law Review*, volume 73, no. 1 (November 1959), pp. 1-35 (finding the decision indefensible on neutrally applied principles and violative of rights of association); Bickel, The Original Understanding, pp. 56-65 (noting the decision could not be defended historically but nonetheless supporting the result because of the progress in racial tolerance, which of course would make *Plessy* a correct decision also since it reflected the state of racial tolerance of its time, and would justify overruling *Brown* if social conditions ever changed); Berger, Government By Judiciary, pp. 151-154, 263-266 (*contra* Bickel argues that the Court should not go beyond the amendment's framers' indisputable intent); Earl M. Maltz, "A Dissenting Opinion to Brown," *Southern Illinois Law Journal*, volume 20, no. 1 (1995), pp. 93-98 (also arguing that *Brown* is not supported by the history of the fourteenth amendment); Earl M. Maltz, "Brown v. Board of Education," in Constitutional Stupidities, Constitutional Tragedies, edited by William N. Eskridge, Jr. and Sanford Levinson, New York: New York University Press, 1998, pp. 207-216.

37.   Generally, on the misuse of the fourteenth amendment contrary to its framers' views see Richard L. Aynes, "Unintended Consequences of the Fourteenth Amendment," in Unintended Consequences of Constitutional Amendments, edited by David

318

E. Kyvig, Athens, GA: The University of Georgia Press, 2000, pp. 110-140.

38.   429 U.S. 190 (1976). See 429 U.S. 190, 210-211 (Powell, J. concurring).

39.   429 U.S. 190, 220-221.   See United States Civil Rights Commission, The Equal Rights Amendment: Guaranteeing Equal Rights for Women Under The Constitution, Washington, DC: U.S. Government Printing Office, June 1981, pp. 24-25.

40.   304 U.S. 144 (1938).

41.   Keynes, Life, Liberty and Privacy, pp. 133-135.

42.   304 U.S. 144, 153.

43.   Thomas Tandy Lewis, "The Ironic History of Substantive Due Process: Three Constitutional Revolutions," *International Social Science Review*, volume 76, nos. 1 & 2 (2001), pp. 21-35.

44.   To be clear Justice Black did not invent the concept of incorporation of the Bill of Rights through the "due process" clause of the fourteenth amendment. In 1925 the Court had used this concept to apply first amendment free speech and free press protections against the state of New York in Gitlow vs. New York, 268 U.S. 652 (1925). However, Black was the foremost proponent of this doctrine, and distinctive in advocating the wholesale incorporation of the entire Bill of Rights.

45.   Berger, Government By Judiciary; Fairman, Does the Fourteenth Amendment Incorporate the Bill of Rights?, pp. 5-139; tenBroek, Equal Under Law, pp. 238-239.

46.   Fairman, Does the Fourteenth Amendment Incorporate the Bill of Rights?, pp. 44-48, 61-64, 69, 72-74, 84-89, 96-116; James E. Bond, "The Original Understanding of the Fourteenth Amendment in Illinois, Ohio, and Pennsylvania," *Akron Law Review*, volume 18, no. 3 (Winter 1985), pp. 435-467.

47.   Michael Kent Curtis. No State Shall Abridge: the Fourteenth Amendment and the Bill of Rights. Durham, NC: Duke University Press, 1987; *contra* see Raoul Berger. The Fourteenth Amendment and the Bill of Rights. Norman, OK: University of Oklahoma Press, 1989. Gingras, Congressional Misunderstandings and the Ratifiers' Understanding, surveys both sides and concludes that, while the two main congressional sponsors, Bingham and Howard, probably did intend that the fourteenth amendment apply the federal Bill of Rights against the States, almost none of the amendment's other supporters in Congress or the ratifying state legislatures understood it to do so.

48.   332 U.S. 46 (1947).

49.   332 U.S. 46, 63.

50.   332 U.S. 46, 65.

51.   Keynes, Life, Liberty and Privacy, pp. 144-205.

52.   Griswold vs. Connecticut, 381 U.S. 479 (1965), 482. (Justice Douglas' disingenuousness should not be too surprising since he was appointed to the Court by Franklin Roosevelt, the master of disingenuity.)

53.   381 U.S. 479, 481.

54.   381 U.S. 479, 484.

55.   381 U.S. 479, 522, 521.

56.   381 U.S. 479, 509.

57.   Louis Lusky. By What Right?: A Commentary on the Supreme Court's Power to Revise the Constitution. Charlottesville, VA: The Michie Company, 1975, pp. 337, 341. More recently even as extreme a progressive as Cass Sunstein has acknowledged that "nothing in the historical materials supports the Supreme Court's modern privacy decisions." Cass R. Sunstein. Radicals in Robes:

Why Extreme Right-Wing Courts Are Wrong for America. New York: Basic Books, 2005, p. 88.

58.   Jamin B. Raskin. Overruling Democracy: The Supreme Court vs. The American People. New York: Routledge, 2003, quotation at p. 6.

59.   Michael J. Phillips. The *Lochner* Court, Myth and Reality: Substantive Due Process from the 1890s to the 1930s. Westport, CT: Praeger, 2001, pp. 41-47, 51, 55.

60.   See, for example, BMW of North America, Inc. vs. Gore, 517 U.S. 559 (1996). A revival of economic substantive due process is now being actively advocated. See David E. Bernstein, "Rehabilitating Lochner: Defending Individual Rights Against Progressive Reform," Chicago: University of Chicago Press, 2011.

61.   Bush vs. Gore, 531 U.S. 98 (2000).

62.   Judith A. Baer. Equality Under the Constitution: Reclaiming the Fourteenth Amendment. Ithaca, NY: Cornell University Press, 1983, pp. 253, 256-257.

63.   Robin West. Progressive Constitutionalism: Reconstructing the Fourteenth Amendment. Durham, NC: Duke University Press, 1994, pp. 9-101.

64.   Over an 18 year period federal district court judge Russell Clark ordered the Kansas City school system to raise taxes and teacher salaries, delved into the details of school construction and even decoration, and mandated curriculum changes, all as part of desegregation. The Supreme Court eventually overturned Judge Clark's management of the Kansas City schools in Missouri vs. Jenkins, 515 U.S. 70 (1995).

65.   Cass R. Sunstein. The Second Bill of Rights: FDR's Unfinished Revolution and Why We Need It More Than Ever. New York: Basic Books, 2004. Sunstein keeps avowing a preference for legislative action, but in the end is willing to use judicial

enforcement, see pp. 5, 149-171, 209-229. However, when discussing conservative actions by the Court, Sunstein suddenly becomes a proponent of judicial restraint! Sunstein, Radicals in Robes, pp. 245-252.

66. H. Jefferson Powell. The Moral Tradition of American Constitutionalism. Durham, NC: Duke University Press, 1993, p. 10.

67. Jacobellis vs. Ohio, 378 U.S. 184, 197 (1964).

68. 381 U.S. 479, 530.

69. 381 U.S. 479, 531.

70. Berger, Government by Judiciary, p. 414 from Felix Frankfurter, "John Marshall and the Judicial Function," *Harvard Law Review*, volume 69 (1955), p. 229.

71. The Papers of Thaddeus Stevens, volume 2, p. 210.

72. Although I arrived at this idea independently, it was also proposed some time ago by Professor Lino Graglia. Lino A. Graglia, "Order in the Court," *National Review*, November 24, 1997, pp. 48, 64.

73. Ashley Montagu. Man's Most Dangerous Myth: The Fallacy of Race. Walnut Creek, CA: AltaMira Press, 1997 (6th edition).

74. Spencer Wells. The Journey of Man: A Genetic Odyssey. Princeton, NJ: Princeton University Press, 2002, pp. 30, 39; Gary Stix, "Traces of a Distant Past," *Scientific American*, July 2008, pp. 60-62.

75. 300 U.S. 379 (1937).

76. Gilbert Y. Steiner. Constitutional Inequality: The Political Fortunes of the Equal Rights Amendment. Washington, DC: The Brookings Institution, 1985, p. 52.

77.   David E. Kyvig. Explicit & Authentic Acts: Amending the Constitution 1776-1995. Lawrence, KS: University of Kansas Press, 1996, pp. 395-419 is a good summary of the history of the Equal Rights Amendment.

78.   Cynthia Harrison, "Heightened Scrutiny: An Alternative Route to Constitutional Equality for U. S. Women," in Women and the United States Constitution: History, Interpretation, and Practice, edited by Sibyl A. Schwarzenbach and Patricia Smith, New York: Columbia University Press, 2003, pp. 347-364, see pp. 354-358.

79.   Jane J. Mansbridge. Why We Lost the ERA. Chicago, IL: University of Chicago Press, 1986, pp. 45-59; Sunstein, Radicals in Robes, p. 250.

80.   See, for example, Credit Suisse Securities (USA) LLC vs. Billing, 551 U.S. 264 (2007), 127 S.Ct. 2383, ruling that lawsuits under the Sherman Antitrust Act (1890) and Clayton Antitrust Act (1914) were superseded by the Securities and Exchange Commission's authority under the Securities Act of 1933 and the Securities Exchange Act of 1934.

81.   Barbara A. Brown, Thomas I. Emerson, Gail Falk and Ann E. Freedman, "The Equal Rights Amendment: A Constitutional Basis for Equal Rights for Women," *The Yale Law Journal*, volume 80, no. 5 (April 1971), pp. 871-985, see pp. 900-902.

82.   Roe vs. Wade, 410 U.S. 113 (1973); Lawrence vs. Texas, 539 U.S. 558 (2003).

83.   Steiner, Constitutional Inequality, pp. 71-74.

84.   Mansbridge, Why We Lost the ERA, pp. 67-84.

85.   Janet K. Boles. The Politics of the Equal Rights Amendment: Conflict and the Decision Process. New York: Longman, 1979, p. 35; Mansbridge, Why We Lost the ERA, p. 129.

86.   Sunstein, Radicals in Robes, pp. 35-36, 100-101, 127-129.

87.   Enormous effort is now being devoted to this issue, which could be resolved far more efficiently (along with so many other issues) by this comprehensive revision of the first section of the fourteenth amendment. For an overview of the controversy over "birthright citizenship," see these articles in "Amendment XIV: Citizenship for All," edited by John Hay, Farmington Hills, MI: Greenhaven Press, 2009: Ron Paul, "The Fourteenth Amendment's Guarantee of Birthright Citizenship Should Be Changed,", pp. 125-128; Dimitri Vasillaros, "Illegal Immigrants Abuse the Fourteenth Amendment by Having Babies in the United States," pp. 135-138; and for a contrary view Priscilla Wang, "Recent Immigrants and Their Babies Are No Threat," pp. 139-142.

88.   United States Commission on Civil Rights. The Equal Rights Amendment: Guaranteeing Equal Rights for Women under the Constitution. Washington, DC: US Government Printing Office, 1981, p. 22.

89.   Bennett vs. Spear, 520 U.S. 154, 173 (1997).

90.   Joe Conason, "Exclusive Bill Clinton Interview: I Would Use Constitutional Option to Raise the Debt Ceiling and 'Force the Courts to Stop Me.'" *The National Memo*, July 19, 2011, http://www.nationalmemo.com/exclusive-former-president-bill-cli nton-says-he-would-use-constitutional-option-raise-debt/; Garrett Epps, "Our National Debt 'Shall Not Be Questioned,' the Constitution Says," *The Atlantic*, May 4, 2011, http://www.theatlantic.com/politics/archive/2011/05/our-ational-debt-shall-not-be-questioned-the-constitution-says/238269/; Jeffrey Rosen, "How Would the Supreme Court Rule on Obama Raising the Debt Ceiling Himself?," *The New Republic*, July 29, 2011, http://www.tnr.com/article/politics/92884/supreme-court-obama-debt-ceiling (all retrieved June 29, 2012).

91.   Laurence H. Tribe, "A Ceiling We Can't Wish Away," *New York Times*, July 8, 2011, p. A23.

92.   Neil H. Buchanan and Michael C. Dorf, "How to Choose the

Least Unconstitutional Option: Lessons for the President (and others) from the 2011 Debt Ceiling Standoff," *Cornell Law School Legal Studies Research Paper Series*, No. 12-09 (2012).

NOTES to Chapter 10

1.   The Writings of Thomas Jefferson, edited by Andrew A. Lipscomb and Albert Ellery Bergh, Washington, DC: The Thomas Jefferson Memorial Association, 1903, volume 16, p. 45 (letter to Major John Cartwright, June 5, 1824).

2.   William Shakespeare, *Henry V*, Act 4, Scene 3.

3.   Stephen P. Halbrook. That Every Man Be Armed: The Evolution of a Constitutional Right. Oakland, CA: The Independent Institute, 1994, pp. 37-54.

4.   Quoted in Saul Cornell. A Well-Regulated Militia: The Founding Fathers and the Origins of Gun Control in America. New York: Oxford University Press, 2006, p. 11.

5.   See generally Cornell's "A Well-Regulated Militia" for a history of the militia and the origins of gun control. Stephen P. Halbrook's "The Founders' Second Amendment: Origins of the Rights to Bear Arms, Chicago: Ivan R. Dee, 2008, gives a comprehensive history of the second amendment from a pro-gun rights perspective and Paul Finkelman, "'A Well-Regulated Militia': The Second Amendment in Historical Perspective,"in The Second Amendment in Law and History: Historians and Constitutional Scholars on the Right to Bear Arms, edited by Earl T. Bogus, New York: The New Press, 2000, pp. 117-147 gives a pro-gun control history.

6.   This historical evolution is described in Cornell, A Well-Regulated Militia, pp. 109-205.

7.   U.S. vs. Cruikshank, 92 U.S 542 (1876), and Presser vs. Illinois, 116 U.S. 252 (1886).

8.   307 U.S. 174 (1939).

9.   See H. Richard Uviller and William G. Merkel, The Militia and the Right to Arms, or How the Second Amendment Fell Silent, Durham, NC: Duke University Press, 2002; Robert J. Spitzer, The Right to Bear Arms: Rights and Liberties under the Law, Santa Barbara, CA: ABC-CLIO, Inc., 2001; and the articles collected in Earl T. Bogus (editor), The Second Amendment in Law and History (see note 5).

10.   Sanford Levinson, "The Embarrassing Second Amendment," *Yale Law Journal*, volume 99, no. 3 (December 1989), pp. 637-659, quotation at p. 642.

11.   Akhil Reed Amar. The Bill of Rights: Creation and Reconstruction. New Haven, CT: Yale University Press, 1998, p. 51.

12.   Levinson, The Embarrassing Second Amendment, p.645.

13.   Amar, The Bill of Rights, pp. 46-52.

14.   William Van Alstyne, "The Second Amendment and the Personal Right to Arms," *Duke Law Journal*, volume 43, no. 6 (April 1994), pp. 1237-1249; Levinson, the Embarrassing Second Amendment, pp. 643-652, quotation at p. 650.

15.   Quoted in Halbrook, The Founders' Second Amendment, p. 253.

16.   Quoted in Halbrook, The Founders' Second Amendment, pp. 262, 266.

17.   Halbrook, The Founders' Second Amendment, p. 275.

18.   The Federalist, edited by Robert Scigliano, New York: The Modern Library, 2000. Quotations from Federalist No. 46, pp. 305-306.

19.   The Law Practice of Alexander Hamilton: Documents and

Commentary, edited by Julius Goebel, Jr., at. al., New York: Columbia University Press, 1964, volume 1, p. 831. In this case, a defense against a libel action, Hamilton argued that, although an army could not overcome an armed populace, liberty could "be subverted...by a pretence of adhering to all forms of law, and yet breaking down the substance of our liberties" by a "servile tribunal [court]."

20.   Van Alstyne, The Second Amendment and the Personal Right to Bear Arms, p. 1250.

21.   Van Alstyne, The Second Amendment and the Personal Right to Bear Arms, pp. 1254-1255; Stuart Banner, "The Second Amendment, So Far," *Harvard Law Review*, volume 117, no. 3, (January 2004), p. 901.

22.   554 U.S. 290 (2008); 128 S.Ct. 2783.

23.   128 S.Ct. 2783, 2817.

24.   Adam Liptak, "Few Ripples From Supreme Court Ruling on Guns," *New York Times*, March 17, 2009, p. A14.

25.   http://www.supremecourt.gov/opinions/09pdf/08-1521.pdf (retrieved September 3, 2010).

26.   Van Alstyne, The Second Amendment and the Personal Right to Bear Arms, p. 1251-1253; Amar, The Bill of Rights, pp. 257-266; Halbrook, That Every Man Be Armed, pp. 107-153.

27.   John Hope Franklin. Reconstruction after the Civil War. Chicago, IL: The University of Chicago Press, 1961, 1994, pp. 61-65.

28.   The Selected Papers of Thaddeus Stevens, edited by Beverly Wilson Palmer and Holly Byers Ochoa. Pittsburgh, PA: University of Pittsburgh Press, 1998, volume 2, p. 381.

29.   See "Gun Control," edited by Tamara L. Roleff, Farmington Hills, MI: Greenhaven Press, 2007, for a one-volume summary of

the issues with articles from both sides.

30.	Andrew Carlson. The Antiquated Right: An Argument for the Repeal of the Second Amendment. New York: Peter Lang, 2002.

NOTES to Chapter 11

1.	The Federalist, edited by Robert Scigliano, New York: The Modern Library, 2000. Quotation from Federalist No. 57, p. 367. Some historians suggest that this essay might have been written by Hamilton, but the majority attribute it to Madison.

2.	James Madison Writings, edited by Jack N. Rakove, New York: Penguin Putnam, 1999, p. 802, (letter to Thomas Jefferson, June 27, 1823).

3.	Federalist No. 43, Modern Library edition, p. 282.

4.	Article I, Section 2, Clause 1.

5.	Article I, Section 2, Clause 3.

6.	George F. Will. "Restoration: Congress, Term Limits and the Recovery of Deliberative Democracy. New York: The Free Press, 1992, pp. 78-80.

7.	Will, Restoration, p. 87.

8.	James Silver, "2004 Map redrawing angers US Democrats," *BBC World News*, October 8, 2004, http://www.news.bbc.co.uk /2/hi/americas/3724372.stm (retrieved June 21, 2010).

9.	Ted Rueter, "Non-Competitive Elections Threaten Democracy," *DePauw University College News*, November 4, 2005, http://www. collegenews.org /x5021.xml (retrieved June 21, 2010).

10.	See reports at http://www.fairvote.org/congressional_elections #dubious_democracy (retrieved July 3, 2016).

11.   Rueter, Non-Competitive Elections Threaten Democracy.

12.   Lani Guinier. The Tyranny of the Majority: Fundamental Fairness in Representative Democracy. New York The Free Press, 1994; Robert Ritchie and Steven Hill. Reflecting All of Us: The Case for Proportional Representation. Boston, MA: Beacon Press, 1995.

13.   A detailed explanation of how to maximize the compactness of electoral districts can be found in George C. Clark, "Stealing Our Votes: How Politician Conspire to Steal Elections and How to Stop Them," Pittsburgh, PA: Dorrance Publishing Co., 2004, pp. 56-101.

14.   A law called the Voting Rights Act requires that certain States redistrict to maximize minority dominated districts. This has often produced polarizing and even perverse results with large numbers of minority voters gerrymandered into often bizarrely shaped districts in a collusion between minority Democratic Representatives who then get a very safe seat and Republicans who use the system to move Democratic-leaning minorities out of neighboring districts. This serves neither the minorities or the nation, for it only ghettoizes their congressional representatives and disincentives other Representatives from having to appeal to minority voters' interests. Under the proposal the Voting Rights Act could remain in place, but its operation would be restricted to the new constitutionally mandated parameters. See David Lublin, "The Paradox of Representation: Racial Gerrymandering and Minority Interests in Congress," Princeton, NJ: Princeton University Press, 1997, pp. 117-133.

15.   "Counts And Undercounts: Fight Over 'Sampling' Continues To Brew," *CBS News*, February 15, 2001, http://www.cbsnews.com/stories/2001/02/15/politics /main272177.shtml (retrieved June 22, 2010).

16.   Wesberry vs. Sanders, 376 U.S. 1 (1964).

17.   Kirkpatrick vs. Preisler, 394 U.S. 526 (1969) and White vs. Weiser, 412 U.S. 783 (1973).

18.   Karcher vs. Daggett, 462 U.S. 725 (1983).

19.   Abrams vs. Johnson, 521 U.S. 74 (1997).

20.   Larios vs. Perdue, 306 F. Supp. 2d 1190 (2003) (72 people) and Vieth vs. Pennsylvania, 195 F. Supp. 2d 672 (2002) (19 people).

21.   Davis vs. Bandemer, 478 U.S. 109 (1986).

22.   Vieth vs. Jubelirer, 541 U.S. 267 (2004).

23.   Baker vs. Carr, 369 U.S. 186 (1962) and Reynolds vs. Sims, 377 U.S. 533 (1964).

24.   Brown vs. Thompson, 462 U.S. 835 (1983).

25.   This is the subject of entire books. See for example Jonathan Winburn, "The Realities of Redistricting: Following the Rules and Limiting Gerrymandering in State Legislative Redistricting," Lanham, MD: Rowman & Littlefield Publishers, Inc., 2008.

26.   Richard S. Katz, "Malapportionment and Gerrymandering in Other Countries and Alternative Electoral Systems" in Voting Rights and Redistricting in the United States, edited by Mark E. Rush, Westport, CT: Greenwood Press, 1998, pp. 245-259, see pp. 250-254.

27.   George Will's "Restoration" presents the argument for term limits on Congress. For an argument against term limits see Victor Kamber, "Giving Up on Democracy: Why Term Limits Are Bad for America," Washington, DC: Regnery Publishing, Inc., 1995. A more recent summary of the term limits issue is in Larry J. Sabato, "A More Perfect Constitution: 23 Proposals to Revitalize Our Constitution and Make American a Fairer Country," New York: Walker & Company, 2007, pp. 41-53.

28.   U. S. Term Limits, Inc. vs. Thornton, 514 U.S. 779 (1995).

29.   See, for example, Mark R. Levin, "The Liberty Amendments:

Restoring the American Republic," New York, NY: Simon & Schuster, 2013, pp. 19-32 (which also argues persuasively for the idea of term limits).

30.   Article II, Section 4.

31.   The Writings of Thomas Jefferson, edited by Paul Leicester Ford. New York: G. P. Putnam's Sons, 1899, volume 10, p. 198 (letter to James Pleasants, December 26, 1821).

32.   Steven G. Calabresi and James Lindgren, "Term Limits for the Supreme Court: Life Tenure Reconsidered," *Harvard Journal of Law and Public Policy*, volume 29, no. 3 (Summer 2006), pp. 769-877, see pp. 778, 782.

33.   L. A. Powe, Jr., "Old People on Good Behavior," in Constitutional Stupidities, Constitutional Tragedies, edited by William N. Eskridge, Jr. and Sanford Levinson, New York: New York University Press, 1998, pp. 77-80, quotation at p. 78.

34.   Sabato, A More Perfect Constitution, p. 110.

35.   Sanford Levinson. Our Undemocratic Constitution: Where the Constitution Goes Wrong (And How We the People Can Correct It). New York: Oxford University Press, 2006, p. 129; Sabato, A More Perfect Constitution, p. 116.

36.   David J. Garrow, "Mental Decrepitude on the U. S. Supreme Court: The Historical Case for a 28th Amendment," *The University of Chicago Law Review*, volume 67, no. 4 (Autumn 2000), pp. 995-1087. See pp. 1050-1052 (Hugo Black), 1052-1056 (William O. Douglas), and 1071-1080 (William Brennan and Thurgood Marshall).

37.   Garrow, Mental Decrepitude, p. 1056; Levinson, Our Undemocratic Constitution, p. 137.

38.   Levinson, Our Undemocratic Constitution, pp. 126-127.

331

39.   William Howard Taft. *Popular Government: Its Essence, Its Permanence and Its Perils*. New Haven, CT: Yale University Press, 1913, p. 159.

40.   Jeff Shesol. *Supreme Power: Franklin Roosevelt vs. The Supreme Court*. New York: W. W. Norton & Company, Inc., 2010, pp. 207-210, 347, 399; Marian C. McKenna. *Franklin Roosevelt and the Great Constitutional War: The court-packing crisis of 1937*. New York: Fordham University Press, 2002, pp. 251-252, 402, 447; Garrow, Mental Decrepitude, pp. 1019-1020, 1023-1026.

41.   Garrow, Mental Decrepitude, pp. 1028-1043.

42.   Garrow, Mental Decrepitude, p. 1086.

43.   Calabresi and Lindgren, Term Limits for the Supreme Court, pp. 819-822, Levinson, our Undemocratic Constitution, pp. 134-135.

44.   Calabresi and Lindgren, Term Limits for the Supreme Court, pp. 824-854.   According to Calabresi and Lindgren, this basic proposal was first made in 1986 by Philip Oliver. It has also been suggested that this proposal be implemented by an act of Congress. See Paul D. Carrington and Roger C. Cramton, "The Supreme Court Renewal Act: A Return to Basic Principles," July 5, 2005, at http://zfacts.com/metaPage/lib/2005-SUPREME-COURT.pdf (retrieved August 27, 2010). However, such an act would likely face a constitutional challenge which would be decided by the very Court it was trying to limit. A constitutional amendment is a much surer means of accomplishing the proposal. Carrington and Cramton's paper does set forth the arguments for the proposal very effectively, and has been endorsed by a wide range of legal scholars.

NOTES to Chapter 12

1.   *The Writings of Thomas Jefferson: being his Autobiography, Correspondence, Reports, Messages, Addresses, and Other Writings, Official and Private*, edited by H. A. Washington. Washington, DC: Taylor & Maury, 1854, volume 7, pp. 15, 16

(letter to Samuel Kerchival, July 12, 1816).

2. The Writings of Thomas Jefferson, volume 7, p. 14 (letter to Samuel Kerchival 1816).

3. The Writings of Thomas Jefferson, volume 7, p. 16 (letter to Samuel Kerchival 1816).

4. The Writings of Thomas Jefferson, volume 4, p. 506 (letter to Wilson C. Nicholas, September 7, 1803).

5. The Writings of Thomas Jefferson, volume 7, p. 14 (letter to Samuel Kerchival 1816, italics in original).

6. Office of Management and Budget. Budget of the U. S. Government, Fiscal Year 2010, Historical Tables, p. 128 at http://www.whitehouse.gov/omb/budget/fy2010/assets/hist.pdf (retrieved March 26, 2010).

7. Edmund L. Andrews, "Wave of Debt Payments Facing U.S. Government," *New York Times*, November 23, 2009, p. A1.

8. Peter G. Peterson Foundation, "Our Real Federal Financial Condition," at http://www.pgpf.org/about/nationaldebt/ (retrieved June 28, 2010).

9. The Writings of Thomas Jefferson, volume 7, p. 216 (letter to C. Hammond, August 18, 1821).

10. The Writings of Thomas Jefferson, volume 7, pp. 297-298 (letter to Judge William Johnson, June 12, 1823).

11. The Papers of Thomas Jefferson, edited by Julian P. Boyd, Princeton, NJ: Princeton University Press, 1956, volume 13, p. 208-209 (letter to Edward Carrington, May 27, 1788).

12. Alexander Hamilton Writings, edited by Joanne B. Freeman, New York: The Library of America, 2001, pp. 863, 864 (from Hamilton's draft of Washington's Farewell Address, July 30,

1796). It might be argued that these words reflected Washington's views rather than Hamilton's. However, we can see that Hamilton was in harmony with this position by looking at his "Report on the Subject of Manufactures." There Hamilton warns that public debt "may be swelled to such a size, as that the greatest part of it may cease to be useful...that the sums required to pay the Interest on it may become oppressive, and...that the resources of taxation, to face the debt, may have been strained too far to admit of extensions adequate to exigencies, which regard the public safety.... And as the vicissitudes of Nations beget a perpetual tendency to the accumulation of debt, there ought to be in every government a perpetual, anxious and unceasing effort to reduce that...as fast as shall be practicable consistently with integrity and good faith." Ibid., p. 685.

13.   Alexander Hamilton, "The Defence No. XI," reprinted in The Papers of Alexander Hamilton, edited by Harold C. Syrett, et al. New York: Columbia University Press, 1973, volume 19, quotation at p. 196 (August 28, 1795).

14.   The Writings of Thomas Jefferson, volume 7, p. 216 (letter to C. Hammond, August 18, 1821).

15.   Owen J. Roberts. The Court and the Constitution. Cambridge, MA: Harvard University Press, 1951, pp . 63, 61.

16.   The Writings of Thomas Jefferson, volume 7, p. 10 (letter to Samuel Kerchival 1816).

17.   Herman Belz. A Living Constitution or Fundamental Law?: American Constitutionalism in Historical Perspective. Lanham, MD: Rowman & Littlefield Publishers, Inc., 1998, p. 261; Noah Feldman, "Imagining a Liberal Court," New York Times Sunday Magazine, June 27, 2010, p. MM41. Brennan's arrogant attitude toward the constitutional text is in full display in a 1985 speech where he declared that the Supreme Court is "the last word on the meaning of the Constitution" which the Court must save from "the anachronistic views of long-gone generations." William J. Brennan, Jr., "The Constitution of the United States:

Contemporary Ratification," reprinted in Interpreting the Constitution: The Debate over Original Intent, edited by Jack N. Rakove, Boston, MA: Northeastern University Press, 1990, pp. 23-34, quotation at p. 33. See also the rebuttal which follows by Lino A. Graglia, "How the Constitution Disappeared," in Interpreting the Constitution, pp. 35-50.

18.   The Writings of Thomas Jefferson, volume 7, p. 256 (letter to William T. Barry, July 2, 1822).

19.   Supreme Court majorities used foreign laws in such recent controversial decisions as Lawrence vs. Texas (539 US 558 (2003)) and Roper vs. Simmons (543 US 551 (2005)) overturning as unconstitutional respectively sodomy laws and capital punishment for juveniles. This approach continues to be advocated on the current Supreme Court. See Justice Ruth Bader Ginsburg's speech "'A Decent Respect to the Opinions of [Human]kind:' the Value of a Comparative Perspective on Constitutional Adjudication," February 7, 2006, available at http://www.supremecourt.gov/publicinfo/speeches/viewspeeches.aspx?Filename=sp_02-07b-06.html   (retrieved January 3, 2011).

20.   Although the wording is my own, this last point on treaties draws on proposals in Randy E. Barnett, "A Bill of Federalism," *Forbes*, May 20,   2009,   http://www.forbes.com/2009/05/20/bill-of-federalism-constitution-states-supreme-court-opinions-contributors-randy-barnett_2.html (retrieved June 29, 2012).

21.   The Writings of Thomas Jefferson, volume 7, p. 9 (letter to Samuel Kerchival 1816).

22.   For summary overviews see Ronald H. Chilcote, Theories of Development and Underdevelopment, Boulder, CO: Westview Press, 1984, pp. 23-47, 60-63, 96-119 and Immanuel Wallerstein, The capitalist world-economy, Cambridge, UK: Cambridge University Press, 1979, pp. 66-94. For a book-length exposition see Purshottam Narayan Mathur, "Why Developing Counties Fail to Develop," London: Macmillan, 1991.

23.   See for example, Jamin B. Raskin, Overruling Democracy: The
        Supreme Court vs. The American People, New York: Routledge,
        2003, Sanford Levinson, Our Undemocratic Constitution: Where
        the Constitution Goes Wrong (And How We the People Can
        Correct It), New York: Oxford University Press, 2006; Andrew
        P. Napolitano, "The Constitution in Exile: How the Federal
        Government Has Seized Power by Rewriting the Supreme Law
        of the Land," Nashville, TN: Thomas Nelson, Inc., 2006, pp.
        239-241; Larry J. Sabato, "A More Perfect Constitution: 23
        Proposals to Revitalize Our Constitution and Make American a
        Fairer Country," New York: Walker & Company, 2007; Randy E.
        Barnett, "The Case for a Federalism Amendment," *Wall Street
        Journal*, April 23, 2009, p. A17; Roger D. Hodge, The Mendacity
        of Hope: Barack Obama and the Betrayal of American
        Liberalism, New York: HarperCollins, 2010, pp. 225-230; Mark
        R. Levin, "The Liberty Amendments: Restoring the American
        Republic," New York: Simon & Schuster, 2013..

24.   Levinson, Our Undemocratic Constitution, pp. 173-180; Sabato,
        A More Perfect Constitution, pp. 198-220; James M. Lemunyon,
        "A Constitutional Convention Can Rein In Washington," *Wall
        Street Journal*, April 1, 2010, p. A19; Lawrence Lessig, "Republic,
        Lost: How Money Corrupts Congress - and a Plan to Stop It,"
        New York: Hachette Book Group, 2011, pp. 290-304.

25.   Ralph Nader and Robert Weissman, "The Case Against
        Corporate Speech: Regulations should limit spending and a
        constitutional amendment should be considered," *Wall Street
        Journal*, February 10, 2010, p, A19; Robert H. Bork, "Our Judicial
        Oligarchy," in The End of Democracy?: The Celebrated *First
        Things* Debate with Arguments Pro and Con, edited by Mitchell S.
        Muncy, Dallas, TX: Spence Publishing Company, 1997, p. 17.

INDEX

original meaning (approach to constitutional understanding), 66-67, 75, 81-85, 88-89, 91-93, 99, 103-104, 107-110, 116, 119, 121, 123, 128-129, 139, 147, 150, 161-168, 173, 176, 181-184, 189-190, 200-201, 210-214, 218, 255

O'Connor, Sandra Day, 109-110

Plessy vs. Ferguson, 31, 161

privacy, 85, 164-168, 171, 174, 258

redistricting, 192, 194-198, 262

regulation, 3-4, 12, 21, 23, 31-33, 36-37, 48-49, 51-59, 61, 99-115, 119-121, 159-160, 171, 174, 177, 183, 186-187, 209-210, 213-214, 241-242, 249-250, 255, 257, 258

Report on Manufactures, 17-18, 64

Republican party, 14, 20-22, 36, 40, 43, 70-71, 100, 153-154, 158, 191

Roberts, John, 87-88, 110

Roberts, Owen, 31-32, 70, 73-75, 77, 102, 108, 110, 160, 162, 170, 212

Roosevelt, Eleanor, 170

Roosevelt, Franklin, 26-37, 70-75, 78, 80, 84-85, 108-110, 121, 122-123, 126, 132-133, 141, 153, 165, 167, 202-203, 211-212

Roosevelt, Theodore, 22, 49, 70

Salatin, Joel, 57

Same-sex marriage, 172-173, 258

Scalia, Antonin 185

Schechter Poultry Co. vs. US, 27, 71

Schumacher, E. F., 44-46, 48, 50, 60

second amendment, 7-8, 85, 108, 164, 179-188, 257

Second World War, 35, 78, 123, 129, 132

Section 8 (of Article I of the Constitution), 19, 64-65, 84, 99-118, 131, 172-176, 181, 223-225, 249, 254

Senate, 27, 38, 40, 87, 92, 97-98, 125, 131, 136, 141, 157, 184, 190, 199, 220-221, 253, 261

separation of church and state, 6, 132-152, (wall of separation metaphor) 6, 85, 134-135, 137-138, 144, 148-150, 152

343